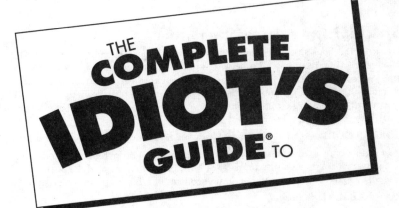

THE **COMPLETE IDIOT'S GUIDE** TO

The NBA

by Steven D. Strauss

ALPHA

All photographs courtesy of NBAE/Getty Images

Ray Amati	287	Kent Horner	127
Victor Baldzon	88	Ron Hoskins	108
Bill Baptist	260	Walter Iooss Jr.	23, 31, 153, 155, 180, 207
Andrew D. Bernstein	52, 54, 78, 114, 125, 143, 148, 160, 200, 247, 276, 290	Robert Laberge	229
		Ken Levin	228
Nathaniel S. Butler	61, 173, 189, 307	Andy Lyons	257
Paul Chapman	94	Fernando Medina	215, 230
Scott Cunningham	245	Jennifer Pottheiser	285, 296, 301
Jonathan Daniel	64, 163	Ken Regan	26
Tim DeFrisco	189	Wen Roberts	134, 166
Garrett Ellwood	198, 261	David Sherman	287
Steven Freeman	295	Catherine Steenkeste	283
Jesse D. Garrabrant	95, 123, 214, 219	Noren Trotman	111
Barry Gossage	64	Jerry Wachter	48
Otto Greule Jr.	138, 150	Rocky Widner	187, 229
Andy Hayt	249, 272, 279		

International Standard Book Number: 0-02-864461-1
Library of Congress Catalog Card Number: 2002166799

05 04 03   8 7 6 5 4 3 2 1

Interpretation of the printing code: The rightmost number of the first series of numbers is the year of the book's printing; the rightmost number of the second series of numbers is the number of the book's printing. For example, a printing code of 03-1 shows that the first printing occurred in 2003.

Printed in the United States of America

Note: This publication contains the opinions and ideas of its authors. It is intended to provide helpful and informative material on the subject matter covered. It is sold with the understanding that the authors and publisher are not engaged in rendering professional services in the book. If the reader requires personal assistance or advice, a competent professional should be consulted.

The authors and publisher specifically disclaim any responsibility for any liability, loss, or risk, personal or otherwise, which is incurred as a consequence, directly or indirectly, of the use and application of any of the contents of this book.

This book is dedicated to the SBA: Larry, GM and coach of 4-2-osity, Spence, GM and coach of Bruddies Bombers; Raph, GM and coach of the gooneys; Jeff, GM and coach of Chickie's Watchin'; Mike, GM and coach of Tiocfaidh ar la, Joe and Zack Meisner, GMs and coaches of Vicious Fishes, John Rodriquez, GM and coach of Tustin Tamales, Gary Silber, GM and coach of Gutman, and Brian Flannigan, GM and coach of Toros Perros.

Let the kvetching begin!

Contents at a Glance

Contents

Part 3: The Greatest Players Ever **145**

11 Great Point Guards **147**

Best of the New Generation 147

   Jason Kidd 147

   The Answer 148

   The Glove 149

   John Stockton 150

Best of the '70s and '80s 151

   Nate "Tiny" Archibald 151

   Dave Bing 152

   Walt Frazier 152

   Magic Johnson 152

   Earl Monroe 153

   Zeke 154

Pioneers 155

   Bob Cousy 155

   Gail Goodrich 156

   Hal Greer 156

   The Big O 157

   Lenny Wilkens 158

12 Great Shooting Guards **159**

New Kids on the Block 159

   Kobe Bryant 160

   Vinsanity 161

   Clyde the Glide 161

   Michael Jordan 162

   T-Mac 164

   Reggie Miller 165

'70s and '80s 165

   George Gervin 165

   Pistol Pete 166

Getting the Ball Rolling 167

   Paul Arizin 168

   Sam Jones 168

   Bill Sharman 169

   Jerry West 169

Introduction

In the past decade, the National Basketball Association has exploded onto the world scene. When the Dream Team won Olympic gold in Barcelona in 1992—the first time that NBA athletes participated in the Olympics—the rest of the world saw what America had known for a long time: NBA players are the most gifted, most athletic, most exciting athletes in the world.

When Michael Jordan retired for the first time shortly thereafter, some were concerned that the league would falter, that there weren't enough new stars to carry on the proud tradition of Wilt Chamberlain, Bill Russell, Magic Johnson, and Larry Bird.

But no one needed to worry. Today's players easily match their predecessors. Stronger, quicker, and more athletic, players like Shaquille O'Neal, Kobe Bryant, Allen Iverson, and Kevin Garnett continue the NBA tradition of crowd-pleasing basketball excellence.

And a proud tradition it is. The NBA is more than 50 years old, and each decade has been different than the one preceding it. From the slow, sleepy league of the early 1950s to the fun, fast-breaking league of the 1980s to the amazing above-the-rim league it is today, the NBA has always found a way to thrill fans.

What's in It for Me?

In *The Complete Idiot's Guide to the NBA*, you get a comprehensive overview of everything NBA. From the beginnings of the league to its greatest stars and memorable moments, *The Complete Idiot's Guide to the NBA* takes you behind the scenes.

Whether you want to know if the 1986 Celtics were better than the 1996 Bulls, whether Wilt was better than Kareem, or who has the most rebounds in NBA history, it's all here.

Part 1, "The History of the NBA," gives you an entertaining decade-by-decade history of the league. From the invention of basketball itself in 1891 to the creation of the NBA to the absorption of four ABA teams to Michael and the Bulls, it's all here.

Part 2, "NBA Teams," is an overview of all 29 teams in the league, including their history and greatest moments. From Reggie Miller's late-game exploits with the Indiana Pacers to Gary Payton's All-Star run with the Sonics, some of the best moments in NBA history can be found here.

Part 3, "The Greatest Players Ever," is a position-by-position analysis of the best of the best. From Bob Cousy to Pete Maravich, from Scottie Pippen to Karl Malone, you'll discover the greatest of all time, and why they are considered the best.

Part 4, "Rounding It Out," is where you learn about the other people and events that make the NBA what it is. What does it take to become a ref in the NBA? What are the most exciting buzzer-beating shots in league history? This is the place to find out.

Part 5, "Inside Stuff," puts it all in perspective. From the NBA All-Star Game (which player appeared in 17 All-Star Games?) to the Hall of Fame, the best players ever share their stories. And if you want to know where the game is headed in the future, this is where to look.

Throughout this book you'll also encounter many more tidbits, which are highlighted by friendly icons. Here's what to expect:

Hoopology

NBA basketball has its own lingo, and it's deciphered here.

Technical Foul

Missteps, mistakes and things to watch out for are flagged for you here.

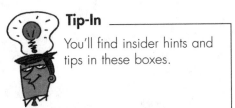

Tip-In

You'll find insider hints and tips in these boxes.

Inside Stuff

Are you ready for an earful of insight from around the league, as well as other interesting facts? Then check out these boxes.

Acknowledgments

I would like to thank Maria for indulging my NBA addiction, and my sweet girls for learning to love professional basketball, whether they wanted to or not. I would also like to thank Lili for always making me laugh, Mai Mai for the joy she gives us all, and Sydney-o for her love and passion for the game.

Larry also learned to love the game and talk trash, even though he was given little choice in the matter. Bruddie has always been a great basketball fan and an endless source of NBA information.

I would also like to thank Mike Sanders, Michael Levine, John Hareas and Marie Butler-Knight for their assistance in getting this book completed.

Finally, I would like to thank my dad for those great season tickets to the Lakers back in the day, and my mom for letting me stay out after dark shooting hoops, even after it was long clear that I would have to be satisfied watching NBA basketball rather than playing it.

Trademarks

All terms mentioned in this book that are known to be or are suspected of being trademarks or service marks have been appropriately capitalized. Alpha Books and Pearson Education, Inc., cannot attest to the accuracy of this information. Use of a term in this book should not be regarded as affecting the validity of any trademark or service mark.

Part 1

The History of the NBA

There's no question that the game of basketball has come a long way from the game that was first played in a YMCA gym in Springfield, Massachusetts. Along the way dozens of local and a few national leagues gave it a go, with the NBA finally coming out on top. The following decade-by-decade recap will fill you in on some of the most memorable moments in league history: The first great franchise (Minneapolis Lakers), the rivalry between Wilt Chamberlain and Bill Russell, the rise of the ABA (the predecessor to the NBA), the emergence of Larry Bird and Magic Johnson, the dominance of Michael Jordan and the Bulls, and finally, Shaq, Kobe and the Lakers.

Chapter 1

1940s and '50s: Roots of the Modern NBA

In This Chapter

- ◆ Meet Dr. James Naismith
- ◆ The birth of the National Basketball Association
- ◆ The first dynasty
- ◆ The 24-second clock to the rescue

The high-flying, above-the-rim, fast-breaking, fun, and exciting game of today's NBA basketball is a far cry from the game of basket ball, as it was called, that was first played over 100 years ago. The score of the first game was 1–0.

The year was 1891, and it would be almost another 60 years before the NBA as we know it would come into existence. In the interim, the game of basketball took many twists and turns, rules and leagues changed constantly, players came and went, all leading to the eventual creation of the Basketball Association of America in 1946, the forerunner to the NBA.

The Good Dr. Naismith

Back in late 1891, what is now Springfield College in Massachusetts was called the International YMCA Training School. It was there that a Canadian-born teacher named Dr. James A. Naismith was asked by his superintendent to create an indoor game that the young men could play in the winter.

It was a request that would change the history of sports, launching what would become one of the most popular sports around the world and arguably the most successful professional sports league of all time.

Naismith accepted the challenge and began to think about what kind of game he wanted. He decided that the game should have very little physical contact. Dr. Naismith also thought that in this new game, players should not be allowed to take the ball and run with it, as they did in football or rugby. He also liked the idea of an elevated goal.

So Naismith asked Pop Stebbins, the janitor at the YMCA, to nail two peach baskets to the school gymnasium's balcony (which happened to be 10 feet high—the same height a basketball basket is today). The school secretary, Mrs. Lyons, typed up the original 13 rules of basket ball.

Inside Stuff

Among Dr. Naismith's 13 original rules of basket ball were: "1. The ball may be thrown in any direction with one or both hands .... 5. No shouldering, holding, pushing, tripping, or striking in any way the person of an opponent shall be allowed; the first infringement of this rule by any player shall count as a foul, the second shall disqualify him until the next goal is made, or, if there was evident intent to injure the person, the whole of the game, no substitute allowed .... 12. The time shall be two 15-minute halves, with five minutes rest between .... 13. The side making the most goals in that time shall be declared the winner. In the case of a draw the game may, by agreement of the captains, be continued until another goal is made."

According to Dr. Naismith, the first game of basket ball had two teams of nine men each. "There were three forwards, three centers, and three backs on each team," he is quoted as saying. History will note that the only player to score a basket in that game, and thus the first player to ever score a basket in the history of basketball, was William R. Chase, who tossed in a 25-foot shot from midcourt.

The date was December 21, 1891, and the game was a rousing success from the first tip-off. For years, play would have to stop whenever a team scored, as the janitor had to climb a ladder to get the soccer ball out of the peach basket (until someone had the bright idea to cut the bottom out of the basket out in 1906). Nevertheless, within a few weeks basket ball began to spread across YMCAs throughout New England.

The Forerunners of the NBA

Five short years later, on November 7, 1896, the first "professional" game ever was staged. At that game, the Trenton YMCA team defeated the Brooklyn YMCA team in a rented Masonic temple by a score of 16–1. Why such a low score? At the time, and until 1937, teams would go to center court and jump for the ball after every basket.

People paid to watch this first game, and the Trenton players each made $15, proving from the start that the game was as enjoyable for the fans to watch as for the players to play, and would likely be a profitable venture to boot. In fact, team captain Fred Cooper received $1 extra in that game and thus became the first "highest paid player" in the game. Little did he know just how profitable the game would become.

The Cagers

Interestingly, this first pro game was played inside a wire-mesh cage. The cage was necessary because, even though Dr. Naismith had envisioned a noncontact sport, basketball had quickly evolved into the opposite, although not in the manner you might suspect.

For reasons unknown to posterity, fans of the early game were an unruly sort. Often hitting and otherwise attacking the players, the fans were ruthless, with an incident of a broken jaw even being reported.

To get away from these "fans," the players decided that it would be safer to play inside a steel-mesh cage. But the players found themselves chasing loose balls and otherwise falling out of bounds, only to end up hurting themselves on the cage that was meant to protect them.

Bloodied but not bullied, the players took to wearing elbow, knee, and shin pads to protect themselves, often to no avail. Indeed, the cage

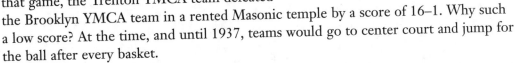

Tip-In

Frank Mahan, a player in the first game, wanted to call the game "Naismith ball," but Dr. Naismith said that "we have a basket and a ball, and it seems to me that it should be named basket ball." The name stuck, although it would be another 30 years before it became one word.

Hoopology

To this day, basketball players are still sometimes called **cagers,** and now you know why.

might have been worse than the fans; the court was often "covered in blood," according to a Hall of Famer from the era, Barney Sedran.

The National Basketball League

The first professional basketball league was called the National Basketball League, formed in Philadelphia in 1898 with six teams. It folded five years later. Other leagues were quickly formed and abandoned, and new teams were created and disbanded.

Teams and leagues were certainly not national at this time, despite the names of the leagues (the Interstate League and the Eastern League, for example). Rather, the forerunners of the NBA were regional in nature.

The one league that did begin to have some success and stability was the second National Basketball League (the NBL), formed in 1937 by General Electric, Firestone, and Goodyear. This league was characterized by its allegiance to the companies who sponsored the teams, such as:

♦ The Akron Firestone Non-Skids.

♦ The Fort Wayne Zollner Pistons.

♦ The Goodyear Wingfoots.

♦ The Oshkosh All-Stars.

> **Inside Stuff**
>
> In 1902, Harry "Bucky" Lew became the first African American to play in a professional basketball game, beating baseball's Jackie Robinson by almost 50 years.

> **Inside Stuff**
>
> Of the 13 teams that formed the NBL, only three remain today: the Fort Wayne Zollner Pistons (now the Detroit Pistons), the Minneapolis Lakers (now the Los Angeles Lakers), and the Rochester Royals (now your Sacramento Kings).

Games back then were played in theaters, high school gymnasiums, and dance halls. According to the late Buddy Jeanette, who played for the Fort Wayne Pistons, usually "you would drive into a town and look for the largest building." That was typically where the game was scheduled; they would clear it out, nail up some hoops, and the game would start.

One thing that the NBL will long be remembered for is the emergence of the marquee-name player—that special hoopster who had both the skills and charisma to change the game, excite the fans, and win the game. Early "shooting" stars included the following:

♦ **Robert McDermott** was named by the NBL as "the best basketball player of all time" and won the NBL MVP for five straight years. He also led his team, the Pistons, to three straight NBL championships.

- **LeRoy "Cowboy" Edwards** lead the NBL in scoring for three straight years.

- **George Mikan** began his career in the NBL before becoming the first superstar in NBA history. *The Associated Press* later named him the "greatest player of the first half century."

Despite the relative success of the league, the game was, for the most part, slow and boring, a problem that would continue for some time. Basketball made one of its biggest leaps forward when, in 1937, it abandoned the *center jump* after every basket, greatly increasing the fluidity of the game.

Hoopology

In basketball's early days, the centers of the opposing teams would go to midcourt and jump for the ball after every basket. In the NBA, the **center jump** occurred only at the beginning of each quarter. Later, the league all but abandoned the center jump altogether, having one jump to start the game, and then alternating possessions at the beginning of each quarter.

The Birth of the National Basketball Association

The changes in the game had created the desired result. Basketball was gaining in popularity, especially at the collegiate level, where a fast-paced running game had evolved. It was clear that fans liked fast-paced basketball.

In an effort to capitalize on this surge in popularity and with World War II now over, a group of hockey and arena owners from some major metropolitan areas got together with the idea of making a new league. Walter Brown, already the owner of the Boston Bruins, organized the group, which included:

- John Harris of Pittsburgh.

- Al Sutphin of Cleveland.

- Ned Irish, owner of Madison Square Garden in New York.

These men were already making money from pro hockey, but their arenas still had open dates that they needed to fill while the hockey teams were on the road. Pro basketball was their answer. And so, on June 6, 1946, inside New York's Commodore Hotel, a competitor for the NBL and the forerunner of the NBA was created, the Basketball Association of America (BAA). The first BAA president was Maurice Podoloff, who was also president of the American Hockey League. He was an immigrant from Russia who was in the ice business.

Tip-In

In 1946, the Rochester Royals won the NBL championship. Among those who played on that team were Red Holzman (later the coach of the 1972–73 NBA champion New York Knicks), Cleveland Brown quarterback Otto Graham, and Chuck Connors (later the star of the TV show *The Rifleman*). The 6' 7" Connors is also famous for being the first player ever to shatter a glass backboard while dunking—during warm-ups! (This happened on November 5, 1946.)

In its inaugural season, the BAA was made up of 11 teams in two divisions:

- Boston Celtics
- Chicago Stags
- Cleveland Rebels (folded after only one year)
- Detroit Falcons (dropped out of the league after only one year)
- New York Knickerbockers
- Philadelphia Warriors
- Pittsburgh Ironmen (dropped out of the league after only one year)
- Providence Steamrollers
- St. Louis Bombers
- Toronto Huskies (dropped out of the league after only one year)
- Washington Capitols

In 1947, after the four teams just mentioned dropped out, the Baltimore Bullets joined the league, making it an eight-team league. The original Bullets disbanded during the 1954–55 season.

The problems with the BAA were evident from the start. The NBL was much more well established, and the stars of the era were playing in that league. Yet, the BAA had larger stadiums and larger population centers. It seemed as if the two leagues would need to merge for professional basketball to survive.

Yet the BAA refused to give up and worked hard at luring some of the NBL franchises to defect to the upstart league. And it worked. At the beginning of the 1948–49 season, four well-established NBL teams decided to jump leagues: the mighty Minneapolis Lakers with that era's equivalent of Shaquille O'Neal, George Mikan; the Fort Wayne Pistons; the Indianapolis Jets; and the Rochester Royals.

By the end of the season, it was apparent that the new league, with its big cities and big-name players, had the edge. The leagues merged, with the six remaining NBL franchises joining the new league.

The name of the new league changed, too. It would now be called the National Basketball Association—the NBA.

> **Inside Stuff**
>
> By 1947, the NBL had teams in cities such as Sheboygan, Wisconsin (the Redskins); Toledo, Ohio (the Jeeps); Youngstown, Ohio (the Bears); and Anderson, Indiana (the Meat Packers).

The First Dynasty: The Minneapolis Lakers

When fans today think of NBA dynasties, they remember the 11 championships won by the Celtics of the late '50s and '60s, or the six won by Michael Jordan and the Chicago Bulls, or Magic and the five he won with the Los Angeles Lakers, but few ever think of the first great dynasty—the Minneapolis Lakers. That team won five titles in six years, which is an amazing accomplishment in any era.

The backbone of the team, and in fact, of the new league, was 6' 10" George Mikan. Mikan would become the first truly dominant big man in a league that would become dominated by dominant big men.

No. 99

In 1947, the Twin Cities had another "professional" basketball team. The St. Paul Saints played in something called the Professional Basketball League of America, a league that folded after a few weeks into the 1947 season.

Players from the now-defunct League of America were absorbed by the NBL, and were subject to an NBL draft. Because the Detroit Gems (soon to be purchased by a Minneapolis businessman and renamed the Lakers) had the worst record in the NBL the previous year, they had the first pick in the draft, and they used it to select the bespectacled George Mikan.

How good was Mikan? Number 99 led the Lakers to the 1947–48 NBL championship while also leading the league in scoring. Not

> **Tip-In**
>
> Mikan was a basketball monster, even in college. A three-time All-American (1944, 1945, and 1946), he led the country in scoring in 1945 and '46 as well. He blocked so many shots while at DePaul, that the NCAA instituted the goaltending rule to slow him down.

only that, but he did so after already winning a championship with the Chicago American Gears of the NBL in 1946–47. In all, Mikan-led teams would win seven professional basketball championships.

Hoopology

Mikan was so great that in his first trip to New York as a professional, the marquee at Madison Square Garden read "Tonight George Mikan versus the Knicks!"

Mikan would go on to lead the NBA in scoring for four years, and was named to the All-Star first team six seasons in a row. He was practically impossible to defend on the offensive end, and in an effort to create some leaguewide parity, the NBA doubled the width of the foul lane in an effort to keep him further away from the basket. Another tactic teams tried in an effort to defeat Mikan and the Lakers was stalling, causing the game to slow down dramatically. The Fort Wayne Zollner Pistons once defeated the Lakers 19-18.

The Championship Lakers

No team can win an NBA championship with just one great player, and the Minneapolis Lakers were no exception to the rule. Indeed, the Lakers had much more going for them than just George Mikan. The team had what would later be four Hall of Famers on the squad: Mikan, Jim Pollard, Vern Mikkelsen and Slater Martin.

Nicknamed the "Kangaroo Kid" because of his extraordinary jumping ability, Pollard was an all-around great player, graced with an equally great shot. The BAA, where he originally played, named Pollard the best player of the era, ahead of even Mikan. Pollard was named to the Basketball Hall of Fame in 1978.

The first true power forward in the game, Mikkelsen had an all-around game, scoring, defending, and rebounding with apparent ease. A six-time NBA All-Star, Mikkelsen was the captain of the Lakers for five seasons.

Although he was only 5' 10", Slater "Dugie" Martin ran the championship Minneapolis team. Playing a position that would later be called the point guard, Martin ran the show. Martin was enshrined into the Hall of Fame in 1982.

Together, these players led the Minneapolis Lakers to NBA championships in 1949, '50, '52, '53 and '54. George Mikan retired at the age of 30 in 1954, and the first NBA dynasty came to an end. He made a come back for half a season (1955-56) but wasn't the same.

The Rule That Revolutionized the Game

Despite the success of the Lakers, the NBA as a whole, by 1955, was in the doldrums. Of the original 17 teams, nine had dropped out by then, leaving it an eight-team, two-division league.

Dolph Schayes was one of the early stars of the new National Basketball Association.

Essentially, the game had become too slow and boring. The up-and-down style that had proved so popular in the college ranks was an anathema to NBA teams. Instead, they had adopted a lumbering, fouling, stalling game plan intended to preserve a lead.

Inside Stuff

The following teams once were part of the BAA or NBA, but are no longer around: Anderson Meat Packers (1949–50); the original Baltimore Bullets (1947–55); Chicago Stags (1946–50); Cleveland Rebels (1946–47); the original Denver Nuggets (1949–50); Detroit Falcons (1946–47); Indianapolis Jets (1948– 1949)/Olympians (1949–53); Pittsburgh Ironmen (1946–47); Providence Steamrollers (1946–49); St. Louis Bombers (1946–50); Sheboygan Redskins (1949–50); Toronto Huskies (1946–47); Washington Capitols (1946–51); and Waterloo (Iowa) Hawks (1949–50).

Because there was no limit on the amount of time a team could keep the ball, NBA teams would look to get a lead and then preserve that lead by stalling. The other team, when faced with the stall, fouled in order to get the ball back. The game became a snail's-paced fouling and free-throw-shooting contest. It was a big bore.

To give you an idea of just how bad things were, consider the following:

♦ In 1953, in a game between the Syracuse Nationals and the Boston Celtics, the two teams shot an amazing 128 free throws.

♦ Maybe the nadir of NBA basketball occurred in 1950 when the Fort Wayne Pistons beat the Minneapolis Lakers by the astounding score of 19–18. Both teams scored a total of eight baskets.

Such games were not atypical.

With the writing on the wall (scores and attendance decreasing every season), one man came up with a solution. His name was Danny Biasone, and he was the owner of the Syracuse Nationals.

Biasone figured that to make the game fun and exciting again, teams should be required to shoot the ball within a specified time frame. That would eliminate the stalling and fouling that was ruining the once-fluid sport. The problem, as Biasone once said, was that "no one would listen to me." He continued, "Baseball has three outs an inning, football has four downs, every game has a limit, except basketball."

Biasone figured that each team really needed to shoot 60 times a game for the game to become high-scoring and exciting again. Thus, the two teams needed to shoot the ball 120 times within the 48 minutes that made up a professional NBA game. One hundred twenty shots in 48 minutes comes out to one shot every 24 seconds. Danny Biasone, therefore, wanted the league to adopt a 24-second clock. The infamous 19–18 game, along with the endless stalling and fouling (there was no limit at the time on the number of fouls a team or player could commit) was simply ruining the game.

Tip-In

The Syracuse Nats, as the Nationals were called, later to moved to Philadelphia and were renamed the 76ers.

After ignoring Biasone's idea for three years, in 1954 the owners and NBA commissioner Maurice Podoloff agreed to consider a clock. Biasone arranged to have the summer owners' meeting held that year in Syracuse, at the Onondaga Hotel.

He got some of the players from his team, along with some local boys, to stage a game for the other owners using the clock in the Syracuse high school gymnasium.

By all accounts the game was fast, furious, and fun—a far cry from the state of the game at that time, which was plodding and ponderous.

The owners approved, and the *24-second clock* was adopted.

The year before the shot clock was instituted, NBA teams were averaging 79.5 points a game. The year the clock was adopted, the point-per-game average jumped to an astonishing 93.1. That year, the Boston Celtics became the first NBA team to ever average over 100 points a game.

Hoopology

Danny Biasone's invention was originally called the **24-second clock**. As time went by however, it was given another, informal name, the **shot clock**.

From the NBA's inception in 1946 until 1963, the commissioner of the league was Maurice Podoloff. In a letter written to Nats' beat writer Bud Vander Veer in 1980, Podoloff had this to say about Danny Biasone's invention:

> *In the entire history of the NBA, Danny is its most important member and will continue to be so even after he is gone. His rule is and will be the most important rule in the entire history of the NBA. In no sport was a rule adopted that had the consequences that Danny's did.*

Appropriately, Danny Biasone's Syracuse Nationals won the 1954–55 NBA Championship, edging out the Pistons 92–91 in a Game 7 thriller.

The Rise of the Mighty Celtics

With Mikan now retired and a new shot clock to keep things moving, the NBA was poised to make a splash. That splash came prior to the 1956–57 season, when the Celtics' coach and general manager Red Auerbach traded All-Star Ed Macauley and draft rights to Cliff Hagan to the St. Louis Bombers for the draft rights to a center out of the University of San Francisco named Bill Russell.

Tip-In

The University of San Francisco basketball team won two NCAA titles with Bill Russell as a player.

Russell joined an established team that already had two future Hall of Fame guards in Bob Cousy and Bill Sharman. Those two had the ability to put the ball in the basket, and Russell, a defensive genius, secured the defense.

In only his first year in the league, Russell, who joined the team late due to the Olympics, led the Celtics to their first NBA championship. It was the beginning of the greatest dynasty any sport has ever known—11 championships over the next 13 years.

Jack Twyman of the Cincinnati Royals drives against the New York Knicks during a game at Madison Square Garden in 1958.

Russell was a defensive, shot-blocking, rebounding phenomenon, the likes of which the NBA had never seen. His uncanny timing and commitment to team basketball made the Celtics a joy to watch. The team routinely had seven or eight players score in double figures, but they also never had an NBA scoring champion among them. They were a team in the best sense of the word.

The Celtics won the NBA Championship again in 1959 and seemed poised to run the table for as far as the eye could see. No one could stop Bill Russell, or so it seemed.

However, on the horizon was, possibly, the greatest player the NBA would ever produce. Seven-foot-one Wilt Chamberlain was an offensive juggernaut who possibly could match Russell's defensive prowess. Who was better? Whose teams would win? The titanic struggles of these two legendary players would shape much of NBA basketball in the 1960s.

Inside Stuff

According to Terry Pluto's book about the early days of the NBA, *Tall Tales*, in Game 3 of the NBA Finals of 1957, Boston was playing at the St. Louis Hawks, with the series tied one to one. Before the game, Bill Sharman was shooting free throws, and they were consistently coming up short. This was odd as Sharman was one of the best free-throw shooters—ever.

Sharman complained to his coach, Red Auerbach, saying that the basket was too high, that it was not the regulation 10 feet. Red walked out to the middle of the court, and was screaming and demanding that the basket be measured. With the crowd watching, the owner of the Hawks, Ben Kerner, came down to the floor to see what was going on.

Kerner was yelling at Auerbach, Red was yelling back, and then, according to Celtics guard Bob Cousy, "as Kerner came closer, [Red] just turned around and leveled him. He really cold-cocked, Kerner." Kerner's nose was bleeding, but he got up, everyone went back to their places, and the game started.

The Least You Need to Know

- James Naismith invented basketball in 1891.

- The Basketball Association of America was created in 1946, and renamed the National Basketball Association in 1949.

- The 24-second clock changed the game.

- The Minneapolis Lakers were the league's first dynasty.

1960s: The Celtics and Their Rivals

In This Chapter

◆ Wilt: The Big Dipper

◆ New players emerge

◆ The Celtics continue to dominate

◆ Challengers to the throne

The '60s were a new era. Gone were Dwight D. Eisenhower and the stuffy '50s. In was JFK and Camelot. The new president had said that this was a new generation, one that had a "rendezvous with history," and almost everywhere you looked, things were changing—new fashion, new ideas, and new politics dominated the landscape.

But throughout the tumultuous decade, one thing remained the same, one thing didn't change, one thing was absolute. The Celtics were the best team in professional basketball, period.

As the decade dawned, they had already won two of the previous three NBA championships, and their core of Bob Cousy, Bill Sharman, Frank Ramsey, Jim Loscutoff, Tom Heinsohn, and Bill Russell seemed poised to run off a string of several more, unless someone, or some team, could stop them.

Wilton Norman Chamberlain

Wilt Chamberlain was dominant! He was a physically intimidating man, with an array of moves around the basket that made him the greatest offensive weapon the NBA had seen to that time, and arguably of all time.

The Little Dipper

Wilt Chamberlain was born on August 21, 1936. By the time he was eight years old, he was so tall that he had to pay for an adult ticket when he went to the movies, and by the time he was done growing, he was 7' 1$\frac{1}{16}$".

Tip-In

Although Wilt once said, "My height has been primarily responsible for my success in life, and I know that," the truth is, Wilt had a lot more going for him than just height.

There are plenty of seven-foot NBA journeymen who never came close to the remarkable success that Wilt had. He combined his height with great skill, passion for the game, a will to win at everything he tried, agility and strength, and a fierce love of competition. Combined, this made Wilt Chamberlain one of the best ever to play the game, and to many, *the* greatest to ever play the game.

Tip-In

During his senior year in high school, Wilt averaged 50 points a game for most of the season.

Tall as he was at such an early age, Wilt naturally gravitated to basketball. He was made a starter on Overbrook High School's basketball team in Philadelphia as a ninth-grade freshman. During the summer, he would work as a bellhop at Kutsher's Country Club in the Catskills. It was there that he first met Red Auerbach, coach of the Celtics. Their paths would cross again many times (probably too many for Wilt).

The Big Dipper

It was clear that Wilt (a.k.a. the Big Dipper), was going to be one for the ages, and Eddie Gottlieb, the owner of the Philadelphia Warriors, didn't want to let the young center get away. So Gottlieb got the NBA to adopt a new rule that allowed teams to draft high school players based upon geography: No matter where they eventually went to college, local boys could be drafted and counted on to fill the seats. So Wilt would begin his career as a Philadelphia Warrior, but in the meantime, college called.

He went to the University of Kansas, and although he never won a championship there, he came close. As a sophomore, his team lost in three overtimes to North Carolina in the NCAA championship game. After three years, he quit (unheard of at the time) and joined the Harlem Globetrotters. The Globies paid Wilt $65,000 that year, at a time when most NBA players were making about $15,000. Playing guard, Wilt loved the travel and antics of the team, but after a year, the Warriors owned his rights, and in 1959, Wilt Chamberlain became an NBA player.

> **Inside Stuff**
>
> Wilt scored 50 or more points seven times in his rookie year, and the Warriors improved by 17 games over the previous season.

There had never been anything like Wilt in any professional basketball league. At 7' 1" and 275 pounds, he was bigger and stronger than everyone else. He was a dunking, scoring, one-man offensive wrecking crew. The NBA record book was in for a major revision once the Big Dipper joined the league.

In his first season, 1959–60, he averaged 37.6 points, and 27 rebounds, per game. To understand just how amazing that second statistic is, consider that in the 2001–02 season, Ben Wallace won the rebounding title with 13 rebounds a game. Wilt was also Rookie of the Year and the league MVP that year.

(However, it must also be noted that the NBA in 1960 was a far different league than the NBA today. Back then, there were only eight teams—four in the East and four in the West—and only about 100 NBA players total. Today there are 29 teams and about 400 players. Player averages are a bit skewed when comparing eras because there are more players but the same number of statistics to go around.)

Yet the new decade began much as the last one ended. The Celtics won the championship again, beating St. Louis four games to three.

The Most Amazing Single-Game Performance, Ever

On March 2, 1962, Wilt Chamberlain's legend grew by leaps and bounds. On that night, in tiny Hershey, Pennsylvania, the Philadelphia Warriors were playing the New York Knicks.

That season, Wilt was already *averaging* 50 points a game, and he had already scored 78 points in one game earlier in the season. So it shouldn't have been much of a surprise that on some night, this night, Wilt would head toward the century mark in points scored.

With only 4,124 people in attendance, Wilt started strong and picked up steam as the game progressed. He had 23 points in the first quarter, and was nine for nine from the free-throw line.

In his book, *Tall Tales*, Terry Pluto quotes Wilt as saying,

> *When I got into the 80s, I heard the fans yelling for 100. I thought, "Man, these people are tough. Eighty isn't good enough. I'm tired. I've got 80 points and no one has ever scored 80." At one point, I said to [teammate] Al Attles, "I got 80, what's the difference between 80 and 100?" But the guys kept feeding me the ball.*

If he was to score 100 on this magical night, Wilt would need 31 points in the fourth quarter. According to broadcaster Bill Campbell (one of the few people who actually saw the game; it is not on film—but a fourth-quarter radio broadcast does exist), "It was something you couldn't believe. As he got closer and closer to 100, he just seemed to will it."

Hoopology

When a player is fouled, he gets a free shot from a line 15 feet from the basket, hence the name **free throw**, or **foul shot**.

It took Wilt playing all 48 minutes of the game, but he did it. With 46 seconds left to play, Wilt scored point number 100. And, maybe most amazingly for him, he hit 28 of 32 from the foul line.

According to Wilt, the fouling, triple-teaming defense that the Knicks used that night was the reason he scored 100. Never one for modesty, Wilt later said, "Scoring 100 points is a lot, but … I maybe could have scored 140 if they had played straight-up basketball." Wilt's Warriors won the game, 169–147.

Al Attles, Wilt's teammate at the time, had a perfect 8–8 night from the field that night, and 1–1 from the free throw line, for 17 points. Attles always remarks about that night: "Wilt and I combined for 117 points!"

As the years have gone by, Wilt's 100-point night has taken on mythic proportions. It is said that before the game, Wilt set records on two pinball machines inside the Hershey arena lobby. Moreover, as Wilt remarked in *Tall Tales*:

> *As I've traveled the world, I've probably had 10,000 people tell me that they saw my 100-point game at Madison Square Garden. Well, the game was in Hershey and there were about 4,000 there. But that's fine. I have memories of the game and so do they, and over the years the memories get better. It's like your first girlfriend—the picture you have in your head is always better than how she looked in real life.*

Box Score of the 100-Point Game

Warriors	Pos.	FGA	FGM	FTA	FTM	Pts.
Paul Arizin	F	18	7	2	2	16
Tom Meschery	F	12	7	2	2	16
Wilt Chamberlain	C	63	36	32	28	100
Guy Rodgers	G	4	1	12	9	11
Al Attles	G	8	8	1	1	17
York Larese		5	4	1	1	9
Ed Conlin		4	0	0	0	0
Joe Ruklick		1	0	2	0	0
Ted Luckenbill		0	0	0	0	0
Totals		115	63	52	43	169

Knicks	Pos.	FGA	FGM	FTA	FTM	Pts.
Willie Naulls	F	22	9	15	13	31
Johnny Green	F	7	3	0	0	6
Darrall Imhoff	C	7	3	1	1	7
Richie Guerin	G	29	13	17	13	39
Al Butler	G	13	4	0	0	8
Cleveland Butler		26	16	1	1	33
Dave Budd		8	6	1	1	13
Donnie Butcher		6	3	6	4	10
Totals		118	57	41	33	147

Legends of the Fall

The 1960s also saw the emergence of several players, aside from Wilt, who would go on to become some of the all-time greatest in NBA history.

Elgin Baylor

Elgin Baylor, a 6' 5" forward from the University of Seattle, was drafted by the Minneapolis Lakers in 1958. Baylor was a new breed of player, foreshadowing the high-flying, above-the-rim style that would later become so popular.

He had an uncanny ability to "hang" in the air, and as more earthbound players dropped to the ground, he would seemingly still be up there, laying the ball in the basket. In his first season, he averaged almost 25 points a game and once scored 55 points in a single game.

Jerry West

In 1960, the Lakers moved from Minneapolis to Los Angeles, and drafted a kid out of Cabin Creek, West Virginia, by the name of Jerry West. West and Baylor were two for the ages, and together they made the Lakers of the 1960s into a powerhouse, albeit the second most powerful powerhouse around.

Hoopology

When a player scores 10 or more points, assists, blocks, or rebounds, he is said to be in "double figures" in that category. When that player has double figures in three categories in one night, he is said to have a **triple double**. It is the sign of an all-around great game for a player.

Jerry West was also known as "Mr. Clutch" for his uncanny ability to hit a game-winning shot just as time ran out. His beautiful style of play and classic jump shot, along with his late-game heroics, made his outline the perfect choice for the NBA logo.

Oscar Robertson: Mr. Triple Double

These days, when a player hits a *triple double*, it often leads ESPN's *SportsCenter*. How good was Oscar Robertson, a.k.a. "the Big O"? In 1961–62, he *averaged* a triple double every game: 30.8 points, 12.5 rebounds, and 11.4 assists. No other player in the history of the NBA has ever duplicated this feat.

Green Reign

Between 1957 and 1969, the Boston Celtics won 11 NBA championships in 13 years; in all likelihood, a feat that will never be duplicated in all of sports. This run included an astounding eight championships in a row, from 1959 to 1966. How talented was this group? In 1960, for example, future Hall of Famers Sam Jones, K.C. Jones, and Frank Ramsey *were not even starters.*

Guided by the legendary Red Auerbach, the Celtics were the ultimate basketball team. Players sacrificed for the good of the whole, they knew and were committed to their role, and winning came before individual statistics or glory. In the end, this combination of skill, tenacity, commitment, teamwork, supreme self-confidence, and basketball smarts defeated almost every challenger on the block.

The Celtics rarely lost during the 1960s.

And because Auerbach was not only the coach but the general manager, too, Red the GM was able to get the players Red the coach wanted. And Red the GM paid them what Red the coach thought they were worth. It was a system that didn't work for everyone, but boy, did it work for the Celtics.

Inside Stuff

(A player today) makes a million dollars, anything after that, it's just numbers. So you have to appeal to his pride, his wanting to win, and you disregard the money. The only thing I did years ago was tell them, "Your salary is dependent solely on what I see with my eyes. Statistics don't matter, contributions matter. Winning matters." You rewarded people that way.

—Arnold "Red" Auerbach

Maybe nothing epitomized the Celtics more than Auerbach's victory cigar. When the game was clearly in hand, when victory was all but assured, and before the final buzzer sounded, the Celtics' coach would light up a cigar in premature celebration of his team's success. Nothing infuriated opponents or typified Celtic bravado more than that damn cigar. But most teams were unable to put it out, either.

Yet, while Red was undeniably a great basketball coach, he was maybe even shrewder as a GM. His first coup was nabbing Bill Russell, and it wasn't easy. Russell had started in the 1956 Olympics in Sydney, Australia, and his team at USF was a championship one (at one point, winning 55 games in a row).

Standing in Auerbach's way were the two teams drafting ahead of the Celtics that year—the Rochester Royals and the St. Louis Hawks. Auerbach explained to Celtics' owner Walter Brown how special Russell was, how the Celtics had to get him, and Brown went to work.

He called the owner of the Royals and told him that if Rochester would pass on drafting "Russ," he (Brown) would make sure that the Ice Capades would stop in Rochester two weeks later. As Auerbach later told *Cigar Aficionado*, "Walter got him the Ice Capades, and [Royal's manager Les Harrison said in return], 'I give you my word that we'll stay away from Russell.'"

With Russell on board, the Celtics won the championship in 1960 (defeating the Hawks). Clearly, teams would have to try something radical if Boston was to be defeated. In 1961, Philadelphia Warrior coach Frank McGuire thought he had the answer: Wilt Chamberlain.

> **Hoopology**
>
> Every year, one coach in the NBA is named the Coach of the Year. The name of the trophy the Coach of the Year receives is the **Red Auerbach Trophy.**

Can Anyone Stop This Team?

McGuire decided that if he let his scoring machine go, really go, his team might just be able to beat Boston. As McGuire said to Wilt at the time:

> **Tip-In**
>
> Maybe even more remarkable than Wilt's 50.4 points per game that season was that he played all but eight minutes of the *entire season*, averaging 48.5 minutes a game (including overtimes).

"We aren't as good as Boston, not with you getting 37, 38 points a game like you did your first two years. We can't get enough scoring out of the rest of our guys to equal them. But if you can score 50, I think the rest of the guys can make up the difference to get us even with Boston."

And so that was the Warriors' game plan. Let Wilt score, and see what the other guys could do. That is why in the 1961–62 season Wilt averaged a never-to-be-repeated, unbelievable, 50.4 points per game.

But it was not enough. In Game 7 of the Eastern Conference Finals that year, the Celtics' *leprechaun* helped Sam Jones hit the game winner over the Warriors with only two seconds left. The Celtics went on to beat the Los Angeles Lakers in seven games to win the championship.

Red Auerbach and his Celtics won the championship again in 1963 (defeating the Lakers), 1964 (defeating the now Golden State Warriors), 1965 (defeating the Lakers), and 1966 (defeating, you guessed it, the Lakers.) The legendary coach hung up his coaching sneakers in 1966, although he would stay on and guide the team from the front office, in one form or another, into the new millennium.

Although Jerry West and Elgin Baylor made a formidable duo, they were not enough to stop the Celtics. Year after year, they came up just short, breaking the hearts of their fans, and vowing that next year things would be different. They never were. (The Lakers wouldn't beat the Celtics in an NBA Finals until 1985.)

The pain of losing to the Celtics was no less for the self-described "Goliath" ("nobody roots for Goliath"), Wilt Chamberlain. Wilt was undeniably the best offensive player the league had ever seen, yet it was Bill Russell whose teams won championship after championship.

The epic battles between these two rivals have become the stuff of legend. There was Wilt, scoring at will, and there was Russ, winning seemingly at will. By the end of the decade, Wilt had been unfairly labeled a "loser." He was determined to change that perception.

The 1966–67 Philadelphia 76ers, who were the ex-Syracuse Nationals, were built to beat the Celtics. Quite a few call it the best team ever assembled. Alex Hannum, one of the great coaches of the era, was brought in. Wilt was teamed with Billy Cunningham and Chet

Hoopology

Boston Celtics' lore has it that a lucky **leprechaun** graced the fabled parquet floor of Boston Garden, tapping in errant shots and otherwise helping the boys in green win games.

Inside Stuff

"I never bought into that whole Internet thing. I don't even own a fax machine."

—Red Auerbach

Tip-In

How different was the NBA in the 1960s? In 1963–64, for example, San Francisco Warrior (the Warriors moved from Philadelphia to San Francisco in 1963) coach Alex Hannum decided that his team needed to focus on defense if it wanted to win games. He was successful, and that year, the Warriors led the league in fewest points allowed—102.6!

Inside Stuff

"Many have called our competition [Russell and Chamberlain] the greatest rivalry in the history of sports. We didn't have a rivalry; we had a genuinely fierce competition that was based on friendship and respect. We just loved playing against each other."

—Bill Russell

Walker, and for the first time in eight years, he did not win the scoring title (although he did win the rebounding title—24.2 a game.)

But it mattered little, because the team was winning. Racing out to an astounding 46–4 start in the first 50 games, the Warriors eventually went 68–13. Facing the Celtics (now coached by Bill Russell) in the Eastern Finals, Wilt finally had his day as his Warriors defeated the Celtics 4–1, ending the Celtics' remarkable eight-year championship run. The Sixers then went on to beat the San Francisco Warriors 4–2.

It was the 1967 76ers who finally stopped the Celtics run.

Old Habits Die Hard

In 1968 (altogether now), the Celtics won the championship again. *Player-coach* Bill Russell proved that he could perform both duties and still dominate a game. The Celtics beat (altogether now, again!) the Lakers in six games. Russell also made history that year, becoming the first African-American coach in the history of the NBA.

Like the '67 76ers, the 1968–69 Lakers were built to beat the Celtics. Joining Jerry West and Elgin Baylor was none other than Wilt Chamberlain. While some observers thought that the Lakers had assembled the greatest team of all time, the three superstars actually didn't mesh together all that well. There were, as they say, not enough basketballs to go around, and when Elgin would drive the lane, he often found Wilt there.

In a dramatic Game 7, Don Nelson hit one of the most improbable shots in NBA history. With the Celtics up by one with seconds remaining, and the ball loose, Nelson grabbed the ball, shot it, the ball hit the back of the rim, went straight up, was tapped by the leprechaun, and went straight in. Celtics win, Lakers lose, and the beat goes on.

With that win, the end was in sight for the aging Celtics. Russell retired after the season, and the dynasty was, happily for the rest of the league, finally over.

Hoopology

A phenomenon of the early NBA was that some players not only played, but coached the team as well. Aside from Bill Russell, these **player-coaches** included Lenny Wilkens, Buddy Jeannette, Dave DeBusschere, Richie Guerin, Paul Seymour, Bobby Wanzer, and Al Cervi.

Inside Stuff

Jerry West had a triple double in that last game—42 points, 13 rebounds, and 12 assists. He was the only player ever in the history of the NBA to be named the Finals MVP, and *play on the losing team.*

The Least You Need to Know

- Wilt Chamberlain, who once scored 100 points in a game, may be the greatest player of all time.
- Jerry West, Elgin Baylor, and Oscar Robertson were also timeless players.
- The Celtics dominated the 1960s.
- The 76ers had a modicum of success against the Celtics, but the Lakers were unsuccessful against them.

1970s: The Calm Before the Storm

In This Chapter

- ◆ New decade, new champs
- ◆ New eligibility rules
- ◆ The ABA emerges
- ◆ A new league

With Russell's retirement, the opposing teams breathed a collective sigh of relief. The dominance of the Boston Celtics was now probably over, a new decade was dawning, and in all likelihood, a new champion would emerge.

What no one knew was that the '70s would be almost the exact opposite of the '60s. Whereas the '60s were a decade dominated by one team, the '70s would be a decade of parity. Eight different teams would win the championship, and the All-Star Game would be split evenly, 5–5, between East and West.

The real news would be made off the court, where challenges and changes in the rules and in the size of the league would have the biggest impact on the game.

The New NBA

The 1969–70 NBA was much different than that of even a few years before. Expansion had brought eight new teams into the league by 1970:

- Seattle SuperSonics
- San Diego Rockets
- Detroit Pistons
- Baltimore Bullets
- Buffalo Braves
- Cleveland Cavaliers
- Phoenix Suns
- Portland Trail Blazers

In 1970, the league also made another significant change that stands to this day. Instead of two divisions (Eastern and Western), the NBA divided itself into two conferences (Eastern and Western), with two divisions within each. By 1970, the new league looked like this:

NBA, circa 1970

Eastern Conference		Western Conference	
Atlantic Division	**Central Division**	**Midwest Division**	**Pacific Division**
New York	Baltimore	Milwaukee	Los Angeles
Philadelphia	Atlanta	Chicago	San Francisco
Boston	Cincinnati	Phoenix	San Diego
Buffalo	Cleveland	Detroit	Seattle
			Portland

The NBA had become a growing league with 17 teams; only five years earlier, it had but nine teams. By 1970, the modern NBA as we know it today was forming.

"A Decade of Parity"

What distinguishes the great teams of this era is that they were in fact great *teams*. The theory in today's NBA is to get two superstars on the same team, add some role players, and shoot for the stars. See, for example …

◆ The Chicago Bulls: Michael Jordan, Scottie Pippen, and Co.

◆ The Los Angeles Lakers: Shaquille O'Neal, Kobe Bryant, et al.

◆ The San Antonio Spurs: Tim Duncan, David Robinson, etc.

But back in the '70s, teams tended to have several very good players, rather than a couple of great ones. The Celtics epitomized this (although it can be argued that they were seven great players deep), and certainly the New York Knicks of 1969–70 exemplified the era.

That was one heck of a team. With Willis Reed anchoring at center, Dave DeBusschere and "Dollar Bill" Bradley on the wings, and Dick Barnett and Walt *"Clyde"* Frazier in the backcourt, the Knicks made for a great basketball team.

Hoopology

Walt Frazier played on the Knicks from 1967 to 1977. His flashy style, which included a Rolls Royce, fur coats, fedora hats, and hip sideburns, made him the toast of the town. Combined with his cool demeanor and clutch play on the court, he came to be known simply as **Clyde**.

Clyde always had style.

The championship that year came down to a clash between the hungry Lakers and the talented Knicks. Although Wilt was slowed by injury, it was Knicks center Willis Reed who tore a muscle in his right thigh in Game 5. He sat out Game 6, Wilt scored 45 points, and the series would come down to another classic Game 7—without Reed.

The Lakers had their chance, finally. No Bill Russell. Celtic Hall-of-Famer John Havlicek couldn't steal the ball, and the center of the opposition, both literally and figuratively, was out. And so, even though the game was in New York's Madison Square Garden, the Lakers and their faithful had reason to hope.

The lights dimmed. The national anthem played. The game was about to start. And just then, hobbling on one leg out of the locker room, was none other than the injured Willis Reed.

The Garden crowd went mad. Reed started the game, gimped his way up and down the court a few times, scored the first two baskets, came out, and the Knicks never looked back. Reed's inspirational play lead New York to an improbable 113–99 victory over the beleaguered Los Angeles Lakers. In that game, Walt Frazier had 36 points and 19 assists and several steals. As Clyde noted, "He [Reed] provided the inspiration and in a way, I provided the desperation."

The Stuff Champions Are Made Of

It would take the retirement of Hall of Famer Elgin Baylor for the Lakers to become the team they always thought they could be. Nine games into the 1971–72 season, Baylor decided that at 37, bad knees and all, he could no longer play up to his standards and hung 'em up. What happened next has never been duplicated in any professional sport, anywhere, anytime.

New coach Bill Sharman (of Celtic fame) placed Jim McMillian into the Laker starting lineup, alongside an aging Jerry West (33) and Wilt Chamberlain (35). Rounding out the starting five were Harold "Happy" Hairston at the other forward, and Gail Goodrich in the backcourt with West.

Thirty-Three Peat

The night that McMillian was placed in the starting lineup, something magical happened to the Lakers. They became one of those great *teams*, maybe the greatest single-season team ever. No longer just the "Big Three," this new Laker team was suddenly a dynamic, unselfish, beautiful basketball machine.

On November 5, 1971, the day after Baylor retired, the Lakers were playing in Baltimore. McMillian scored 22 points and pulled down 13 rebounds, and the boys from L.A. won 110–106.

Inside Stuff

By the time Elgin Baylor retired, he was considered an offensive genius. He was an 11-time All-Star, averaged 27.4 points per game (ppg) for his career, averaged 30 or more ppg three different times, averaged 38.3 ppg in 1961–62, and was the first NBA player ever to score more than 70 points, lighting the Knicks up for 71 on December 11, 1960.

What they didn't know, what no one could know, was that they would not lose again for a long, long time, until well into the next calendar year. Here are some highlights of that winning streak:

◆ The next night, Jerry West scored 30 points, and the now running-and-gunning Los Angeles Lakers beat up the Golden State Warriors 105–89. Showing also how different the NBA today is, then the Lakers played a now-unheard of third night in a row, and beat the Knicks on November 7.

◆ In Chicago on November 9, they won again. *The Los Angeles Herald-Examiner* says that one can "sense that a trend is developing."

◆ After the next win in Philadelphia, Coach Sharman offered to cancel practice the next day, but the players declined the offer. On November 12, the Lakers won their sixth in a row as role player Pat Riley played six minutes against the Seattle SuperSonics.

◆ The Lakers won their eleventh game in a row on November 21, beating the NBA Champion Milwaukee Bucks, despite 39 points by Kareem Abdul-Jabbar. Says Kareem, "The Lakers seem to have jelled."

◆ On November 28, the Lakers won yet again against the Seattle Supersonics (number 14). Riley started for an ill McMillian, and the Lakers finish the first unbeaten month in NBA history.

◆ Up until now, the most wins in a row for any NBA team was 20, by the 1970–71 Bucks. On December 10, the Lakers matched that record, beating the Phoenix Suns in *overtime*.

Hoopology

An NBA game is 48 minutes long. If the score is tied at the end of that time, the teams play a five-minute **overtime** period. They continue to do so until one team wins. (The most number of overtimes in any NBA game ever is six—Indianapolis at Rochester, January 6, 1951.)

Tip-In

After winning their twenty-seventh game in a row, now the longest win streak in professional sports history, Laker Wilt Chamberlain wasn't that impressed. Said Wilt, "I played with the Harlem Globetrotters and we won 445 in a row … and they were all on the road!"

♦ The Lakers won their 25th game in a row on December 19, beating the Philadelphia 76ers 154–132. That night, Wilt scored 32 points and pulled down an astounding 34 rebounds.

♦ In 1916, baseball's New York Giants won 26 games in a row, a record that stood throughout the twentieth century. But on December 22, 1971, the Lakers shattered that record, too, beating the Baltimore Bullets 127–120.

♦ On January 7, 1972, the streak reached 33 games in a row, as the Lakers beat the Atlanta Hawks by 44 points.

All good things must come to an end, and finally, on January 9, the Lakers' win streak was stopped at 33 by Kareem and the champion Bucks. The Lakers had not lost since Halloween night.

The 33-game win streak is a record that still endures, in all of professional sports.

Finally!

That Laker team went on to win 69 games that season, a number that would go unmatched for almost 25 years. The finals that year came down to a rematch of two years before—the Lakers against the Knicks. But this time, for the first time, Los Angeles had all the right ingredients. After seven unsuccessful trips to the NBA Finals, Jerry West and his Los Angeles Lakers finally won it all, beating New York four games to one.

The 1971-72 Lakers won 33 games in a row; a record that may never be matched.

Changes off the Court as Well

While it was heartening for many to see the Lakers finally get their due, legal changes off the court would have a far more long-lasting impact on the league.

The NBA Eligibility Rule

Up until 1971, NBA rules stated that a high school player had to wait for four years after graduation before he could be drafted by an NBA team. Although the rule did not require that a player go to college, that was certainly its intent.

Spencer Haywood was a gifted athlete who played on the 1968 U.S. Olympic team and who then played in the ABA with the Denver Nuggets for the 1969–70 season. He led the ABA in scoring (29.5) and rebounding (19.5) and won Rookie of the Year and MVP honors.

 **Hoopology**

A player must sign a contract with a team before he can step foot on the court. When he does put his name on the dotted line, he is said to have **signed,** and can now officially play for that team.

The problem was that four years had not passed since Haywood had graduated high school. The NBA said that Seattle's signing of Haywood violated league rules, and it threatened sanctions against the team.

Spencer Haywood thought that the rule was illegal, that he had the right to play for whomever wanted his services, whether or not four years had passed since he graduated high school. Haywood and his lawyers challenged the NBA's four-year eligibility rule, arguing in the courts that it violated the Sherman Antitrust Act.

Dawn of a New Era

The U.S. District Court for the Central District of California ruled in Spencer Haywood's favor. The court said that Haywood had the right to play in the NBA if Seattle wanted him, that the NBA's four-year eligibility rule violated the Sherman Antitrust Act, and that the NBA could not sanction the Sonics.

Spencer Haywood joined the Sonics near the end of the 1970–71 season, averaging 20 points over the last 33 games. Over the next five years, he made the All-Star team four times and the All-NBA First Team twice.

Inside Stuff

The Sherman Antitrust Act was passed into law in 1890 as a way to restrain the behemoth corporation of the time, Standard Oil. The intent of the law is to prevent companies from thwarting competition, trade, and commerce while also outlawing monopolies.

The NBA is subject to the antitrust laws because the agreements by and between the owners could conceivably be considered anticompetitive. That was Spencer Haywood's argument.

Technical Foul

"The real superstar is a man or a woman raising six kids on $150 a week."

—Spencer Haywood

Because of Haywood's successful lawsuit, the NBA had to change its eligibility rules. The end result is what you see today—high school graduates like Kevin Garnett of the Minnesota Timberwolves and Kobe Bryant of the Los Angeles Lakers can declare themselves eligible for the NBA Draft. And if teams like them, they can draft them.

The Late, Great American Basketball Association

In 1965 the American Football League and the National Football League were on the verge of a merger. The mayor of Buena Park, California, Dennis Murphy, wanted to get an AFL franchise into the area quickly so that when the merger came, they would have an NFL team. But the merger happened faster than Murphy anticipated, and they had no team in place.

Murphy looked around and noticed that there was only one basketball league. He concluded that even though his plan to create an AFL franchise that would be absorbed by the NFL didn't pan out, a similar tactic could work in basketball. Murphy knew some people, made some calls, garnered some interest, and before too long a nascent league was forming that was supposed to challenge the NBA.

Inside Stuff

Who is the youngest player ever to play in the NBA? None other than Kobe Bryant. Kobe was drafted out of high school and entered his first NBA game at the tender age of 18 years, 2 months, and 11 days.

Needing a commissioner with some stature, they decided to see if they could tap the legendary George Mikan, who had played for the Minne-apolis Lakers, for the job. Mikan, now an attorney living in Minneapolis, was interested. As ABA executive Mike Storen later put it, "[Mikan's] credibility was something you couldn't buy." So in 1967, the ABA was born. Mikan was its commissioner, and its innovations many.

Some Healthy Competition for the NBA

Although the ABA was created in the late '60s, its impact on the NBA really occurred in the 1970s and beyond.

How to describe the ABA between 1967 and 1976? It was the Wild West show of basketball, the anti-NBA, and street ball, all rolled into one. It was wild hair, a wild ball, and wilder shots. And it was responsible for the above-the-rim, up-and-down, fast-break style of ball you see in the NBA today.

NBA agent Ron Grinker, in the great book about the ABA, *Loose Balls* by Terry Pluto, is quoted as saying that the ABA was "glitzy, get the ball out and let's run and jump … and we'll make things up as we go along." According to Billy Cunningham, who played in both the NBA and the ABA, "The ABA had a huge impact on the NBA. The ABA players and coaches forced a faster pace of the game, they pushed the ball up the court, they created a more exciting brand of basketball."

Technical Foul

The ABA never patented the red, white, and blue ball, and consequently, could never license it. Any company that wanted to could create and sell a red, white and blue ball, and did.

The Red, White and Blue Ball

The first, and most striking, difference was the ball. Says Mikan in *Tall Tales*, "The ABA had a red, white, and blue ball because I said it would have one. We wanted our own identity, and the ball is the symbol of basketball, isn't it? To this day, you hear ABA, and people talk about the ball."

Although some people in the new league hated the ball, by and large, it was a huge hit. Kids were playing with a red, white, and blue ball wherever you looked; it gave the *American Basketball Association* an identity; and besides, it was cool.

The Three-Point Shot

Contrary to popular belief, the ABA was not the first professional basketball league to adopt a three-point shot. In 1961, Abe Saperstein, founder of the Harlem Globetrotters, created the American Basketball League (ABL). Existing for only 19 months, the ABL did have one lasting thing about it—it was the first to use a three-point shot.

ABA founder Dennis Murphy always liked the idea of a three-point shot. "It is exactly what our league was supposed to be about," Murphy later said, "something wild, a little out of the ordinary …."

The three-point line is 22 feet from the basket in each corner, and 23 feet, 9 inches from above the key. The genius of the shot is two-fold:

◆ First, it opens up the game. Without the three-point shot, teams were clogging the middle of the lane, knowing that the longer shot was harder to make. Adding an extra point for a distance shot forced defenses to be more honest and guard everyone.

◆ Second, the three-point shot is awfully exciting. Seeing someone shoot from that far out is always fun, and, when combined with the its ability to allow a team to catch up quickly, it makes the shot the basketball equivalent of a home run, as Mikan put it.

It didn't take the NBA long to realize the value of the three-point shot—the league adopted the shot for the 1979–80 season. History will note that Chris Ford of the Boston Celtics made the first three-point-shot ever in the NBA. That season, the NBA Champion Lakers *only* made 20 three-pointers *all season*.

The Slam Dunk Contest

Another ABA innovations was the Slam Dunk contest, which was held at the ABA All-Star Game and was designed to get the league noticed and get fannies in the seats. The first contest, held in 1976, featured five of the best dunkers around, in any league:

◆ Julius "Dr. J" Erving

◆ David Thompson

◆ Artis Gilmore

◆ George Gervin

◆ Billy Cunningham

Although Thompson did the first 360-degree dunk, it was *Dr. J* who stole the show. Julius Erving took one of those red, white, and blue balls, started at the other end of the court, ran toward the basket, and when he hit the free throw line, took off, dunking the ball after flying 15 feet in the air.

The NBA adopted the Slam Dunk contest in 1984.

Hoopology

Julius Erving, one of the greatest to ever play the game, is usually called by the nickname he earned while at the University of Massachusetts, **Dr. J**, or simply, the Doctor.

The ABA Challenge

While the new league was fun and wild, it never seemed to represent much of a threat to the NBA—that is, until some top-name talent bolted to the new league. Aside from Dr. J, Gervin, Gilmore, and Thompson, other great players that played in the ABA at one time or another include Rick Barry, Connie Hawkins, Dan Issel, and Spencer Haywood.

Yet, despite raiding the NBA's players (and coaches and refs, too), the ABA was always a league on the verge of collapse. Arenas would be lucky to be half full, teams moved or collapsed, and players were often a misbegotten lot.

Although the league had begun play in 1967 with 10 teams, by 1976, the ABA was down to only six. The league folded and four teams joined the NBA: the Indiana Pacers, the Denver Nuggets, the New York Nets, and the San Antonio Spurs. The Kentucky Colonels and the Spirits of St. Louis went to that great playground in the sky.

To get in the NBA, each of the remaining four ABA teams had to pay the NBA $3.2 million, although the Nets had to pay the Knicks $4.8 million more for infringing on the Knicks' territorial rights.

Those players whose teams didn't join the NBA were subject to a dispersal draft. Picks number one and two were Artis Gilmore—to the Chicago Bulls—and Maurice Lucas—to the Portland Trail Blazers. The biggest name in the ABA, Julius Erving, went to Philadelphia when the Nets were forced to sell his contract to help pay off its debt to the Knicks.

Tip-In

Bob Costas got his first job in sports as the radio announcer for the Spirits of St. Louis, at the age of 22, in 1974.

At the 1977 NBA All-Star Game, 10 of the 24 players were from the once high-flying, unconventional, late, great ABA.

Rounding Out the Decade

That same season, 1976–77, saw the emergence of an unlikely NBA champ. The Portland Trail Blazers had only been in existence for six years. But the team had drafted Bill Walton with the first overall pick in the 1974 draft, and then picked up Maurice Lucas in the ABA dispersal draft. Under new coach and future Hall-of-Famer Jack Ramsay, the Blazers posted their first winning record (49–33) and made it to the playoffs for the first time in franchise history.

Portland met the Sixers and their new star, Dr. J, in the Finals. The Blazers lost the first two games and things looked bleak for the Cinderella team. But Walton, Lucas, and Co. proved to be too much, beating Philly four straight to take the series 4–2, and in the process, creating Blazermania inside Rip City.

The '70s ended with the Washington Bullets and the Seattle SuperSonics meeting for the championship two years in a row. Washington won in 1978, and Seattle paid them back in 1979.

At 6'7", Wes Unseld proved that you don't have to be tall to dominate under the boards.

The decade of parity was now over. With the addition of the four former ABA teams, the NBA now had 22 teams. It seemed poised for the next level.

What came next, the NBA of the 1980s, would come to be viewed by many as the Golden Age of NBA Basketball.

The Least You Need to Know

- The Los Angeles Lakers finally slew their demons in 1972.
- Spencer Haywood's legal challenge changed the league, allowing players to join the NBA right out of high school.
- The emergence of the ABA changed the NBA in many ways.

4

1980s: The Golden Era

In This Chapter

- ◆ Magic and Larry revive the league
- ◆ The Celtics and Lakers, revisited
- ◆ The battle continues
- ◆ The Pistons Rev Up the NBA

As the 1980s dawned, the NBA was changing in many ways. The popular three-point shot was now part of the NBA game, the New Orleans Jazz moved to Utah, and teams began to play interdivision rivals more. But the biggest change came with the emergence of two players who would catapult the league into worldwide prominence.

Magic and Larry, Together Again

In 1979, the Michigan State Spartans went up against the Indiana State Sycamores in the NCAA championship game. Michigan State was led by a 6' 9'' charismatic point guard named Earvin "Magic" Johnson. Indiana State had its own very special player in Larry Bird.

Inside Stuff

The term *March Madness* has come to be equated with the NCAA basketball tournament, but the term is actually pretty old. March Madness was first used in a 1939 *Illinois Interscholastic Magazine* article to describe the state's crazed, annual high school basketball tournament. The moniker stuck, and was later adopted by the NCAA.

The hype going into the game was unbelievable. Almost single-handedly, these two great players turned the NCAA basketball tournament into a cultural phenomenon, on par possibly with the Super Bowl and the World Series. "March Madness" had become a national event.

The game, when it was finally played, was won by Magic and Michigan State 75–64, surprising because Indiana State was unbeaten until then. Although it was the first time these two great players met in a championship game, it would by no means be the last. Theirs would be a rivalry that would reshape sports.

The Magic Man Emerges

Earvin Johnson was born on August 14, 1959, in Lansing, Michigan, the sixth of 10 children. Earvin became obsessed with basketball at an early age, often sleeping with his first basketball. Neighbors found him playing ball before school, after school, and into the night. They dubbed him "June Bug" because he was always flitting around the court.

But the nickname that stuck came when Earvin was 15 years old, playing as a sophomore for Everett High School. That night, Earvin …

- ◆ Scored 36 points.
- ◆ Pulled down 18 rebounds.
- ◆ Passed off for 16 assists.

A local sportswriter who was covering the game dubbed him "Magic," and that his been his name ever since.

Tip-In

In his three seasons on the team, Magic Johnson led Everett High School to a 73–5 record.

As a high school senior, one of his closest friends died in a car accident. The team dedicated the season to him, vowed to win the state title in his memory, and did. In the championship game, Magic scored 34 points and grabbed 14 rebounds.

Johnson's next stop was Michigan State. Proving that he had the ability to win wherever he went, Magic transformed the 10–17 Spartans into a team that would win its first Big Ten title in 19 years.

The next year, his team beat Bird's Indiana State team, and Magic decided to turn pro.

Inside Stuff

Magic and Bird competed in many ways. In 1979, Bird was named the Naismith College Basketball Player of the Year, but Johnson was named the NCAA Final Four MVP. When Johnson was signed by the Los Angeles Lakers the next year, he received the most amount of money ever for a rookie. When Bird signed a short time later, the Boston Celtics gave him a higher salary. Bird was named Rookie of the Year that year, but Johnson was named the NBA Finals MVP.

Larry Legend

Larry Joe Bird, the fourth child of Joe and Georgia Bird, was born on December 7, 1956, in French Lick, Indiana. Growing up, Bird didn't seem to be the natural athlete that Johnson was, but by his senior year at Springs Valley High School, he was averaging 30.6 points and 20 rebounds a game. And whatever Bird may have lacked in foot speed and leaping ability, he more than made up for in court savvy, killer instincts, and an uncanny shooting ability.

Bird initially opted to attend Indiana University and play for Bobby Knight, but after only 24 days, he decided that the campus was too big, and headed home, back to French Lick. He hitchhiked home and spent the next nine months working as a garbage collector and playing ball for the Northwood Institute.

Finally, with basketball beckoning, Bird decided to go to Indiana State, but because of eligibility rules, he had to sit out the first season. He was finally able to join the Sycamore squad in 1976, where he quickly became arguably the best collegiate basketball player in the country.

As fate would have it, Bird was ending his college career the same year that Magic decided to leave college. They would enter the NBA together, and together they would change that league.

> **Tip-In**
>
> The population of French Lick, Indiana, is about 2,000 people. It might surprise you to learn, then, that Larry Bird is not the only person from the tiny town to make it to the NBA. Sacramento Kings executive and former coach Jerry Reynolds also hails from French Lick.

The State of the Game

It was a good thing, too, because the league needed some changing. NBA basketball at this time was certainly not "fan-tastic!" Indeed, the opposite was more accurate. Although the '70s had seen the league grow, it had also gone stale, as the following facts indicate:

◆ The stars of the '60s—Wilt, Russell, Havlicek, West—had long since retired. The parity of the '70s had done nothing to replace them, and the ABA had done much to steal the NBA's thunder. The league seemed old.

◆ At the start of the 1977–78 season, Kareem Abdul-Jabbar punched Kent Benson in retaliation for an elbow two minutes into the first game, broke his hand, and was out for two months. In December, Kermit Washington hit Rudy Tomjanovich so hard that Rudy was out for the season and had to have his jaw, eye, and cheek reconstructed.

> **CAUTION**
> **Technical Foul**
> Indicative of the rough style of play in 1977–78, the NBA Finals were not even broadcast on prime-time television. Instead, games were taped and aired at 11:30 P.M.

◆ The conventional wisdom of the time was that all you had to do was turn on the "last two minutes" of a game and you would see all you needed to see; the rest was superfluous.

So it was fortuitous that Larry Bird and Magic Johnson came upon the league when they did. The league needed them, badly.

The Celtics and Lakers, Round Two

It was Red Auerbach who shrewdly nabbed Bird in the draft. While Larry was still a junior at Indiana State, Auerbach used the Celtics' draft pick (No. 6, 1978) to select the forward, knowing full well that Bird would be playing his senior year and wouldn't be coming to the Celtics for another year. No one had thought of doing that before. Bird joined the Celtics for the 1979–80 season.

The Lakers were more lucky than shrewd. In 1976, the Lakers lost an aging Gail Goodrich to the Jazz in free agency, and pursuant to league rules of the time, the Jazz thereafter owed Los Angeles a future *first-round* pick.

Inside Stuff

Who was drafted ahead of Larry Legend that year?

◆ The Portland Trail Blazers took Mychal Thompson with the first pick.

◆ Phil Ford went No. 2 to the Kansas City Kings.

◆ The Indiana Pacers picked Rick Robey third.

◆ The New York Knicks used the fourth pick to grab Micheal Ray Richardson.

◆ The Golden State Warriors used the fifth pick on Purvis Short.

In 1979, the Lakers were finally able to use that pick. A coin toss was held with the Chicago Bulls (who was tied with the Jazz for the worst record the year before), and the Lakers won the flip. They drafted Magic with the first overall selection in the draft.

The two players energized their respective teams—and the league—almost immediately. Magic had an enthusiasm for the game and that infectious grin—he was a sight for sore eyes. Bird was incredibly competitive and had a great feel for the game and big play. Ending up on opposite coasts, on teams that were already one of the greatest rivalries in sports, made their debut all the sweeter.

A Bird in Boston

Larry Bird's arrival in Boston couldn't have come at a better time. The season before he came to town, John Havlicek had retired and the Celtics had stumbled to a 29–53 record.

Bird teamed up with Dave Cowens at center, Cedric Maxwell in the frontcourt, and Nate "Tiny" Archibald and Chris Ford in the backcourt. With Bird on board, the team won 32 more games than the year before, posting a 61–21 record. As noted previously, Bird was named the NBA's Rookie of the Year.

Hoopology

When players want to join the NBA, they enter a draft. The NBA drafts players based on team records from the year before, with the worst teams getting the best chance to draft first. The best players available are, obviously, drafted in the **first round** of the draft. Additional players are drafted in the second round.

Hoopology

The Celtics played in the **Boston Garden** from 1946 until 1995. With its fabled parquet floor and rafters full of championship banners and retired numbers, the Garden was one of the most difficult places in the NBA for opposing teams to play.

Bird's ability to hit the game-winning shot, to score almost at will (from both inside and outside), his refusal to quit, and his court sense and presence gave the Celtics a new star the likes of which the team hadn't seen in quite awhile. The leprechaun was laughing again, and *Boston Garden* was hopping again.

Larry Bird always seemed to make the big play when it was needed most.

In the 1979–80 Eastern Conference Finals, the Celtics (who hadn't even made it to the playoffs the year before) were matched up against Julius Erving and the Philadelphia 76ers. The Sixers beat the Celtics in five games and advanced to the Finals.

Magic in La La Land

Magic Johnson had the same effect on the Lakers that Bird had on the Celtics. Teaming up with Kareem Abdul-Jabbar, Magic and his infectious style of basketball revived the now-mediocre franchise.

He was unlike anything the NBA had ever seen: A 6' 9" point guard who would rather win than look good, and who seemed to have *fun* while he played. He created a style of game in Los Angeles that they dubbed "Showtime." It was a run-and-gun, fast-breaking basketball extravaganza that caught, not just L.A., but the country by storm.

L.A. won 60 games that year (13 more than the year before), and came in first in the Pacific Division. They would meet the Philadelphia 76ers for the NBA Championship.

A Finals to Remember

After five games, the Lakers were up 3–2 in the finals, but Kareem twisted an ankle in Game 5 and couldn't make the trip to Philly for Game 6. With no center, the Lakers decided to try Magic at the position. He went on to have one of the most memorable games in NBA Finals history.

Besides center, Magic ended up playing every position at one time or another during the game. When later asked what position he played, because he seemed to be playing them all, Johnson said, "Well, I played center, a little forward, some guard. I tried to think up a name for it, but the best I could come up with was CFG-Rover."

In that memorable game, Magic scored 42 points, had 15 rebounds, and made 7 assists as the Lakers won the title with a 123–107 victory.

Tip-In

After his amazing performance in Game 6, Magic Johnson became the first rookie ever to be named the MVP of the finals. He was also only the third player ever to win NCAA and NBA titles back-to-back. The others were Bill Russell and Henry Bibby.

Our Turn!

The 1980–81 season was the first in which the Celtics' "Big Three" played together. Bird teamed up with new center Robert Parish and forward Kevin McHale to form probably the best frontcourt in NBA history. That first year together, the Celtics' Big Three led Boston to a record of 62–20, setting the stage for what would hopefully be the first NBA Championship in Boston in well over a decade.

Inside Stuff

Beware of Red Auerbach bearing a trade! Auerbach was undoubtedly one of the sharpest judges of basketball talent around and had a well-deserved reputation for picking the pockets of those with whom he traded. His trade for Bill Russell was but one example, but his trade for Parish and McHale cemented the deal.

In 1980, the Celtics had the first and thirteenth picks of the draft. Auerbach traded those to the Golden State Warriors for four-year veteran Parish and the third pick, which Red used to nab McHale. The Warriors used the first pick on Joe Barry Carroll and the 13th pick on Rickey Brown.

In the Eastern Conference Finals, the boys from Boston met up with the Sixers, battling Philly over a dramatic seven-game series. Game 7 ended with the Celtics beating the Sixers 91–90, to advance to the NBA Finals for the first time since Bill Russell retired in 1968–69.

The Celtics faced the Houston Rockets in those finals, and in Game 1, Bird hit one of his most memorable shots ever. He took a jumper from the right wing, saw that it would miss, raced in for the rebound, grabbed it on the left side of the basket, and as he was practically falling out of bounds, switched the ball to his left hand and canned a 10-footer. This guy was the real deal.

> **Tip-In**
> "No matter how good I am, I'm still just a hick from French Lick."
> —Larry Bird

The Celtics went on to win the championship 4–2, the franchise's 14th NBA title.

No, It's Our Turn!

The NBA was back, indeed! With the Lakers winning in 1980 and the Celtics in '81, with Bird and Magic providing a needed jolt of juice, and with teams playing up-and-down team basketball again, the NBA had become fun again. And when the NBA is fun, people watch.

One thing they saw was that both the Lakers and the Celtics seemed to be on a collision course with one another. It was only a matter of time before they would meet in the finals, a place where the Lakers had never beaten their archenemy.

During the 1981–82 season, the Lakers got a new coach. Paul Westhead had instituted a slower offense than the team generally, and Magic Johnson specifically, liked. Eleven games into the season, Westhead was sacked and one-time Laker player and *color analyst* Pat Riley was made head coach.

> **Hoopology**
> The person who calls the game on radio or TV is the play-by-play announcer. His sidekick, the one who is supposed to add flavor, context, and "color" to the broadcast, is the **color analyst**.

Riley reinstituted the Showtime offense and a tough, often underrated defense, and the team went on to win the Pacific Division again with 57 wins.

Boston won 63 games in the East, and the showdown loomed. But faced with another dramatic seven-game series with the 76ers, the Celtics lost this time, and Philadelphia met the Lakers instead. L.A. went on to win their second championship in three years, beating the 76ers 4–2. And wither the 76ers? Would these talented team ever win it all?

Yes

The Sixers had been expecting a title since Dr. J had arrived in 1977, but something always seemed to be missing. In the 1982–83 season, they thought they had found the missing ingredient—center Moses Malone.

By the time his career was over, Malone would be a 12-time All-Star, would lead the league in rebounding six times, would average more than 20 points a game 11 times, and would be MVP of the league three times. Moses Malone was a player.

The 1982–83 76ers suddenly became a great team. They won 65 games that year, and would have been the odds-on favorite to win it all, if the mighty Lakers hadn't stood in the way.

Yet the Sixers were not to be denied, not this time. They steamrolled through the playoffs, beating the Knicks in four straight, and then trouncing Milwaukee 4–1, to send them to the finals against you know who.

The Lakers were slowed by injury that year. Forward James Worthy had broken his leg in the last week of the season and Norm Nixon and Bob McAdoo were also hurt during the 1982–83 finals. The 76ers beat them 4–0. Dr. J finally had his NBA *championship ring*.

The Battle

It was during the next season, 1983–84, that the showdown that had been looming since Magic and Bird first battled in college was finally at hand. The Lakers had won the West, the Celtics the East, but only one could win the NBA Finals. Insiders had to give the edge to the Celtics because they had *home-court advantage*.

Tip-In

Moses Malone led Petersburg High School in Virginia to 50 straight wins and two state titles. He graduated in 1974 and the next year played for the Utah Stars of the ABA. He joined the Buffalo Braves of the NBA in 1976.

Hoopology

Every year, each member of the team that wins the NBA Championship gets a **championship ring,** commemorating the event.

Hoopology

Playoff series are always odd numbers, either best of five or best of seven. That means that one of the two teams will get to play at least one more game on their floor. That is called **home-court advantage.** Out of the two teams involved in a series, the team that gets it is the one that won more regular season games.

The rivalry between the Lakers and Celtics electrified the basketball world.

L.A won the first game at Boston, but Boston won the next game at home. The Lakers won Game 3 at home, but Boston won Game 4. Boston won Game 5 and L.A. won Game 6, tying the series at 3–3. It came down to Game 7.

The Lakers, who had never beaten Boston in a championship series and who had never won a Game 7 on the road, lost again. Despite all of their recent success, the Lakers couldn't get the Boston leprechaun off their back. The Celtics were champs again.

Skeletons

Eight losses in eight tries to the Celtics left that crop of Lakers hurting. They were bent on revenge, but beating Boston's Big Three was no easy feat. That year, 1984–85, the Lakers won 62 games, but the Celtics won 63. A rematch seemed inevitable.

Although Kareem was nearing the end of his career at 38 years of age, he and his sky-hook were still two of the greatest offensive forces in league history. This Lakers team was on a mission, and they played like it. Older, wiser, seasoned, and hungry, they were a well-oiled instrument.

But no matter how well the Lakers executed, they were not ready for what came to be known as the "Memorial Day Massacre." The Lakers had rolled (11–2) through the Western Conference on the way to their rematch with Boston. But Game 1 was a blowout for Boston, as the Celtics out-showtimed the Lakers, fastbreaking to a lopsided 148–114 romp.

Coach Pat Riley later called the thrashing "a blessing in disguise." The Lakers used the humiliating defeat to their advantage, and finally beat the dreaded Boston Celtics in an NBA Finals series, four games to two. The ghost of Christmas past was finally gone. Maybe sweetest of all, the Lakers won on the fabled parquet floor of Boston Garden.

> **Inside Stuff**
>
> 1984 was also memorable for its rookie class, which included Akeem Olajuwon, Charles Barkley, John Stockton, and a fellow out of North Carolina by the name of Michael Jordan.

Rubber Match

The Celtics won the championship the next year, after winning an astounding 67 games in the regular season. That meant that during the 1980s, the Celtics and the Lakers had each won three championships. Another showdown seemed inevitable. It truly was a fan-tastic era for the NBA enthusiast.

Adding to the interest in the league was the emergence of Michael Jordan. Not since the early days of Wilt's career, a quarter-century earlier, had a player put on such an offensive display as *MJ*. He …

> **Hoopology**
>
> Michael Jordan has been given many nicknames over the years, but **MJ**, Air Jordan, and His Airness are the most common.

- Scored 40 or more points 37 times—at one stretch, nine games in a row.

- Scored 50 or more points eight times.

- Scored 61 points once.

The inevitable occurred once again as (have you heard this before?) Boston and L.A. met in the NBA Finals.

One mark of the great player is that he (or she) is always trying to add a new facet to his game. It might be a three-point shot, or better defense, or something else. For years, Magic had watched Kareem's virtually unstoppable skyhook. He asked the big guy to teach it to him, and the Lakers' captain obliged.

So it shouldn't have been a big shock to see that Magic pulled that rabbit out of his hat when the team needed it most. Leading the series 2–1 in Boston, in Game 4 the Lakers found themselves down by one point with only a few seconds left to play. Magic got the ball, drove the lane, and tossed in what he called a "junior, junior sky-hook" for the win. The Lakers went on to win the series 4–2.

Tip-In

"You're probably going to get beat (by Los Angeles) on a skyhook, but you don't expect it from Magic."

—Larry Bird

At the victory parade in Los Angeles a few days later, Riley shocked everyone, his team especially, when he publicly "guaranteed" that the Lakers would win it again the next year. No team had won back-to-back championships since the Celtics of the '60s.

Pat Riley knows something about coaching. The Lakers did win it again, their fifth title of the '80s, beating the Detroit Pistons 4–3 in 1988. But the Pistons would have their day in the sun, too.

When Magic Johnson entered the Hall of Fame in 2002, it was Larry Bird who introduced him.

Detroit Revs Up the NBA

Surprisingly, the '80s ended without either the Lakers or the Celtics winning the championship. Instead, almost with no one noticing, the Detroit Pistons had assembled a great team of their own.

The team, whose main components were Joe Dumars, Bill Laimbeer, Isiah Thomas, and Dennis Rodman, won 63 games that year. They met Los Angeles in the NBA Finals. But Byron Scott tore a hamstring before Game 1, and Magic Johnson was injured in Game 2. The self-proclaimed "Bad Boys" would not let this golden opportunity pass them by. They beat the Lakers and became the NBA Champs, 4–0.

The year 1989 would also be NBA scoring leader Kareem Abdul-Jabbar's last season. But waiting in the wings, waiting for his chance, was another scoring phenom.

The Least You Need to Know

- Magic Johnson and Larry Bird revived the NBA.
- The Lakers and Celtics battled throughout the decade.
- The Pistons won the last championship of the '80s.

Chapter 5

1990s: The Running of the Bulls

In This Chapter

- ◆ Michael Jordan and the Bulls takes over
- ◆ Zen and the art of the Triangle Offense
- ◆ The ingredients are in place
- ◆ Three-peating, twice
- ◆ MJ retires

The Detroit Pistons won the NBA Championship again in 1990, and in defeating the Blazers, it was the first time since 1979 that neither the Lakers nor the Celtics reached the NBA Finals. Back-to-back (and back!) championships, once thought a thing of the past, made a roaring comeback in the '90s.

This would be the decade of Michael. Although NBA watchers for some time had been wondering whether anyone could possibly replace Magic Johnson and Larry Bird, they needn't have worried. Michael Jordan proved a more-than-adequate successor to the throne; indeed, he would take the game to a whole new level of popularity and excitement.

Knocking on the Door

If you want to become the NBA Champion, history proves that you will need to come up short several times before you slay your demons and have that breakthrough season.

For example, the Detroit Pistons had most of the pieces in place well before they won their first championship. Yet, in 1987, Boston beat them in the Eastern Conference Finals in seven games. The next year, 1988, they beat Boston in the same series, and met the Lakers for the championship, but lost in seven games. Finally, the next year, 1989, they beat the Lakers to win the championship.

The same pattern held true for the Bulls. The Pistons beat them in the Eastern Conference Semifinals in 1988, 4–1. Detroit beat them again in the Eastern Conference Finals in 1989, 4–2. Detroit beat them *again* in the Eastern Conference Finals in 1990, 4–3. Every year the Bulls got a little better, and yet, every year, the Pistons beat them in the playoffs.

> **Tip-In**
>
> The Lakers won five NBA Championships during the 1980s, and the Celtics won three. By the end of the decade, Magic Johnson and his Showtime teammates came to be known as "the team of the '80s."

Finally, in 1991, after knocking for so many years, the door finally opened for the Chicago Bulls. That year, they swept the Pistons in the Eastern Conference Finals, and went on to beat the Lakers for the NBA crown, 4–1.

For the Lakers, it would be the end of their amazing championship run. Another decade would pass before they would get back to this lofty perch.

In the meantime, the Chicago Bulls would become one of the greatest, and maybe the greatest, team ever assembled. So what changed?

The Dominance of MJ

Michael Jordan was born on February 17, 1963, in Brooklyn, New York, the fourth of five children. While still a young boy, Michael's father, James, and mother, Delores, moved the family to Wilmington, North Carolina.

Like most great players you read about in this book, Jordan began to play the game at an early age and showed a fierce competitive instinct (although Jordan's may have been a bit more fierce than others). Losing always had the effect of spurring MJ on, even as a youngster.

He played for Laney High School in Wilmington, but as a sophomore, he was cut from the varsity squad. As the world would later see, this was the sort of thing that fired him up. Determined to get back on the team, MJ practiced more than ever. "Whenever I was working out and got tired and figured I ought to stop, I would close my eyes and see that list in the locker room without my name on it," Jordan later said, "and that usually got me going again." Eventually, Jordan made the team again and led it to the state championship.

He was offered and accepted a basketball scholarship to the University of North Carolina, where he played for the disciplined Dean Smith. It was mere foreshadowing when, in the 1982 NCAA Championship game, freshman Michael Jordan hit the game-winning shot at the buzzer.

> **Inside Stuff**
>
> Dean Smith was one of the greatest college coaches of all time. Between the time he started coaching at UNC in 1962 and when he finished in 1995, his teams had won the Atlantic Coast Conference title 17 times, reached the NCAA Final Four 11 times, and had won the national championship twice, in 1982 and 1993.

> **Inside Stuff**
>
> The term *slam dunk* was invented by the great Los Angeles Lakers broadcaster Chick Hearn, who died just prior to the 2002–2003 season. Among the many now-ubiquitous terms that the broadcasting legend invented were *airball* (a shot that missed everything), and *finger roll* (explaining a certain kind of shot where the ball rolls off the fingers into the basket).
>
> Other phrases that Chick Hearn used that have become part of NBA jargon include:
>
> ◆ Caught with his hand in the cookie jar.
>
> ◆ The mustard's off the hot dog.
>
> ◆ Ticky-tack.
>
> ◆ No harm, no foul.
>
> ◆ Faked him into the popcorn machine.
>
> ◆ The game is in the refrigerator, the door is closed, the light is out, the eggs are cooling, the butter is getting hard, and the Jell-O is jiggling.
>
> But maybe even more than his ability to coin a phrase, Chick will be remembered for a record that will likely never be broken in sports: From November 21, 1965, until December 16, 2001 (three days before he underwent heart surgery), Chick never missed calling a Laker game—3,338 consecutive broadcasts!

Michael Goes Pro

The Sporting News named Jordan the College Player of the Year in 1983 and in 1984. After his junior year, he declared himself eligible for the NBA Draft, and was chosen third overall by the Chicago Bulls, after the Rockets took Akeem Olajuwon with the first pick and the Blazers took Sam Bowie with the second pick.

No one really knew how good Jordan was because, playing as he had for the Tar Heels, he had been confined by Dean Smith's structured offense. The NBA game is different than the college game because, for one thing, the offenses are much more open. Players have more room to innovate; and if Michael Jordan is anything, he's an innovative ballplayer.

So when Jordan burst onto the NBA scene in the 1984–85 season, few were ready for his high-flying acrobatics. At 6' 6", Jordan seemingly played faster, jumped higher, hung longer, and slam-dunked better than anyone around. He was a one-man basketball wrecking crew, here to rewrite the records and destroy basketball complacency.

Averaging 28.2 points per game that season, Jordan was named Rookie of the Year. But maybe more significantly, his presence helped the team win more games, as the following statistics reveal:

- The year before he arrived, Chicago had won only 27 games.

- In Jordan's rookie season, the team won 38 games.

- By 1988, it was winning 50 games a season.

- In 1990, it won 55 games.

- In 1991, the year they won their first championship, the Bulls won 61 games in the regular season.

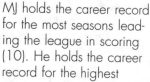

Tip-In

MJ holds the career record for the most seasons leading the league in scoring (10). He holds the career record for the highest points-per-game average (31.7). He holds the career record for most seasons leading the league in field goals made (9), and he shares the career record for most seasons with 2,000 or more points (10).

The Phenom

In his second year, Michael broke his foot, an injury that sidelined him for 64 games that year. Even so, he cemented his rapidly growing reputation as an offensive player to be reckoned with when, in a first-round playoff game against Boston, he scored an NBA playoff-record 63 points.

Michael Jordan took the game to new heights, in more ways than one.

By the next year, people had really begun to take notice—this Michael Jordan kid was going to be something special. That year he averaged 37.1 points, and he would lead the league in scoring for the next seven years in a row, something only the great Wilt Chamberlain had done before.

Yet, despite Michael's unquestionable individual greatness, questions remained. Could he win? Could he lead his team to a championship? Was he all about his own glory and not the greater good of the team?

Those questions began to be answered when the Bulls brought in a new head coach, a gangly, ex-hippie, ex-*CBA* coach with a penchant for Zen Buddhism named Phil Jackson.

Hoopology

Players who are not yet ready for the NBA have choices. For instance, they can play in the European leagues, or in the NBDL—The NBA Development League.

They Call Him the Zen Master

Phil Jackson won two championships as a player for the New York Knickerbockers, in 1970 and in 1973. But far more than a player, Phil Jackson was a thinker. He liked books and liked to expand his mind. Recalls teammate Walt Frazier, "He could have been a better player if he had applied himself to it more, as much as he applied himself to his books. He read those weird books. They were weird to us, anyway. No one else ever read them, anyway."

After he retired from playing the game, Jackson continued his spiritual quest, and it is that side of him that is often used to explain why Jackson became a very successful basketball coach.

Tip-In

While Phil Jackson is certainly one of the greatest coaches of all time, he was considered a superb role player in the NBA. Playing for 12 years (10 with the Knicks and two with the Nets), Jackson averaged 6.7 points per game, 4.3 rebounds per game, and 1.1 assists per game. His best year as a pro was 1973–74, when he averaged 11.1 ppg and 5.8 rpg.

For one, he meditates every day, a practice which he says has influenced his coaching style. In an interview with online magazine Salon.com, Jackson said, "The tighter your mind is, the more you try to force your thinking into a constricted space or direction ... I certainly believe in boundaries, but I want my boundaries to be spacious enough to allow for extreme flexibility. So when I'm coaching, I try not to let myself get too rigid."

Jackson continued, "My own personal tendency is to be fairly tight, precise, and dogmatic, but a dictatorial coach can frighten his team. My daily meditation practice frees me from habitual behavior, allows me to be a little loose, to be open to having fun, and to react more to the breath of the moment."

His love for the game could not keep him away long, and by 1984, he had won another championship—as the coach of the CBA Albany Patroons (where he was also the driver of the van that took the team from town to town).

Yet even with this notch under his belt, Jackson still existed on the outskirts of professional basketball. It was then, as Jackson was coaching a summer league in Puerto Rico, that Chicago Bulls GM Jerry Krause persuaded Bulls head coach Doug Collins to hire Jackson as an assistant coach.

Back in the Saddle Again

The Bulls were growing and developing as a team. Yet, the measuring stick was the Detroit Pistons, and the Bulls always fell short against the two-time defending NBA champs in their playoff matchups.

As a way to take the next step, the Bulls tabbed Phil Jackson to replace Collins as head coach of the Chicago Bulls and their young superstar.

When offered the job, Jackson says that "it was also made clear that I could use whatever system or style of play that suited me … there was no question in my mind that the Triangle was … the very system I'd been seeking for so long."

The Triangle

While there is no need to go into sophisticated NBA offensive and defensive schemes here, suffice it to say that the Triangle Offense that Jackson instituted was unlike anything else run in the NBA. Jackson learned this offense from Bulls assistant coach and former Kansas State head coach Tex Winter, who wrote a book called *The Triple Post Offense.*

In it, the offense ends up looking like a triangle, with one man at the top of the key and the others on either wing, cutting back and forth in a fluid rhythm designed to find the open man and keep the defense off-kilter.

According to Winter, the purpose of the Triangle is to create what he calls the Seven Principles of Sound Offense. It states that a sound offense …

- ◆ Must penetrate the defense.

- ◆ Must utilize end-to-end, fast-break play.

- ◆ Provides proper floor spacing.

- ◆ Provides player and ball movement with a purpose.

- ◆ Provides strong rebounding and defensive position.

- ◆ Provides the player with the ball an opportunity to pass to any of his teammates.

- ◆ Utilizes the abilities of the individual players.

Jackson calls these "almost biblical requirements."

But because the Triangle was essentially untried at the NBA level, Michael Jordan was, as Phil

> **Tip-In**
>
> It's what I call the Tai-Chi, finding out what the flow of the other team is … where's their strength, what they are trying to do, and beating that because you're sucking them in and defeating them where their weakness is— ultimately what they're hiding.
> —Phil Jackson in *Brentwood Magazine*

> **Inside Stuff**
>
> "It's so easy for the media to call me a 'Zen Master'," Jackson has said. "[It] is certainly nothing I'd ever be so presumptuous to call myself. But they think that the label gives them a handle on me. In truth, who I really am is a mediator who's sitting at the edge of this culture and looking in."

Jackson put it, "dubious" about the new scheme, despite the fact that the team had started to win at a record clip. For a player with such tremendous individual skills, an offense that allowed everyone an equal chance to score seemed like a sacrifice.

Tip-In

As usual, Jordan dominated in 1990. He led the league in scoring (33.6 ppg), and scored the most he ever would in any single game, 69, in an overtime win against the Cleveland Cavaliers.

Despite Michael's reservations, that first season together, Jackson, Jordan, and the Triangle meshed. Phil Jackson's unique coaching style—blending respect, intelligence, books, movie clips, and a new offense—worked. The team went 55–27 that year, the best any Bulls club had done since 1972.

With the new coach on board, with Michael leading the way, with an offense that clicked, everything seemed ripe for a championship run. All that was needed were a few last pieces of the puzzle.

Phil Jackson led the Bulls to six championships in eight years.

The Last Few Pieces

Scottie Pippen joined the Bulls at the same time Phil Jackson did, but it wasn't until Jackson became head coach, and Pippen embraced the Triangle, that the forward's true basketball brilliance came through.

Whereas Jordan took to the Triangle slowly, Pippen, says the coach, "was a much easier sell. Scottie eagerly immersed himself in the intricacies of the Triangle—so much so that he became the organizer of the offense."

By the 1990–91 season, the Bulls had matured to the point where they were ready for a legitimate championship run, and the credit has to go to Pippen and Jordan.

By this time, the world knew who Michael Jordan was, knew he could light up the scoreboard at will, and knew that he was also a defensive specialist. Although "greatest ever" was not attributed to him then as it is today, there was little doubt that he was in the top ten already.

But to get to that next level, Jordan had to win a championship, plain and simple. He knew it, and so did everyone else. The greatest players, the very best of the best, only get that recognition after they have led their team to a championship, or two or three. That was Jordan's next challenge.

To do that, to get there, he would have to sacrifice his individual game and stats for the team. That was where the Triangle came in, that is where great coaching came in, and that is what Jordan was willing to do. The result was that the 1991 Bulls were a threat to win it all.

By the same token, Pippen came into that year ready to make a statement as well, averaging 18 points, 7 rebounds, and 6 assists that year. Says Jackson, "He became a dominant force."

The Bulls swept New York in the *first round*, beat Philly 4–1 in the *second round*, swept the rival Pistons in the *third round*, and stomped on the Lakers 4–1 to win the first of what would be six championships over the next eight years. Only the Celtics of the '60s had a better run.

> **Hoopology**
>
> The NBA Playoffs are four rounds deep. The **first round** is a best-of-five series. The **second round** is also known as the semifinals (Eastern or Western) and is best-of-seven set. The remaining three rounds are a best-of-seven series called the conference semis and finals, and the best-of-seven final round is called the NBA Finals.

Back-to-Back-to-Back

The 1991–92 season started off on a very somber note when Magic Johnson called a press conference and stated "Because of the HIV virus I have obtained, I will have to announce my retirement from the Lakers today."

Technical Foul

Magic made one comeback in 1996 and retired for good at the end of that season, and went on to become a highly successful businessman and entrepreneur. He had won five championships, and had been named league MVP three times.

Hoopology

The Houston Rockets won NBA titles in 1994 and 1995. San Antonio became the first former ABA team to win a title (1999).

Inside Stuff

For as great as he was during the regular season, Michael Jordan was always able to turn up the proverbial notch in the playoffs. When he retired from basketball in 1993 as a three-time Finals MVP, Jordan's career playoff average of 34.7 was the best in NBA history.

It became apparent very early in the season that the Bulls were no fluke. Although Jordan was scoring less (if you can call 30.1 ppg less), his teammates were scoring more, and the Bulls were on a serious roll. They won 67 games in the regular season, and then beat the Portland Trail Blazers 4–2 to win their second straight title.

Not since the Minneapolis Lakers of the '50s and the Celtics of the '60s had any team won three NBA Championships in a row. That was the task and challenge that now lay before Michael and the Bulls.

This was a team that thrived on challenges. The coach liked to create them, the star player lived for them, and the rest of the team blossomed when confronted with them. To *three-peat* was a challenge unlike any other.

Michael was 29, at the prime of his career and athletic abilities, and no one was going to stop him now. The Bulls, though they only won 57 games in the regular season, came into the playoffs like a team on a mission. They lost but two games as they marched through the Eastern Conference Playoffs, and then beat Phoenix in the NBA Finals, four games to two.

One reason that this Bulls team was so good was that, triangle offense aside, they were great defensive teams. Michael and Scottie particularly were perennial all-defense players. And, as they say, "defense wins championships."

They had done the seemingly impossible—they had won three championships in a row—and then the improbable happened.

Michael Jordan retired from basketball.

While the Cat's Away

Jordan reassessed his life after a personal tragedy and came to the conclusion that he had nothing left to prove in basketball.

By this time, Jordan was routinely acknowledged as probably the best to ever play the game. He had won three championships, three NBA Finals MVP awards, and seven scoring titles in a row. He was so good at this point in his career that his play seemed effortless, almost too easy, and he seemed a bit bored.

Wanting a new challenge, Jordan stunned the world when he announced, just before training camp, that he would retire. He eventually pursued his childhood love, baseball. At age 30, Michael Jordan attempted to break into the majors.

Meanwhile, the rest of the NBA took advantage of MJ's departure, as the league was suddenly wide open. Seattle posted an impressive 63– record, but in one of the great upsets in NBA history, was tossed out of the playoffs in the first round by eighth-seeded Denver.

It was the Houston Rockets who would emerge from the West, and with Jordan now gone, the Rockets' Hakeem Olajuwon was clearly the most dominant player in the league. That year, he won the regular season MVP award, as well as the finals MVP and a championship ring, as the Rockets defeated the Pat Riley–led Knicks in a thrilling seven-game series.

> **Inside Stuff**
>
> Michael Jordan signed with the Chicago White Sox and was sent down to the minors to play for the Birmingham Barons of the Southern League. He batted .202, in 127 games.

> **Tip-In**
>
> Seattle's loss in that playoff series was all the harder to take because they led the best-of-five series 2–0 and then proceeded to lose three straight.

The Cat Is Back

The next season began with the Rockets looking for that seemingly ever-elusive NBA requirement—respect. To some, their title was tainted because it was won with Jordan out of the league. But that would soon change.

On March 18, 1995, with roughly a month left in the season, Jordan faxed his intentions to the press with a short statement: "I'm back." He had decided to unretire and return to the Bulls. But by then, the team had become Pippen's, and incorporating MJ back into the fold took some time. The Bulls won only 47 games that year, and were knocked out of the playoffs in the second round against the Orlando Magic, who featured Shaquille O'Neal and Anfernee Hardaway.

The Rockets, meanwhile, erased whatever notions people had about an asterisk, and won back-to-back championships, trouncing Shaquille O'Neal and the Orlando Magic 4–0.

Inside Stuff

By the time MJ returned to the Bulls, the organization had already retired his number (23) and had erected a statue of him in front of the United Center. So Jordan donned a jersey with the number 45 on it, the number he had worn in junior high and on the baseball field.

In his fifth game back from his retirement, MJ was playing the Knicks at Madison Square Garden, where he poured in 55 points. He was right; he *was* back.

Strange Bedfellows

The 1995–96 season was the best of many great ones for Chicago basketball. That year, the team posted a record 72 wins (eclipsing the 1972 Lakers record of 69 wins), and romped their way across the NBA landscape.

Inside Stuff

Dennis Rodman was a rebounding monster on the court. He once had 34 rebounds in a game against the Pacers in 1992 and averaged more than 13 rebounds per game for his 14-year career.

There are two reasons for that incredible season. First, MJ likes a challenge (as we all have learned), and his longing to be remembered as one of the NBA's all-time greatest basketball players fueled his desire to prove the skeptics wrong.

Second, the Bulls traded for former Piston Dennis Rodman. Now, Rodman was unquestionably one of the greatest rebounders the league had ever seen. He was a lean, leaping, rebounding machine. But just as true, Rodman was a free spirit. His ever-changing hair and ever-increasing number of tattoos made him an odd match for the more boardroom-like MJ.

But Phil Jackson, Michael Jordan, and Scottie Pippen were able to keep Rodman in check, and the team ran off victory after victory. The inevitable occurred late in the spring of 1996 when the Bulls won the championship yet again.

The two-year respite enjoyed by the rest of the league was over, very over.

Jordan Retires

The Bulls won the championship again in 1997, and again in 1998, three-peating for a second time. Had Jordan not retired for the better part of two years in the middle of this amazing run, they could have added to their championship trophy collection—perhaps even winning in eight in a row.

The Chicago Bulls: Six championships in eight years. Pictured here are the 1995–96 Bulls.

In his last game as a Chicago Bull, Jordan scored 45 points, and hit the game-winner (after stealing the ball, natch) with 6.6 seconds left. Would MJ's shot over Utah's Bryon Russell be his last? Jordan often said that he would play for no other coach than Phil, and there was talk in Chicago about rebuilding for the future.

So Jordan hit that last shot, won the game, and rode off into the sunset, retiring once again. The amazing 1990s run of the Bulls was officially over.

The Least You Need to Know

- ◆ The '90s were the decade of the Bulls.
- ◆ Michael Jordan emerged as the greatest player of the decade.
- ◆ Phil Jackson instituted the offense that allowed the Bulls to win.
- ◆ Houston won NBA titles in 1994 and 1995 while San Antonio won in 1999.

Chapter 6

New Millennium: A New Dynasty

In This Chapter

- ◆ Putting the pieces in place
- ◆ Shaq and Kobe
- ◆ L.A. Lakers: The first one is the hardest
- ◆ Lakers: Again and again

The '90s ended with two significant events. First, due to a lockout the 1998–99 season was 50 games long, as opposed to the regular 82-game schedule. Secondly, the San Antonio Spurs became the first former ABA team to win the NBA Championship.

As a new decade and a new millennium dawned, with Michael and the Bull's championship reign now a thing of the past, it seemed that the league was once again wide open, that anyone could win the championship. But that changed when, right before the 1999–2000 season, Los Angeles Lakers general manager Jerry West hired none other than Phil Jackson to coach the team. Would Jackson and his six championship rings from his Chicago days make a difference? Absolutely.

Architect of a Championship

Yes, Jerry West was one of the greatest guards to ever play the game, but that may not be what he will long be remembered for; West is considered one of the greatest general managers in the history of the NBA.

Although his title with the Lakers was "executive vice president of basketball operations," the job was essentially that of a GM: to find talent and put together the best team possible.

In that role, West is virtually unmatched. After retiring from the Lakers as a player in 1974, he came back to coach the team in the 1976–77 season, a job he held for three years. But West found that he had neither the temperament nor the personnel to match his lofty expectations. The Lakers then hired him as a "special consultant" for a few years, before finally elevating him to GM in 1982. Although the foundation was already in place for their run through the '80s (notably Magic and Kareem), West made the moves that allowed the run to continue for as long as it did. From 1995 until 2000, when he retired from the Lakers, West was the executive vice president of the club. One year later, the challenge of building another team into a championship contender was too great for West to pass up. He was named president of basketball operations of the Memphis Grizzlies, hoping to turn that team's fortunes around.

> **Tip-In**
>
> In the 1965 playoffs, Jerry West averaged 40.6 points per game, and a record 46.3 ppg over a six-game series with the Bullets.

It won't be the first time West has had to start from scratch with a basketball team. After Kareem retired in 1988, and Magic followed suit in 1991 (more or less), West was faced with *rebuilding* his squad. It is never easy to rebuild a team, but it is even more difficult to rebuild a team that has won a few championships—the expectations are almost always too lofty.

> **Hoopology**
>
> To win in the NBA, teams normally need to give their best players a few years to play together in order to gel as a unit. After that, they need a few more years to make their run.
>
> Inevitably, the best players on the team, those that stuck around the longest, will retire or will get traded away near the end of their careers. When that happens, the team must start again, and find some young new talent to begin the process over. This process is called **rebuilding**.

How bad was the fall? The last year Magic played, 1991, the Lakers had won 58 games. In the 1992–93 season, they skidded to a record of 39–43, losing in the first round to the Phoenix Suns. The next year, the once-mighty Lakers won but 33 games (and no, they were not in a row). To West's credit, that was the only season the team missed the playoffs under his watch. The next few seasons saw the team try to make the ascent to the NBA Finals, but they always fell short. The franchise needed to make personnel changes.

West had to do something, and something he did.

West's One-Two Attack

What Jerry West did first was to land center Shaquille O'Neal and guard Kobe Bryant, in the same summer. Not a bad off-season! While it was a potent start for a Laker rebirth, it was not quite enough—the right coach would still be needed.

Inside Stuff

When the NBA turned 50 years old in 1996, it asked an elite group of hoops experts to select the 50 greatest basketball players in NBA history. The annoucement was made on October 29, 1996 at the Grand Hyatt Hotel in New York, the same location where, 50 years before, a group of businessmen met to start a new basketball league in what was then known as the Commodore hotel.

The Diesel

Shaquille O'Neal is one of those once-in-a-generation players, the type who can impact a game, a team, a division, even a league. He is that good, that special. In 1996, when the league celebrated its 50th season, O'Neal was voted as one of the 50 Greatest Players in NBA History. He had only played in the NBA for four seasons up to that point.

Shaquille Rashaun O'Neal was born on March 6, 1972. Lucille O'Neal raised him as a single mother and Shaq found a surrogate father when she married Phillip Harrison.

Tip-In

Shaquille Rashaun ironically means "Little Warrior" in Islam. Like MJ, Shaq is one of those players who inspires many nicknames—Shaq, Diesel, the Big Aristotle, Shaq Daddy, Big Daddy, and Shaq Fu are but a few. But whatever you call him, make sure you say it nicely. At 7' 1", 315 pounds, he is a *very* big man.

Harrison, an army man, adopted Shaquille, and soon his son was living the life of an army brat. Says Shaq about himself at the time, "I was bad. Anything outside of drugs and killing someone, I'd do it. I stole. I lied. I cheated. I broke into cars to steal tapes."

By the age of 13 and now living on an army base in West Germany, Shaq was 6' 7", and naturally, he discovered basketball. The family moved back to the States soon after, and by the time he was a senior, Shaq had shaped up and was leading his high school to the state championship in Texas.

He entered Louisiana State University the next year, and was named the College Basketball Player of the Year his sophomore year. He decided to go pro after his junior year, was drafted first by the Orlando Magic in 1992, and signed a lucrative three-year contract. After playing three years in Orlando—despite getting swept out of the finals in 1995—when Shaq became a free agent, every team in the NBA wanted him. Why? Shaq combines height (7-footers are always at a premium), strength (Kobe Bryant tells the story of the time Shaq got so mad that he ripped a steel door off its hinges), and agility (he is as graceful a 7', 315-pound man as you will ever see).

Jerry West, like every other GM in the league, knew a *franchise player* when he saw one. West thought he had something to offer the Big Diesel that other teams did not—a great basketball tradition in general, and a great center lineage in particular:

- **George Mikan,** the first NBA superstar and first dominant center, played for, and won championships with, the Lakers when they were still in Minneapolis.

- **Wilt Chamberlain,** the most dominant offensive player ever, played for, and won a championship with, the Los Angeles Lakers.

- **Kareem Abdul-Jabbar,** the greatest scorer in the history of the game, played for, and won championships with, the Los Angeles Lakers.

Hoopology

There are players, good players, great players, superstars, and then there are **franchise players**. A franchise player is the best of the best—the one guy you want to build your entire team around. Larry Bird was a franchise player. Bill Russell was a franchise player. Shaq is a franchise player.

Inside Stuff

The Lakers have retired the numbers of seven players:

No. 13: Wilt Chamberlain

No. 22: Elgin Baylor

No. 25: Gail Goodrich

No. 32: Magic Johnson

No. 33: Kareem Abdul-Jabbar

No. 42: James Worthy

No. 44: Jerry West

West's argument to Shaq was clear: Play for the Lakers and you will inherit this unique lineage, you will win championships, and you will come to be known as one of the best centers, ever.

And so, on July 18, 1996, Shaquille O'Neal signed a lucrative seven-year contract. Afterwards, the Lakers went back in their winning ways, as the team went 56–26, their best record since 1991.

Out With the Old

To make room for Shaq, Jerry West had to trade his current starting center, Vlade Divac, a 7'1" Serb who played with grace and skill. Knowing that he had to move Vlade, West looked around the basketball landscape to see if another piece of the puzzle might be available.

Sometimes an NBA GM has to be conservative, and sometimes, he has to take a risk. Without taking a calculated risk at times, it is almost impossible to break away from the pack. The danger is that the risk may not pan out, and the team will get stuck with some deadwood for some time. But that's the nature of the NBA.

In 1996, West was ready to make a deal. He knew that the L.A. fans were a fickle bunch, and that he needed to get his team back to championship levels if he wanted the team to be the talk of the NBA. So West was in a risk-taking mood.

The one player who really intrigued him was a kid out of Lower Merion High School in Pennsylvania named Kobe Bryant. Taking a risk is one thing, but trading an All-Star-caliber center like Vlade for a 17-year-old prodigy is quite another. But that is just what West was prepared to do.

Jerry West had his reasons.

In With the New

Kobe Bryant was born on August 23, 1978, in Philadelphia, Pennsylvania. Kobe comes from NBA stock; his father was Joe "Jelly Bean" Bryant, a player for the Philadelphia 76ers, San Diego Clippers, and Houston Rockets.

Kobe Bryant spent much of his youth in Italy, as his dad played in the Italian leagues after his NBA days were over. But by the time Kobe was old enough for high school, the family was back in the United States, settling in Pennsylvania.

Kobe played for Lower Merion High School, and by his senior year, he was considered a hoops phenom. He was voted both the *USA Today* and *Parade* magazine High

Tip-In

Joe "Jelly Bean" Bryant began his career in Philadelphia in 1975, averaging 7.4 ppg his rookie year. He spent four years with the 76ers before joining the Clippers when they played in San Diego. He averaged a career-high 11.8 ppg for the Clips in 1981–82.

Inside Stuff

At the 1997 Rookie Game at the NBA All-Star Weekend, Kobe set a new record, scoring 31 points. He also won the Slam Dunk contest.

School Player of the Year, and averaged 30.8 points, 12 rebounds, 7 assists, and 4 blocks per game his senior year. He became the leading scorer in southeastern Pennsylvania history, beating the previous record held by a guy named Wilt Chamberlain.

In the 1995–96 season, Kevin Garnett had successfully jumped from high school to the pros, not an easy task by any measure. Yet, because he did do it, Garnett gave hope to a legion of kids who would come after him who thought that they, too, were good enough to skip college and go straight to the NBA. Most weren't, but Kobe Bryant was.

Kobe announced that he would be forgoing college and would be making himself eligible for the NBA Draft. In the first round of the 1996 NBA Draft, Kobe was selected by the Charlotte Hornets with the 13th overall pick.

The next month, he was traded to the Lakers for Vlade Divac.

The Best-Laid Plans of Mice and Men

Jerry West thought he had done it. He had captured the biggest prize of the free-agent market for that, or any, year—Shaquille O'Neal. He had also traded a center he no longer needed for an incredibly athletic, high-scoring, NBA protégé.

But Kobe and Shaq didn't mesh well or quickly. Although the team was significantly improved, the hoped-for championship never arrived; indeed, it wasn't even in the vicinity:

- They lost to the Jazz 4–1 in the Western Conference Semifinals in 1997.
- They lost to the Jazz 4–0 in the Western Conference Finals in 1998.
- They lost to the Spurs 4–0 in the Western Conference Semifinals in 1999.

Along the way, the team added and eventually let go of rebounding machine Dennis Rodman, and went through assorted coaches, endured off-court bickering, and generally seemed overtalented and underwhelming.

Shaq and Kobe, although they sure looked good on paper, had a hard time communicating and playing together. Who was "the man"? Whose team was this? Distrust and poor play ran rampant.

There were no answers, only questions, one of which was: Did Jerry West have any more tricks up his sleeve?

Zen Master to the Rescue

Indeed he did. After the Bulls won that last championship in 1998 (see Chapter 5), Phil Jackson decided that he needed some time off to recharge his batteries. Although Jackson officially "retired," few expected him to stay away from the game for long. By the time the 1999–2000 season was rolling around, the Zen Master seemed ready to coach again.

Although he had already been contacted by several NBA teams, none of the jobs felt right. When a call came in from the Lakers, however, both the timing and the situation struck a chord. He was willing to listen.

So, as the new millennium dawned, the Lakers hoped the last ingredient they had been looking for was finally in place. They had the best center in a generation in Shaquille O'Neal, an acrobatic, flamboyant scoring machine in Kobe Bryant, and a coach with an amazing winning pedigree in Phil Jackson.

The only was question that remained was: Would these three big egos, these big talents, explode, or would they implode?

Inside Stuff
"My father always played with a great love for the game, and that's one of the things he always taught me, especially after I made the jump to the NBA. He told me to not let the pressure or the expectations take away from my love for the game, and I think that's the best advice anyone's ever given me."   —Kobe Bryant

Maybe This Time, for the First Time

When Jackson joined the Lakers, he says that he explained to them that if the team wanted to win a championship, they would have to do the following things:

- They would have to play much better defense.
- Shaq would need to rebound and block shots more than ever before.

- They would have to run the Triangle Offense; ball and player movement would be their hallmark.

- Kobe would have to mature and develop as a player.

Shaq and Kobe: A formidable duo.

Yet, Jackson noticed something peculiar as he talked to his new team for the first time: They couldn't or wouldn't pay attention to what he was saying. "There were blank looks on their faces," the coach later explained. The coach knew that explaining a new offense and a new system wouldn't be easy, that there would be a natural learning curve. What no one knew was how quickly they would learn to pay attention, and how well they would learn this new system.

Showdown

The Lakers came out of the gate in the 1999–2000 season a much-improved team. But they were not the only kid on the block. The Portland Trail Blazers, now featuring Scottie Pippen, seemed an equal match for the Lakers.

For much of the season, the Blazers had the best record in the league, and a February showdown between the two teams found both entering the game with 11-game winning streaks. The Lakers won that game, and bad blood between the teams ensued.

They would meet for a far more important showdown in the Western Conference Finals. Although the Lakers quickly took a 3–1 series lead, the Blazers roared back, tying the series at 3 apiece.

In a thrilling Game 7, Portland had a 15-point lead in the fourth quarter, but suddenly went cold. They couldn't buy a basket. The Lakers came roaring back and won the game, advancing to the NBA Finals for the first time in a decade.

The Champs

The Lakers met the Larry Bird–coached Indiana Pacers in the NBA Finals. In what seemed to be an anticlimactic series after the thriller with Portland, Shaq and the Lakers finally lived up to their potential and won the championship 4–2.

Along the way, this new Laker team had become a strong unit, as opposed to the individual play of five guys for which they had been noted in previous years.

Also along the way, they seemed to develop a confidence, a championship swagger.

Three-Peating

In the 2000–01 season, the Lakers looked to repeat. Though they looked anything but stellar during the season, and the bickering, both public and private, between Shaq and Kobe reached record levels, the team caught fire when they needed to most.

They won their last eight games of the regular season, clinching the second straight Pacific Division title. They then swept Portland, the Sacramento Kings, and San Antonio, meeting the 76ers and Allen Iverson in the finals. Although Philadelphia won Game 1, Los Angeles won the next four, capping a record 15–1 post-season run, the best in NBA history.

Tip-In

Shaquille O'Neal was named NBA Finals MVP after averaging 33.0 ppg and 15.8 rebounds against the 76ers.

In the 2001–02 season, with the focus on the two-time champion Lakers, the Sacramento Kings felt they had something to prove to the rest of the teams in the league, especially out West.

Kings GM Geoff Petrie certainly had assembled a great team:

◆ Forward Chris Webber, with his big paws and deft shooting touch, anchored the team.

- Point guard Mike Bibby was a steady and calming presence, as opposed to previous point guard Jason Williams.

- Center Vlade Divac (the NBA is a small universe) was still one of the top centers in the league.

- Sharpshooting forward Peja Stojakovic reminded a few of Larry Bird.

The Kings and Lakers battled it out all season, with the once-lowly Kings winning the Pacific Division crown in the last week of the season.

Inside Stuff

In the late '80s and early '90s, the Sacramento Kings were certainly struggling. The team routinely ended up in last place, couldn't quite win 30 games a season, and at one point, lost a record 37 games *in a row* on the road.

Indicative of their bad fortunes at the time was the 1993–94 season. That year, the Kings had drafted a much-heralded point guard out of Duke named Bobby Hurley, the NCAA career assists leader who had led Duke to two NCAA titles. But 19 games into the season, Hurley was involved in a horrific life-threatening car accident. Although he came back the next year, he was never the same player.

The Kings' fortunes began to turn around when Geoff Petrie, the former Senior Vice President of the Blazers, was hired in 1994. Petrie rebuilt the Kings, hired Rick Adelman in 1998 and then, at the end of the decade, Joe and Gavin Maloof bought the team. The new blood turned things around, finally.

The Kings and Lakers met again at the Western Conference Finals, and engaged in an epic seven-game series. Although many observers felt that the Kings should have won, in the end, it was the Lakers who prevailed. They went on to sweep the Nets in the NBA Finals, capturing their third championship in a row.

For Phil Jackson, the win was especially sweet as it made him the only coach ever to three-peat with two different teams. The championship gave him nine as an NBA coach, tying him with the legendary Red Auerbach for the most in NBA history.

The Least You Need to Know

- Jerry West is not only one of the greatest players in NBA history, but also one of the league's greatest general managers.

- Shaquille O'Neal and Kobe Bryant of the Los Angeles Lakers became one of the NBA's most feared combos.

- Phil Jackson brought order to the Laker house.

- The Lakers have won three consecutive championships (for a total of 14 in franchise history).

Part 2

NBA Teams

The NBA is made up of 29 teams, and in the following chapters you'll find out what makes each one of them unique. In the East, traditional Atlantic Division powerhouses like the New York Knicks and the Philadelphia 76ers battle it out with the New Jersey Nets and Orlando Magic, among others. In the Central Division, we look at the past—and peer into the future—of teams like the Indiana Pacers, Detroit Pistons, and the Toronto Raptors.

In the Midwest Division, a trio of Texas teams (the San Antonio Spurs, Houston Rockets, and Dallas Mavericks) compete against the Utah Jazz, Minnesota Timberwolves, Memphis Grizzlies, and Denver Nuggets. Finally, we look at the tough Pacific Division where the Los Angeles Lakers, Sacramento Kings, and Portland Trail Blazers are but a few of the teams who play out West.

Chapter 7

Atlantic Division

In This Chapter

- Boston Celtics
- Miami Heat
- New Jersey Nets
- New York Knicks
- Orlando Magic
- Philadelphia 76ers
- Washington Wizards

The NBA is divided into two conferences; each featuring two divisions.

The Eastern Conference, which includes the Atlantic and Central Division, has a reputation for being the tougher, more physical of the two conferences. Out West, teams in the Midwest and Pacific Divisions tend to play with more flash and flair, but in the East, slow-it-down, pound-it-in basketball is the tradition.

The Atlantic Division certainly lives up to this reputation. With great rivalries and a long tradition, teams in the Atlantic form the roots of the NBA.

Boston Celtics

Needless to say, the history of the NBA and the history of the Celtics are intertwined. Indeed, much of this book recounts the glory days of Celtic basketball.

The Celtic franchise calls itself "the most successful franchise in professional sports history," and with good reason. Its two amazing title runs netted the franchise 16 NBA Championships, a record that is yet unmatched in basketball (the New York Yankees have 26 baseball championships while the Montreal Canadiens have 24 in hockey.)

By the same token, the team has seen some of the greatest players in NBA history pass through its doors. Boston has retired a record 21 numbers:

- No. 1: For the founder of the team and first owner, Walter Brown
- No. 2: In honor of coach and GM Red Auerbach
- No. 3: Dennis Johnson
- No. 6: Bill Russell
- No. 10: Jo Jo White
- No. 14: Bob Cousy
- No. 15: Tom Heinsohn
- No. 16: Tom "Satch" Sanders
- No. 17: John Havlicek
- No. 18: Dave Cowens
- No. 19: Don Nelson
- No. 21: Bill Sharman
- No. 22: Ed Macauley
- No. 23: Frank Ramsey
- No. 24: Sam Jones
- No. 25: K.C. Jones
- No. 32: Kevin McHale
- No. 33: Larry Bird
- No. 35: Reggie Lewis
- No. 00: Robert Parish
- "Loscy": Jim Loscutoff

So the Celtic organization certainly has plenty to be proud of, not the least of which is that the team played in a game that has come to be known as "the greatest game ever played"—Game 5 of the 1976 NBA Finals against the Phoenix Suns.

In that game, the Celtics amassed an early 20-point lead, but the Suns kept chipping away at it. By the end of regulation, the Suns had tied it up. The score was tied at the end of the first overtime as well.

In the second overtime, John Havlicek hit a shot at the buzzer, seeming to give the Celtics a one-point win. But referee Richie Powers said that one second actually remained on the clock, and so the Suns took a timeout to draw up a play. The problem was that the Suns were out of timeouts.

According to the rules, a *technical foul* was called on the Suns, and Boston hit the free throw, now giving them a two-point lead.

Here's how Suns announcer Al McCoy explained what happened next: *"In it goes to Heard, here's his jump shot … GOOD! It's GOOD! We will go to a third amazing overtime. I've got to take a breather,"* McCoy shouted, adding, *"I've got to tell you, some-body up there is on our side."* But the lucky leprechaun was on the Celtics' side, as Boston finally won arguably the greatest game ever played, in triple overtime, 128–126.

So yes, the Celtics have a rightfully proud place in NBA lore.

Tip-In

Jim Loscutoff requested that his number (18) not be retired so that a future Celtic could wear it. It was later worn by, and retired for, Dave Cowens.

Technical Foul

According to the NBA Rulebook, "a **technical foul** is the penalty for unsportsmanlike conduct or violations by team members on the floor or seated on the bench. It may be assessed for illegal contact which occurs with an opponent before the ball becomes live."

Miami Heat

Although the Heat do not have near the history of the Celtics, their consistent ability to improve and win is impressive.

In the mid-1980s, producer Zev Buffman and Philadelphia 76er legend Billy Cunningham led a move to get an NBA team into south Florida. In 1987, the NBA Board of Governors voted to expand the league, and the Miami Heat (along with the Charlotte Hornets) were admitted for the 1988–89 season.

The Miami Heat played their first game on November 5, 1988, against the Los Angeles Clippers. History will note that it was a sellout crowd of 15,008 that saw Rory Sparrow hit the first basket in Heat history, as the team lost 111–91.

As with all expansion teams, the Heat won little their first few years in the league. However, in only its fourth year in existence, in the 1992–93 season, the team made the playoffs. Although that was in itself impressive, the team had little chance against the Michael Jordan–led Chicago Bulls.

> ### Inside Stuff
>
> To enter the NBA, a new team must pay an entry fee to the league. The Miami Heat's entry fee was $32.5 million.

> ### Tip-In
>
> That first year in Miami, Alonzo Mourning led his team in scoring (23.2 points per game) *and* in rebounding (10.4 per game).

The Heat made the most important move in their history when, on September 2, 1995, they hired Pat Riley to be the team president and head coach. Riley's teams had never failed to make the playoffs, and besides his four championships in L.A., he also had four 50-plus-win seasons in New York. Riley is one of the best coaches in NBA history.

Almost immediately, President Riley began to build a team that Coach Riley would like. On November 3, he landed All-Star center Alonzo Mourning from the Hornets in a six-player deal. Riley's next deal netted him guard Tim Hardaway.

Riley had coaching success in Los Angeles and New York before arriving in Miami.

The next season, 1996–97, the Heat were the surprise of the NBA. The team won 61 games that year (19 more than the year before), and won the Atlantic Division title. But for the second year in a row, Michael and the Bulls tossed the Heat out of the play-offs, although this time in the Eastern Conference Finals.

Yet the Knicks were the Heat's biggest rivals. A series of intense regular-season games, combined with the fact that Riley used to coach the Knicks and a heated seven-game series the year before, all added fuel to the fire.

In the 1998 playoffs, things got even more "heated." In the first round of the playoffs that year, the Knicks and Heat split the first four games, 2–2. Tempers had flared throughout the hardfought series and had reached the boiling point. As emotions ran high, Mourning got off the bench during the fight. Pursuant to the rules, the center was suspended for the fifth and deciding game of the series. New York won.

The next year, the Heat won the Atlantic Division again, met New York in the playoffs again, and once again lost. How did they lose? In the most heartbreaking of ways: With 0.8 seconds left in Game 5, Knick guard Allan Houston hit a running shot, giving the Knicks a 78–77 victory.

But things were put into perspective when, during the 2000–01 season, the team's heart and soul, center Alonzo Mourning, was diagnosed with the kidney disease focal glomerulosclerosis.

The good news is that Mourning came back strong the very next season, proving just how strong his heart is.

> ### Inside Stuff
>
> During the 2000–01 season, Heat head coach Pat Riley had his 1,000th career win. He became the second coach in NBA history to accomplish this feat. Lenny Wilkens was the first. That year was also the 19th year in a row that Riley-led teams made the playoffs, another record. The previous number of consecutive playoff appearances was 18, by Red Auerbach.

New Jersey Nets

In 1967, the Nets were one of the 11 original ABA teams, although at the time they were known as the New Jersey Americans. The ragtag bunch played in a converted armory in Teaneck, New Jersey. The ABA, desperate for a team in the nation's number-one media market, took what it could get—and the New Jersey Americans were all it could get.

The next season, the New Jersey Americans became the New York Nets (so as to rhyme with the Mets and Jets). The team's next change occurred in 1970, when it lured Rick Barry to the team. The ABA finally had a superstar player playing in the country's major media market.

Inside Stuff

The Americans went 36–42 that first season, tying them with the Kentucky Colonels for the fourth and final playoff spot. The ABA scheduled a single-elimination game to decide which of the two teams would play the Minnesota Muskies in the first round of the playoffs, but problematically, the Teaneck Armory was booked for a circus that night.

New Jersey owner Arthur Brown hustled to find an alternate venue, and finally landed the Commack Arena in Long Island. However, when the teams showed up for the game, the Colonels refused to play. The floorboards of the arena were unfastened, bolts were loose and unscrewed, and the basketball stanchions were unpadded. ABA commissioner George Mikan ruled that the Americans had forfeited the game and Kentucky had won. And so it is that New Jersey lost its first-ever playoff game without ever playing.

But the biggest turning point for the Nets franchise occurred in 1973, when it traded for Dr. J, Julius Erving. The good doctor was only 23 years old at the time and was at his gravity-defying best. The Nets suddenly had fans and championship aspirations. And in fact, they won the ABA Championship in 1974 as Dr. J walked off with the MVP award.

In 1975–76, the last year of the ABA, the Nets won the championship again, but soon thereafter, the league folded (see Chapter 3). The Nets sold Dr. J's contract to the 76ers for $3 million. This marked the beginning of a steep decline for the ball club. They would not get back to championship-caliber play for over a quarter-century.

In 1981, three-time ABA Coach of the Year Larry Brown was made coach of the Nets. As he has done many times since, the coach turned the team around, and by the 1982–83 season, the Nets went 49–33. However, with six games remaining in the season, it was announced that Brown had signed to coach the Kansas Jayhawks the next season. The Nets' fortunes declined again. Beginning in 1985 and continuing on for the next seven seasons, the team never topped the .500 mark.

Inside Stuff

The fortunes of the Nets may have hit the bottom when, in 1993, New Jersey star and Euro-pioneer Drazen Petrovic was killed in a car accident. He had just come off his best season, averaging 22.3 ppg. Petrovic was only 28 years old and was very popular with the fans.

The up-and-down fortunes of the Nets went up again when former Piston head coach Chuck Daly took over the team. With Derrick Coleman up front and Kenny Anderson running the offense, the Nets made the playoffs again in 1994, but as usual, soon faded away, and stayed that way for the next few years.

Things definitely changed for the better when the team hired Rod Thorn in 2000 to run the front office. One of Thorn's first moves was to hire ex-Laker guard Byron Scott to coach the team. One season later, the team traded All-Star guard Stephon Marbury for Jason Kidd. In a little over a year, Thorn reshaped the Nets, setting the stage for a very special season.

In 2001–2002, the Nets won a franchise-record 52 games, as well as the Atlantic Division Championship, thanks in large part to Kidd's MVP-caliber all-around play. After defeating Indiana, Charlotte, and Boston, the Nets went on to meet the Lakers in their first-ever trip to the NBA Finals. Although they lost to Los Angeles, the 2001–2002 campaign was a magical season and will go down in Nets history as one of the best ever.

New York Knicks

New York has a basketball tradition as old and rich as the Celtics:

♦ The Knicks and the Celtics are the only two charter members of the National Basketball Association still in their original cities. The third, the Warriors, now play in Oakland instead of Philadelphia.

♦ The first NBA game (or BAA, as it was known back then) occurred on November 1, 1946, when the Knicks played the Toronto Huskies. The Knicks won that game 68–66, and Leo "Ace" Gottlieb was New York's high scorer with 12 points.

♦ The first actual NBA Finals occurred after the 1950–51 season; the Knicks played in the series, despite their 36–30 record and a third-place finish in the East. The Knicks lost to the Rochester Royals in seven games.

♦ One of the first African-Americans to play in the NBA—Nat "Sweetwater" Clifton—played for the Knicks that same season that Earl Lloyd became the first African-American player to play in the NBA.

Although the Knicks don't have as many championships as the Celtics, they have been a dominant team in the East for as long. In the league's early years, the Knicks played for the title three times. In the '70s, they won it twice, and in the '90s, they made it back to the NBA Finals twice (1994 and 1999). It's an impressive legacy.

Inside Stuff

Just what is a Knickerbocker, you ask? The terms comes from the Dutch settlers who came to New York in the 1600s. Their pants, rolled up below the knee, were known as knickerbockers. Since then, the term has become synonymous with the Big Apple.

The first organized baseball team (circa 1845) was named the New York Knicker- bockers, a.k.a. "the Knickerbocker Nine."

When the Basketball Association of America (the forerunner to the NBA) was formed in 1946, New York was given a charter franchise. The men in charge of the new team put their various choices for a team name in a hat. When they pulled the names out, most said "Knickerbockers," and founder Ned Irish thus named the team the New York Knickerbockers.

Throughout the years, the Knicks have had some of the very best players in the league on the team, including …

- Walt Frazier
- Dick Barnett
- Earl Monroe
- Dick McGuire
- Willis Reed
- Dave DeBusschere
- Bill Bradley
- Bernard King
- Patrick Ewing

And it's not just these sorts of legendary players that make New York basketball so special, it's the executives and other off-court personnel.

For example, before Chick Hearn ever called a Laker game, before Johnny Most became the Celtic play-by-play man, Marty Glickman was calling Knick basketball games and inventing basketball lingo. Some of the phrases created by the legendary Marty Glickman are …

- The lane
- The key
- Top of the key
- Swish

And of course, Marty's most famous protégé is current Knick broadcaster Marv Albert.

So Knick basketball is a veritable "Who's Who" of NBA basketball itself, a rich tradition that is sure to continue.

Orlando Magic

In 1986, Pat Williams and Jimmy Hewitt teamed up to try and bring an NBA franchise to Orlando. Williams at the time was a member of the Philadelphia 76er family, but, he says, "I knew deep within that the adventure and risk involved in trying to start up a team was really something I had to pursue."

And pursue it he did. Williams became the driving force behind the Magic. What are the greatest moments in the team's history? Here are Pat Williams' Top 10:

1. The press conference on June 19, 1986, during which Williams, Hewitt, and their associates announced that they were going to try and get a basketball team into central Florida.

2. April 22, 1987: The NBA Board of Governors announced that Orlando would get an expansion franchise in 1989, *if* 10,000 season tickets were sold 10 months before tip-off.

3. The 10,000th ticket was sold on December 22, 1988. Says Williams, "I'll never forget the day …. A Volkswagen repairman came in off the street and plunked down the money for four season tickets."

4. The Magic's first preseason game, October 13, 1989. The team was playing the world champion Detroit Pistons. Williams says of the excitement that first night, "You would have thought it was the seventh game of the NBA Finals."

5. The team's first regular-season game. November 4, 1989, versus the New Jersey Nets. The Magic lost.

6. The DeVos family buys the team.

7. The team wins the *NBA Draft Lottery* in 1992, gaining the right to draft Shaquille O'Neal. Says Williams, "I'll never forget the total shock, the feeling of being absolutely overwhelmed with joy and excitement."

Tip-In

Where did the name *Magic* come from (aside from the obvious fact that the team played in the same city as Disney's Magic Kingdom)? The *Orlando Sentinel* held a naming contest; 4,296 entries were received, and the team chose the Magic.

Hoopology

Every year, the 13 teams that had the worst record in the league compete for the right to pick first in the **NBA Draft Lottery,** the method by which college and international players are brought into the league. The lottery is weighted in favor of the teams with the most losses. The lottery began in 1985.

8. The 1993 NBA Draft Lottery. With only one chance out of 66, the Magic are magic again, winning the lottery two years in a row. That year, they drafted Chris Webber, and then promptly traded him on draft day for Penny Hardaway and a boatload of future draft picks to Golden State.

9. The 1995 NBA Finals. After only six years in the league, the Magic made it to the finals. Impressive.

10. The summer of 2000. The team signed free agents Grant Hill and Tracy McGrady—not a bad off-season at all.

T-Mac chose Orlando over a host of other suitors.

Philadelphia 76ers

The storied Philadelphia 76er franchise can trace its roots back to the old NBL. It was there, in 1946, that the Syracuse Nationals were born. In 1955, the Nats won the NBA Championship.

In 1963, the Nats were sold by Dan Biasone, the inventor of the 24-second shot clock, to Irv Kosloff and Ike Richman. The new owners petitioned the league to move the franchise and change its name, and the request was granted. As the Philadelphia Warriors had moved to San Francisco in 1961, the Nats moved to Philly and were renamed the 76ers.

In 1965, one of the most significant moves in NBA history occurred when the Sixers acquired Wilt Chamberlain for three players and some cash. Wilt paid immediate dividends, leading the team to a 55–25 record and the Eastern Division title in 1965–66.

The next season was the extraordinary one. New coach Alex Hannum told Wilt that he would have to shoot less and pass more if the team wanted to win. He did and they did, winning the championship that year.

Although the Sixers fortunes declined shortly thereafter, they rose again in 1976 when Julius Erving joined the team. Erving led them to another championship in 1983. In 1984, the team added a new rookie to the mix named Charles Barkley. The "round mound of rebound" (as he was known) would pick up where Dr. J left off, as Erving retired after the 1987 season.

Barkley remained in Philly until 1993, when he was traded to Phoenix. Yet the Sixers wouldn't be without another star player for long.

> ### Inside Stuff
>
> In 1965–66, Wilt averaged 33.5 ppg, but in 1966–67, he averaged only 24.1 ppg. Although it was the first time in eight years that Wilt didn't win the scoring title, he nevertheless was quite effective: He ended up first in field goal percentage (.683), first in rebounding (24.2 rpg), and third in assists (7.8 per game).

Allen Iverson brought new life to the Sixers.

The team drafted Allen Iverson in 1996. Billed as "The Answer," AI had it all: explosiveness, spunk, quickness, and scoring ability and took home NBA Rookie of the Year honors. In 1998–99, Iverson won the NBA scoring title, averaging 26.8 ppg.

Although Iverson and Coach Larry Brown clashed from time to time, the 2000–01 season was a special one. Iverson went on to lead the Sixers to a 56–26 record as he took home MVP honors. Brown was named Coach of the Year as he guided Philly to the NBA Finals before succumbing to the Lakers in five games.

Washington Wizards

The early days of the Washington Wizards were a wild time when the team changed cities and names what seemed like every year:

- In 1961–62 they were the Chicago Packers

- In 1962–63 they were the Chicago Zephyrs

- From 1963 to 1973 they were the Baltimore Bullets

- From 1973 to 1974 they were the Capital Bullets

- From 1974 to 1997 they were the Washington Bullets

- And in 1997 they became the Washington Wizards

In the 1967 NBA Draft, the Baltimore Bullets selected a 6' 3" guard out of Winston-Salem State College named Earl "The Pearl" Monroe. The Pearl was a flashy, exciting player who served as an inspiration for players such as Pete Maravich. A creative scorer and great passer, Monroe was named Rookie of the Year in 1968.

Tip-In

How different was the NBA in 1968? Center Wes Unseld was 6' 7".

The Bullets struck gold twice when, in 1968, drafting second again, they selected Wes Unseld, a center out of Louisville. Unseld became only the second player in NBA history (Wilt was the other) to win NBA Rookie of the Year honors and be named the MVP the same year. Unseld would play for the team for the next 13 years, and afterwards, coached the team for seven years.

Although Earl Monroe was traded to the Knicks in 1971, the Bullets traded for forward Elvin Hayes the next year, creating the foundation for a championship run. In 1978, under head coach Dick Motta, the team did in fact win the championship, with Unseld being named the finals MVP.

But what followed were some years of pretty mediocre basketball. Although some great players walked through the doors, winning basketball was in short supply for much of the '80s and '90s.

In 1996, the team made it to the playoffs again, behind the play of Chris Webber, Juwan Howard, and Rod Strickland. But this dynamic trio was not together long enough to see what they could do. In 1998, Webber was traded to the Sacramento Kings for All-Star guard Mitch Richmond.

The biggest, most dramatic change in Wizards history may have come on January 19, 2000, when owner Abe Pollin named Michael Jordan as president of basketball operations. Jordan looked around and realized what he needed most was an impact player if he was to kick-start the franchise.

That was when it hit him. Who was the most dynamic player in the history of the NBA? So Michael Jordan hired himself. He unretired for a second time on September 25, 2001, and donned the uniform of the Washington Wizards.

The Least You Need to Know

- The Boston Celtics, New York Knicks, and Philadelphia 76ers are as old as the NBA itself.

- The Miami Heat history is one of success.

- After years of struggle, the New Jersey Nets made it to the NBA Finals in 2002.

- The Orlando Magic struck lottery gold twice in acquiring Shaquille O'Neal and Anfernee Hardaway.

- The Washington Wizards have reason for optimism.

Chapter 8

Central Division

In This Chapter

- ◆ Atlanta Hawks
- ◆ Chicago Bulls
- ◆ Cleveland Cavaliers
- ◆ Detroit Pistons
- ◆ Indiana Pacers
- ◆ Milwaukee Bucks
- ◆ New Orleans Hornets
- ◆ Toronto Raptors

The NBA's Central Division is home to some storied franchises in the league. Not only do the six-time NBA Champion Bulls battle it out there, but so do ex-champions Hawks, Pistons, and Bucks. It's a powerhouse in the Eastern Conference.

Atlanta Hawks

It may surprise you to learn that the Atlanta Hawks franchise is one of the oldest in the league. The team's history dates back to 1949, when it was known as the Tri-Cities Blackhawks. What Tri-Cities, you ask?

- ◆ Davenport, Iowa
- ◆ Moline, Illinois
- ◆ Rock Island, Illinois

Later, the team moved to Milwaukee; later still, St. Louis; and finally, Atlanta. While playing in St. Louis, the Hawks won their only NBA Championship.

Your NBA Champion St. Louis Hawks

The 1956–57 season got off to a bad start. Coach Red Holzman was fired after 33 games, and then player-coach Slater Martin quit coaching after eight games, so reserve forward Alex Hannum was named head coach halfway into the season.

It was a fortuitous decision, as Hannum would go on to be one of the great coaches in NBA history and would be enshrined in the Hall of Fame as a coach. The team went on to tie with the Lakers and Pistons for first in the Western Conference. The Hawks then upset the heavily favored Lakers in the Western Conference Finals, actually *sweeping* the Lakers out of the playoffs. The Hawks went on to meet the even more heavily favored Boston Celtics in the NBA Finals.

Game 7 was a classic. It was on national TV (a new phenomenon), and was a tight game throughout. Bob Pettit of the Hawks sank two free throws at the end of regulation to send the game into overtime. A shot at the end of overtime by the Hawks sent the game into double-overtime. At the end of that extra period, Boston forward Jim Loscutoff sank a free throw in the last few seconds, giving Boston a 125–123 victory, and the first of many NBA Championships.

Tip-In

The last game of that series had an amazing ending: After Boston's Jim Loscutoff sank that free throw near the end of the game, Hawks coach Alex Hannum devised a bold play where his team would inbound the ball and throw it the full length of the court—off the backboard—where Pettit would grab the rebound and then hopefully sink the winning shot. Amazingly, the play almost worked! Pettit got the ball about 10 feet from the basket and quickly let the shot go—it rimmed out and the Celtic celebrated their first ever NBA title.

The 1957–58 Hawks played like a team on a mission. They tore through the regular season and met the Celtics again for a rematch of the previous year's finals.

Fortunately for St. Louis, Boston's young center, Bill Russell, suffered an ankle injury in Game 3. Hobbled but still playing, Russell could do little to slow down Hawks All-Star Bob Pettit. Pettit scored a then-record 50 points in Game 6, and the Hawks won the game 110–109 and the series, earning them their first—and so far, only—NBA title.

Great Hawks Through the Ages

The Hawks have seen more than their share of great players through the years. Among the most beloved are …

- **Bob Pettit:** The 1955 NBA Rookie of the Year, Bob Pettit was a banger. With both inside and outside moves to his game, Pettit was the best power forward of his era. At a time when power forwards were mostly rebounders, Pettit redefined the position, adding scoring to the mix. Pettit was a two-time NBA MVP and a 10-time All-**NBA First Teamer**. Pettit also was a four-time All-Star MVP.

- **"Sweet Lou" Hudson:** A six-time NBA All-Star, Lou Hudson was a deadly shooter who averaged over 20 points per game for his career. Former NBA referee Ken Hudson (no relation) called Lou Hudson "one of the great offensive players ever to play in the NBA, as good a pure shooter as you will ever see."

- **Dominique Wilkins:** With one of the great nicknames in all of sports history— The Human Highlight Film—Dominique Wilkins was also one of the great players of his era. Throughout the '80s, although Larry Bird and Magic Johnson got the lion's share of the press, Wilkins followed close behind.

Tip-In

The Hawks' history:

- Tri-Cities Blackhawks: 1949 to 1951
- Milwaukee Hawks: 1951 to 1955
- St. Louis Hawks: 1955 to 1968
- Atlanta Hawks: 1968 to the present

Hoopology

At the end of the season, the NBA picks the five best players in the entire league—one for each position. These best of the best are called the **All-NBA First Team**. There is also an All-NBA Second Team and Third Team.

Tip-In

Dominique Wilkins wasn't the only Atlanta Hawk to win the Slam Dunk Contest during the '80s. In 1986, his diminutive teammate Anthony "Spud" Webb became maybe the most amazing winner of all time. Why? Spud is only 5' 7".

He was a unique talent; a high-flying, acrobatic, dunking machine. Winning the NBA All-Star Slam Dunk contest in 1985, Wilkins was beyond impressive, he was drop-your-jaw amazing.

Chicago Bulls

We all know about the Bulls' championship run through the 1990s (we gave you the details in Chapter 5). The untold story is how they got there.

History of the Bulls

Chicago has always been a great basketball town. Prior to the Bulls entering the NBA in 1966, the city had two other professional basketball teams.

The Chicago Stags were a charter member of the Basketball Association of America, the forerunner to the NBA. Although the team folded in 1950, a new team, the Chicago Packers, debuted in 1961. The next season, they changed the name of the team to the Zephyrs, and one year later still, that team moved to Baltimore and became the Washington Wizards.

The Chicago Bulls joined the NBA in 1966. On October 15, 1966, the Chicago Bulls franchise earned its first-ever victory when it beat the St. Louis Hawks, 104–97. That first Chicago team was coached by Johnny "Red" Kerr, and the team's opening light lineup was as follows:

- Len Chappell
- Bob Boozer
- Don Kojis
- Jerry Sloan
- Guy Rodgers

The expansion Chicago Bulls had a very successful first season, finishing with a 33–48 record. The team made the playoffs, Kerr was named NBA Coach of the Year, Erwin Mueller made the NBA All-Rookie Team, Rodgers led the NBA in assists, and Rodgers and Sloan were both named All-Stars.

In the early '70s, a hard-nosed, defense-oriented, competitive team took to the floor. Coached by Dick Motta, the team featured such players as the following:

- Bob Love

- Chet Walker

- Norm Van Lier

- Jerry Sloan

- Tom Boerwinkle

Technical Foul

The Chicago Bulls lost the 1979 coin flip to the Los Angeles Lakers for the No. 1 overall pick in the NBA Draft. The Lakers took Magic Johnson. The Bulls, drafting No. 2 overall, selected David Greenwood out of UCLA.

Aside from the nice run this group had, the Bulls for the most part were a mediocre bunch before Michael Jordan, Scottie Pippen, and Phil Jackson arrived.

Cleveland Cavaliers

Cleveland joined the NBA family for the 1970–71 season, as part of the expansion that also brought in the Buffalo Braves and Portland Trail Blazers. The Cavs, though they started slow, came on strong by the late 1980s to become a consistent Central Division contender.

The first group to play for the Cavs included not-so-memorable names like Luther Rackley, Johnny Egan, Larry Mikan (son of George Mikan), Gary Suiter, Walt Wesley, and John Warren.

Their coach was a new guy out of the college ranks named Bill Fitch. After looking over the roster, Fitch is said to have said, "Just remember, the name is Fitch, not Houdini."

Fitch knew what he was talking about. That team started out 0–15, and in the middle of that streak, Fitch was quoted as saying, "I phoned Dial-a-Prayer, but when they found out who it was, they hung up."

Tip-In

The Cleveland Cavaliers played their first seven games ever on the road because the Cleveland Arena was booked for the Ice Capades.

That first season in Cleveland was certainly memorable, but not for the usual reasons people want to remember things. The team went 2–34, and then 3–36 before embarking on an unprecedented three-game winning streak. They finished the season 15–67.

The next year, a player who would become a mainstay of the Cleveland franchise came to town when Fitch traded for Seattle guard Lenny Wilkens. Lenny was also now the new coach. Yet even so, the team was still bad, and would be bad for some time.

Inside Stuff

Battle of the expansion teams: In a game against its expansion rival Blazers, Cleveland's John Warren made a layup—in the wrong basket! Not to be outdone, Blazers center LeRoy Ellis tried to block it.

Finally, on April 10, 1976, the Cavs clinched the Central Division Championship (along with its first trip to the playoffs) by beating the Knicks. The team finished that season at 49–33.

But the next decade saw the team decline again, a road that it would continue to go down until the 1986 draft, when the team drafted two players who would turn the tide: center Brad Daugherty and guard Mark Price.

Those changes would turn the once-hapless Cavs into contenders. In the 1987–88 season, Cleveland faced the Chicago Bulls in a first-round playoff matchup, the beginning of what would become many memorable series between these two teams.

In that great five-game series, Michael Jordan scored 50 or more points twice (becoming the first player in NBA playoff history to do so), and 38, 44, and 39 points in the other three games. His average of 45.2 points for the series set an NBA playoff record for a five-game series.

Inside Stuff

Jordan's buzzer-beating shot over Cleveland's Craig Ehlo has come to be considered one of the great moments in NBA playoff history, and is now known as "The Shot."

Figuring out how to stop MJ became a bit of an obsession in Cleveland (among other places). In 1989, the team faced the Bulls in the opening round of the playoffs again. In an epic Game 5, Jordan hit a 16-foot jump shot at the buzzer to win the game, 101–100.

Tip-In

At the 1998 NBA All-Star weekend, four Cavs were selected for the Rookie Game: Cedric Henderson, Brevin Knight, Zydrunas Ilgauskas, and Derek Anderson. Ilgauskas was named the game's MVP.

How good was this team? Consider that in the 1990 season, Mark Price, Brad Daugherty, Larry Nance, and Co. once beat the Miami Heat 148–80, setting the NBA record for margin of victory. In Wilkens' seven seasons as head coach of the Cavs, Cleveland made the playoffs five times.

But as good as this team was, it had the misfortune of playing in the East at a time when the Celtics were strong (albeit descending), and the Bulls were even stronger (and ascending). Always the bridesmaid but never the bride—that was this Cleveland team. They were in the same boat as the Cincinnati Royals in the early to mid-1960s with Oscar Robertson, who could never get past the Celtics.

Detroit Pistons

As you may recall, the Detroit Pistons is the oldest team in continuous operation in the league, dating back to the franchise's inception as the Fort Wayne Zollner Pistons of the National Basketball League in 1941. The team joined the NBA in 1949 and moved to Detroit in 1957.

Then, as now, the Central Division teams were a tough lot, including the dynastic Minneapolis Lakers and the tough Rochester Royals. The closest the franchise came to a championship back then was a loss to the Syracuse Nationals in 1955. The Pistons lost Game 7 when the Nats' George King, in what would later become vintage Havlicek style, stole the ball with but a few seconds left. The Pistons made it to the finals again the next year, and were again rebuffed by the Philadelphia Warriors. They would not have another shot at a championship for almost 35 years.

Although the team might have struggled, fans nevertheless saw some great players play.

Great Pistons of the Past

There have always been great Piston players:

- In 1959, the team drafted Bailey Howell. Howell averaged more than 20 points a game and made the All-Star team four times in his five years as a Piston.

Inside Stuff

Although Dave DeBusschere is best known as an essential cog in those great New York Knick teams of the '70s, he has two other distinctions for which is he less well known.

First, long before Michael Jordan began his baseball detour, DeBusschere actually played in the Majors, pitching in 36 games for the White Sox in 1962 and 1963 (ironically, the same franchise Jordan played for).

Second, while still only 24 years old, DeBusschere was made the player-coach of the Pistons during the 1964–65 season. He thus became the youngest coach in league history.

◆ In 1962, the Pistons drafted Dave DeBusschere, a three-time All-Star while a Piston.

◆ In the 1966 draft, Detroit selected what would become one of the most popular players in Piston history, Dave Bing. The 1967 Rookie of the Year and future All-Star and Hall of Famer, Bing was a scrappy 6' 3" guard who became synonymous with Detroit Piston basketball.

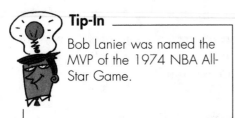

Tip-In

Bob Lanier was named the MVP of the 1974 NBA All-Star Game.

◆ The Pistons continued to draft impressively when, in 1970, the team selected a 6' 11", 265-pound former All-American from St. Bonaventure named Bob Lanier. Throughout the '70s, Lanier and Bing made a formidable duo.

Championship Seeds Are Sown

With the second pick of the 1981 draft, the Detroit Pistons selected Isiah Thomas from Indiana University. The electrifying guard had just led IU to the 1981 NCAA Championship and had been named MVP of the Final Four.

Isiah made the NBA All-Star team as a rookie, and would make it for the next 12 years in a row.

Inside Stuff

In point guard Isiah Thomas, the Pistons put in place the first essential piece of their championship puzzle. It is difficult to say which of the five positions on an NBA team are the most important, but the point guard is definitely a contender.

The point guard on a basketball team is often compared to a quarterback in football, and it is easy to see why. The point guard directs the offense. He's the one who passes the ball and is a surrogate coach on the court. Without a great point guard, a team can sputter or otherwise appear directionless.

The next step in the long Detroit quest for a championship happened the next year when the team traded for center Bill Laimbeer from Cleveland. The center had a surprisingly soft shooting touch, especially when considering his intense on-court persona.

Step Three: Get a great coach. The Pistons did just that when, in 1983, they hired Chuck Daly to be their coach. Daly, once a high school coach in Pennsylvania, had worked his way up the coaching ladder. Daly coached eight years in college—two at Boston College and six at Pennsylvania. Daly also coached the Cavaliers for part of the 1981–82 season.

The last critical piece of the championship-building process for Detroit occurred in 1985 when it drafted Joe Dumars out of McNeese State, kept him, and then traded for forward Rick Mahorn.

Tip-In

In 1984 and 1986, Isiah Thomas was named MVP of the NBA All-Star Game.

The Pistons looked to be title contenders in 1986–87 as their aggressive, no-nonsense play earned them the nickname the "Bad Boys." That team finished the regular season 52–30, and for the first time in a long time, made it to the Eastern Conference Finals.

In Game 5 at fabled Boston Garden, the Pistons had a one-point lead and the ball with five seconds left. But, as Isiah Thomas inbounded the ball, Bird stole the pass and tossed to teammate Dennis Johnson, who made a layup, and Boston pulled out another improbable victory.

The next year—1988—Detroit lost to the Los Angeles Lakers in seven games in the NBA Finals. Although two heartbreaking losses in a row left the Pistons huffing and puffing, they would soon blow the house down. In 1989, Detroit Pistons clinched the championship when they defeated the Lakers in the 1989 NBA Finals. In 1990 they repeated the feat, this time defeating the Portland Trail Blazers.

Indiana Pacers

Basketball and Indiana are almost synonymous, and from their run as an ABA power-house to the present-day heroics of Reggie Miller, the Indiana Pacers have been integral to that state's love affair with the game.

Love affair or not, the team was decidedly average after they joined the NBA, and would continue that way for a while. The team's fortunes began to change, as is often the case with NBA franchises, when it made an astute draft pick.

Tip-In

Reggie Miller has good genes. His brother Darrell was a Major League catcher, and his sister Cheryl is one of the greatest women's basketball players of all time.

With the 11th pick in the 1987 NBA Draft, the Indiana Pacers chose Reggie Miller, a 6' 7" guard from UCLA. Miller combined deep, deep range with a killer instinct.

Reggie Miller for threeeee!

The next year, the team drafted well again, picking 7' 4'' Rik Smits with the second pick. Although the team would win only 26 games that year, a solid nucleus was now in place.

Hoopology

In basketball, each position is assigned a number, and a player of that position is often called that number. The point guard is a 1, the shooting guard is a 2 (or **2-guard**), the small forward is a 3, the power forward is a 4, and the center is a 5.

By 1990, Reggie Miller was developing into one of the best *2-guards* in the league.

In the 1991 playoffs, the Pacers met the Celtics in the first round, extended Boston to five games (after not-a-little trash talking by Pacer Chuck Person), but lost in the end. Boston knocked Indiana out of the playoffs for a second year in a row the next year, and they made another quick exit the year after that, too (1993).

If anything is certain in the NBA it is this: When a team is expected to win and doesn't, the coach will get fired. And so, after the 1992–93 season, Indiana fired Coach Bob Hill and hired Larry Brown.

Larry (I)

At Indiana, Larry Brown continued his amazing streak of turning around ball clubs. The team went 47–35, beat Orlando in the first round, upset the Atlanta Hawks in semifinals, and then met the New York in the Eastern Conference Finals.

The Pacers won two games at Market Square Arena after the Knicks had won the first two games in New York. In Game 5, at Madison Square Garden, Reggie scored an astounding 25 points *in the fourth quarter*, as the Pacers beat the Knicks. Although the Knicks eventually won the series, Reggie Miller became an NBA star that series.

This Indiana team, consisting of Miller, Smits, Dale Davis, Antonio Davis, and newly acquired Mark Jackson would remain one of the best in the NBA for the next several years.

But despite this success, the Pacers could never seem to get over the final obstacle: to advance to the NBA Finals. Although Larry Brown twice had taken the team to within one game of the finals, more was expected. So the Rule of Coaches was enforced, and Brown resigned. Another coach, another Larry, would have to do that job.

Tip-In

Reggie Miller always seems to do his best when the light shines brightest. One of the most memorable events in playoff history occurred in 1995. In that game, with the Knicks up by six and time running out, Miller somehow scored 8 points in the 8.9 seconds remaining, and the Pacers won.

Larry (II)

For the 1997–98 season, Indiana native and NBA legend Larry Bird became the head coach of the Pacers. Bird led the team to its best record ever, 58–24, and again, the team came within one game of making it to the NBA Finals.

Finally, in the 1999–2000 season, the Indiana Pacers crossed the threshold and won the Eastern Conference Championship to advance to the NBA Finals for the first time ever. Although the team lost to the Lakers in six games and would begin rebuilding after that, its run as a Central Division powerhouse had been impressive.

Milwaukee Bucks

To understand the Bucks' history, maybe all one need do is look at the players who have played there and whose numbers the Bucks have retired. Therein lays the story of the franchise.

No. 33, Kareem Abdul-Jabbar: The Bucks joined the NBA in 1968, and as expansion teams often do, they came in last. The Suns also came in last in the West, and so the two teams had a coin flip to see which one would draft first in the 1969 draft. The Suns called heads, the coin was tails, and Milwaukee had the first pick.

Fortunately for the Bucks, 1969 was the year Kareem (then still known as Lew Alcindor) graduated from UCLA. The Bucks wasted no time in drafting the amazing center. The Bucks won 56 games that year, and Abdul-Jabbar was, not surprisingly, named Rookie of the Year. The next year, the Bucks won 66 games, and Kareem was named the MVP of the league.

Hoopology

Prior to Kareem, a hook shot was shot with an arc—up, then down. But because of his size (7' 2") and the fact that he jumped when he shot it, Kareem's hook shot was often going down toward the basket from the moment he released it. It was thus dubbed the **skyhook** because it looked like it was coming down from the sky.

That year, 1970–71, the big guy averaged 31.7 ppg and 16 rpg, and the Bucks romped through the playoffs, winning their only NBA Championship.

No. 1, Oscar Robertson: The difference between a good Bucks team and a great Bucks team was the Big O. Teaming up with Kareem gave Oscar a chance to win that elusive ring. With Kareem scoring at will from the inside with his *skyhook* and Oscar passing and shooting from the outside, the two made for a scary alliance.

Robertson played with the Bucks for three more years, and even though Kareem was now playing in L.A., the Bucks won no fewer than 59 games while Oscar ran the show.

No. 12, Junior Bridgeman: Bridgeman was acquired with Brian Winters in the trade that sent Kareem to the Lakers. He played for the team over two different stints, has played in more Bucks games than any other player, and is among the leading scorers and rebounders in Bucks history.

No. 32, Brian Winters: The other major part of the Kareem trade, Winters played for the Bucks for eight years. Like Junior Bridgeman, Brian Winters ended up being one of the best Bucks ever, being one of the top players in team history in assists, scoring, games played, and steals.

No. 4, Sidney Moncrief: After the Kareem and Kareem-trade eras, the Bucks of the 1980s became a very good team, too. They won 50 or more games seven seasons in a row, and made it to the playoffs 10 years in a row. Integral to that success was Sidney Moncrief. "Mr. Everything" was selected fifth overall in the 1979 draft and could score, rebound, pass, and defend.

No. 14, Jon McGlocklin: An original member of the team, "Johnny Mac" has been both a beloved player and broadcaster for the organization for years.

No. 16, Bob Lanier: Though Lanier played for nine seasons in Detroit, Milwaukee still remembers fondly his four years he spent with the Bucks.

Don Nelson, head coach: One of the NBA's greatest coaches, Nelson led Milwaukee to seven straight division titles in 11 seasons and seven straight 50-win seasons.

> ### Inside Stuff
>
> Hall of Famer Bob Lanier is currently the special assistant to NBA Commissioner David Stern and is very active in the NBA's Read to Achieve program. Lanier has worked in the league office since 1995.

Ray Allen of the Bucks lights 'em up.

New Orleans Hornets

The Charlotte Hornets joined the NBA in the 1988–89 season, and in only its fifth year in existence, the team made the playoffs behind the muscle of Larry Johnson and Alonzo Mourning.

Although the team was originally stocked with veterans, the most important development for Charlotte was the emergence of a short young point guard, Muggsy Bogues. At 5' 3", Muggsy was both amazingly quick and equally effective; causing opponents as much of a matchup problem as they caused him.

Inside Stuff

Why the "Hornets"? Charlotte's minor-league baseball team had been known as the Hornets, and its World Football League team was also known as the Hornets, so the name has historical significance to Charlotte.

Even more importantly, the Hornets won the 1991 NBA Draft Lottery, which they used to select a stud power forward from the University of Nevada-Las Vegas, the College Basketball Player of the Year, Larry Johnson. LJ became the focal point of the team, the franchise player they needed. Johnson was named NBA Rookie of the Year that year.

The next year, picking second, the Hornets selected another franchise player when they acquired Alonzo Mourning. It seemed as if the basketball gods had smiled on Charlotte, and the team was ready for a long run deep into the playoffs.

In 1993, the Hornets made their playoff debut in the first round against the Boston Celtics. Somehow, this young team found a way to beat the Celtics in only four games (before losing to the Knicks in five in the next round).

By the 1995–96 season, the team had decided that it needed to go in a new direction. It traded LJ to New York and Mourning to Miami, and began to rebuild. In 1997, even Muggsy Bogues, an original Hornet, was traded (to Golden State).

Bogues' replacement was David Wesley. Shooting guard Bobby Phills joined Wesley in the backcourt. Once again, the team posted a 50-win season (51–31).

 Tip-In

After the 1993 season, the Hornets signed Larry Johnson to a 12-year contract, the biggest in league history up to that point. But Johnson hurt his back the next year, and was never again the explosive power player who had signed that lucrative contract.

Phills was a very popular player among his teammates and the fans, and so it was especially hard when he was killed in an automobile accident on January 12, 2000. The Hornets retired his number 13 on February 9, the first number to be retired by the team.

Although the Hornets continued to make the playoffs, the air had gone out of the ball in Charlotte, for a variety of reasons, not the least of which was the inability of the owners to get financing for a new arena. And so, after 14 years in the NBA, the team in 2001 asked the league if it could move.

Although the NBA is very reluctant to permit franchises to change cities (the last time a team had moved was in 1985 when the Kings left Kansas City for Sacramento), the NBA is a business, and a business has to make money. The Hornets relocated to New Orleans for the 2002–03 season.

Toronto Raptors

The Toronto Huskies had been a charter member of the old BAA, but the team folded at the end of the first season. NBA basketball would not return to Canada for almost 50 years.

When the league finally did decide to expand into Canada again, it determined that Toronto and Vancouver were the cities that would most likely be successful, and both ended up getting an NBA franchise.

Needing a name, the new franchise created a nationwide "Name Game" contest. The game generated more than 2,000 entries, some of which were "Raptors," inspired by the hit movie of the time, *Jurassic Park*.

With a city and name in place, the hard work began. The Raptors would need players and coaches who could win. One of the first things the team did right was to hire Isiah Thomas as vice president of basketball operations.

In the 1995 NBA Draft, the Raptors first-ever draft pick was guard Damon Stoudamire from Arizona. The seventh pick would go on to earn Rookie of the Year honors.

The team started slowly, a seeming requirement of expansion, but gained steam quickly. In 1998, the team made a move that put it on the NBA map. In a draft day deal with the Golden State Warriors, the Raptors sent Antwan Jamison and cash for Vince Carter.

Tip-In

Aside from the desire on the part of the league for international expansion, there was another reason that the NBA wanted to be back in Canada. Basketball inventor James Naismith was Canadian.

Inside Stuff

The first player ever signed by the Toronto Raptors was Vincenzo Esposito, a forward from the Italian League.

Like Michael Jordan, Carter had played at North Carolina (as did Jamison; they were roommates), and also like MJ, no one knew how good he would be in the pros because of NC's structured approach to the game. Finally, like Jordan, it turned out that the pro game suited Vince just fine. "Vinsanity" was another air-walking, slam-dunking phenomenon. Needless to say, he was named Rookie of the Year that year.

Vince Carter: Air Canada.

The Least You Need to Know

◆ The Atlanta Hawks, Chicago Bulls, Detroit Pistons, and Milwaukee Bucks franchises have all won NBA Championships.

◆ The Indiana Pacers have come close and the Cavaliers are searching for their first NBA Finals berth.

◆ The New Orleans Hornets and the Toronto Raptors are newer teams on their way up.

Midwest Division

In This Chapter

- Dallas Mavericks
- Denver Nuggets
- Houston Rockets
- Memphis Grizzlies
- Minnesota Timberwolves
- San Antonio Spurs
- Utah Jazz

The rugged Midwest Division also has its share of ex-NBA champions and champion hopefuls. The steady, sturdy Utah Jazz play here, as do the up-and-coming Dallas Mavericks. Toss in the Spurs and Rockets, and the stage is set for one tough division.

Dallas Mavericks

The Mavs have again become one of the most exciting teams in the NBA. With managment ready to bring in great players, the Mavericks stand poised to join the NBA elite.

Dallas was a charter city of the old ABA, with the Dallas Chaparrals playing in that league from 1967 to 1973. The next season, the team moved to San Antonio and became the Spurs. Dallas would be without a basketball team for the next seven years.

The Dallas Mavericks joined the NBA in the 1980–81 season. The team soon became a powerhouse, as Dallas and basketball became synonymous throughout most of the 1980s.

> **Inside Stuff**
>
> The expansion fee price for the Dallas Mavericks was $12 million.

> **Technical Foul**
>
> Why did the Chaparrals leave Dallas? On March 26, 1973, the team played its last home game against the Carolina Cougars. Attendance: 134.

The '80s

NBA basketball got off to a rough start in Dallas when the Mavs' first-ever draft pick, Kiki Vandeweghe, held out, refusing to play for an expansion club. The team eventually traded him for two future first-round draft choices, which were spent on Rolondo Blackman and Sam Perkins. Over the next few years, those two would be joined by …

- Derek Harper
- Mark Aguirre
- Detlef Schrempf
- Roy Tarpley
- Brad Davis

Aguirre played for the Mavericks for more than seven seasons, averaging 24.6 points per game. Blackman went on to become the team's all-time scoring leader, averaging 19.2 ppg over 11 seasons.

In only its fourth season in existence, 1984, Dallas made the playoffs, coming in an impressive second in the Midwest Division and making it to the semifinals. By 1988, the team made it to the Western Conference Finals before losing in seven to the Lakers.

Sadly though, this would be the high-water mark for the ball club. The next season, the team began to crumble as Roy Tarpley was suspended for violating the NBA's antidrug policy. Eventually, he was banished from the league.

After the Tarpley distraction finally played itself out, the Mavs found themselves at the bottom of the division, having gone from the pinnacle to the nadir in short order. In 1992, for example, they won only 22 games.

The "Three Js"

If there is any good news in being bad, it is this: You get to draft early. The next few years found the Mavs drafting three excellent players whom they hoped would foster a turnaround: Jim Jackson, Jamal Mashburn, and Jason Kidd.

But almost as quickly as they arrived, the three Js were gone. Their styles of play collided. New coach Don Nelson decided that wholesale changes were in order and so …

- Kidd was traded to the Suns for, among others, Michael Finley.

- Mashburn was traded to Miami.

- Jackson was traded to New Jersey in one of the biggest trades in NBA history.

> **Inside Stuff**
>
> On February 17, 1997, Dallas and New Jersey entered into an almost unprecedented nine-player swap. Dallas traded Jim Jackson, Sam Cassell, Eric Montross, George McCloud, and Chris Gatling for the Nets' Shawn Bradley, Ed O'Bannon, Robert Pack, and Khalid Reeves.

A New Era

In January of 2000, Mark Cuban purchased the team. That, when combined with some shrewd moves by Don Nelson, allowed the Mavs to remake their roster with the likes of Finley, Dirk Nowitzki, and Steve Nash. As a result, another golden era of exciting Maverick basketball began.

Denver Nuggets

The Denver Rockets were an inaugural ABA team, changed their name to the Nuggets in 1974, and became one of only four ABA teams to join the NBA in 1976. The team has always been known as a fun, loose, high-scoring unit. To understand the history of this franchise, it may be best to look at some of its greatest players.

Spencer Haywood: As you may recall, Haywood broke the professional basketball eligibility barrier when he joined the ABA after only two years in college, in 1969.

His presence was immediately felt:

- On November 13, he garnered 31 rebounds, a club record that still stands.

- In April 1970, he scored 59 points in a game.

- He averaged 30 points and almost 20 rebounds a game that year.

Tip-In

The team was renamed the Denver Nuggets before the 1974–75 ABA season.

Tip-In

Dan Issel was elected to the Basketball Hall of Fame in 1992.

Inside Stuff

In 1984, near the end of the Cold War, Alex English starred in a great movie called *Amazing Grace and Chuck*. In it, English plays "Amazing Grace" Smith, an NBA player who gives up his career, like his Little League friend Chuck, in support of global nuclear disarmament.

David Thompson: "Skywalker" was a 6' 4" athletic player who once scored 73 points in a single game. Thompson, along with Dr. J, helped revolutionize basketball, inventing much of the above-the-rim game you see today.

Thompson may best be remembered for his battle with George Gervin of the Spurs on the final day of the season, 1979. The two men were in a dead heat for the scoring title. That day, Thompson erupted for 73 points, the third most in NBA history (behind only Wilt Chamberlain's marks of 100 and 78). By the end of the game, Thompson was in the lead and the scoring title looked to be his. However, later that same day, Gervin took to the floor, and he, too, erupted in dramatic fashion, scoring 63 to take the scoring title away from David Thompson (27.22 to 27.15).

David Thompson's number was retired by the franchise in 1984.

Dan Issel: Issel has been part of Nugget basketball for more than a quarter-century. The forward had played for a few years previously with the Kentucky Colonels, helping the team win an ABA championship. "The Horse" was always a strong, durable player for the Nuggets, missing only 24 games in his 15-year career.

Issel helped take the team into the NBA, making it a winning franchise from the start.

Alex English: During the 1979–80 season, the Nuggets acquired Alex English, a smooth small forward who would play for the team for 11 years and retire as the all-time Nuggets scoring leader. In fact, he was the highest scorer in the NBA for the decade of the 1980s. This team of English, Thompson, and Issel made for some great NBA basketball.

Kiki Vandeweghe: When Vandeweghe refused to play for the expansion Mavericks, he joined this exciting Nugget squad in 1981–82. The solid forward out of UCLA helped Denver average an all-time NBA high of 126.5 points per game. Although the squad rarely made it far in the playoffs, they sure were fun to watch.

Dikembe Mutombo: With the fourth pick of the 1991 NBA Draft, the Nuggets selected a 7' 1" shot blocker and rebounder out of Georgetown named Dikembe Mutombo. By 1992, Deke was an All-Star.

Mutombo, sharp-shooting guard Mahmoud Abdul-Rauf, and new coach Paul West-head brought high-scoring basketball back to Denver. This was the team that upset the strong Sonic team in the first round of the 1994 playoffs.

Antonio McDyess: In the grand Nugget tradition, McDyess was a strong, athletic, exciting, high-scoring player who, despite an *ACL injury*, still managed to light 'em up.

McDyess was drafted by Denver, spent his first two years as a pro there, played a year in Phoenix, and then returned to the Nuggets as a free agent. He was later dealt to the Knicks in another rebuilding effort.

Although the Nuggets are an up and down squad (in more ways than one), they are also usually an exciting club to watch.

Hoopology

The main ligament that holds the knee in place is the anterior cruciate ligament. Tearing it, or suffering an **ACL injury**, can be a career-ending disaster for hoopsters.

Houston Rockets

The San Diego Rockets joined the NBA for the 1967–68 season and the first draft pick in Rockets history was Pat Riley out of the University of Kentucky. Ending up with the worst record that year, the Rockets were given the first overall pick in the following year's draft and selected a center out of the University of Houston named Elvin "Big E" Hayes. Hayes went on to lead the league in scoring in the 1968–69 season and helped transform the club.

The drafting of Hayes would signal the beginning of a tradition: Great centers would play for the Rockets.

In 1971 the team moved to Houston, and the next year Hayes was traded. But big basketball returned to the Rockets soon after when they acquired Moses Malone. Malone, who would later lead the 76ers to a championship, ironically led the Rockets to the Eastern Conference Finals in 1977 against the Sixers (the Rockets lost in six).

Although Moses was traded to Philadelphia in 1982, the seas parted for the Rockets once again when they drafted 7' 4" Ralph Sampson in 1983 and 7' 0" Akeem Olajuwon the next year. The Rockets were once more stocked with quality big men.

The "Twin Towers" made for a formidable front line, leading the team to the NBA Finals

Tip-In

Moses Malone averaged 31 ppg in the 1981–82 season and won the Most Valuable Player Award for the second time.

in 1986. They didn't win, Sampson hurt his knee, and for the next few years, the team made some early exits from the playoffs.

But with the arrival of former Rocket Rudy Tomjanovich as the head coach in 1992, the squad once again became championship material. With Robert Horry (and later Clyde "The Glide" Drexler) coming on board, Olajuwon transforming into one of the most dominant players in the game, and point guard Kenny "The Jet" Smith running the ball club, the Houston Rockets became a team to be feared.

The team won back-to-back titles in 1994 and 1995. But it was not able to three-peat, and so Charles Barkley was brought in 1996. Although this core of Barkley, Hakeem, and Drexler made it to the Western Conference Finals, they never were able to grab the brass ring together.

All three retired or left the team over the next few years, and the Rockets started to look toward the future. But they need not have worried. The prize of the 2002 NBA Draft was a 7' 5" (!) center from China named Yao Ming.

Was there any doubt that the Rockets, with their history of quality big men and draft luck, would win the draft lottery and select a center as tall as a tree? No, not really.

Memphis Grizzlies

The Grizzlies are one of the newer ball clubs in the NBA and don't have nearly the history or tradition of other teams. But with the arrival of Laker legend Jerry West as the team's new president of basketball operations in 2002, good times should certainly be ahead for this ball club.

The Grizzlies joined the league for the 1995–96 season as the Vancouver Grizzlies (along with the Toronto Raptors), as the NBA expanded internationally into Canada. Although the club always was able to get some high lottery picks and draft some quality players, the team has been unable to make the playoffs. Among those drafted by the Grizzlies were …

- ◆ 1995: Bryant "Big Country" Reeves from Oklahoma State (sixth overall).

- ◆ 1996: Shareef Abdur-Rahim from UC Berkeley (third overall).

- ◆ 1997: Antonio Daniels out of Bowling Green (fourth overall).

- ◆ 1998: Mike Bibby out of Arizona (second overall).

- ◆ 1999: Steve Francis from Maryland (second overall, draft rights traded to Houston).

- 2000: Stromile Swift from Louisiana State (second overall).

- 2001: Shane Battier from Duke (sixth pick overall).

- 2002: Drew Gooden from Kansas (fourth pick overall).

In 2001, the Grizzlies were also able to trade Shareef Abdur-Rahim to Atlanta for the third pick in the draft, Pau Gasol. Gasol was later named the "got milk?" NBA Rookie of the Year.

> **Inside Stuff**
>
> Gasol was a star in Europe long before he ever joined the NBA. He helped his team, FC Barcelona, win the 1998–99 Spanish National Championship and he helped Spain win the gold medal at the 1999 World Junior Championship.

Yet, despite this array of lottery talent, the Grizzlies were never able to put a winning ball club on the floor. That, combined with low attendance meant that the team had to look elsewhere. In 2001 the franchise moved to Memphis, Tennessee.

An even bigger coup for the franchise came in 2002 when it was able to hire Jerry West to run the show. West had retired from the Lakers the year before, grew restless, and was looking for a new challenge when the Grizzlies called.

According to West:

> "I decided to end my retirement and join the Grizzlies for three reasons. One, this opportunity gives me a challenge to do something unique. After being a part of the Lakers success for so many years, I have always wondered how it would be to build a winning franchise that has not experienced much success. I want to help make a difference.

> Two, who you work for makes a huge difference in enjoying your job, and I have been so impressed with [owner] Mike [Heisley]. He wants to win so much and is committed to creating a winner for Memphis.

> And three, retirement is not what I thought it would be. Watching NBA games in the last year has rekindled my interest, and I am excited again about being involved in basketball—something that I love to do so much."

Translation: The rest of the NBA better watch out.

Minnesota Timberwolves

The state of Minnesota has a rich basketball legacy; after all, the Minneapolis Lakers won five NBA Championships there. So, when that team moved to Los Angeles in

1960, it left a big hole—a hole that was finally filled by the Minnesota Timberwolves joining the league in 1989. NBA basketball was back in the Gopher State.

When the Twin Cities were finally able to land an expansion NBA franchise, they needed a name for the team. The team held a regionwide contest, and 6,076 entries featuring 1,284 different nicknames were submitted. The two finalists were "Timberwolves" and "Polars." As Minnesota is home to the largest timberwolf population in the lower 48 states, it seemed an apt nickname.

A Slow Start

The T-Wolves played their first NBA game on November 3, 1989, against the Seattle SuperSonics. Their starting lineup was as follows:

◆ Sam Mitchell

◆ Tod Murphy

◆ Brad Lohaus

◆ Tony Campbell

◆ Sidney Lowe

Mitchell made the first bucket in Timberwolves history, but the team lost that first game, 106–94. It would lose a lot more before it would ever begin to win consistently. Yet even though it lost 60 games that first season, the team proved what a great basketball state Minnesota is by setting an all-time NBA record for attendance, averaging more than 26,000 people per game that season.

The next few years found the team mired in bad basketball. Indeed, by 1995, the T-Wolves set the dubious record of having the most 60-loss seasons in a row (four).

The Turnaround

As is always the case in the NBA, the right people, whether they are management, coaches, or players, make the difference. In the case of the Wolves, the team's turnaround began in 1995 when they hired Celtics great and Minnesota's favorite son Kevin McHale to be the new vice president of basketball operations.

McHale immediately made an impact when he boldly used the Wolves '95 draft pick (fifth overall) to draft high school phenom Kevin Garnett. No high school player had ever been selected so high in the draft, but McHale's gambit soon would pay off; Garnett was the real deal.

The final piece of this triumvirate came when Phil "Flip" Saunders was made the head coach the next year. With McHale making savvy personnel moves, Garnett emerging as one of the great players in the game, and Saunders showing them how to win, the Timberwolves were no longer an NBA laughingstock.

By 1997, the team won a record (for them) 40 games and made the playoffs for the first time in their history. Point guard Stephon Marbury and Kevin Garnett made for a great one-two combination, and the Wolves started to win more and more.

But despite their newfound success, the team could not make it out of the first round of the playoffs, a new frustration.

Kevin Garnett helped turn around the T-Wolves.

San Antonio Spurs

As one of only four ABA teams to join the NBA, and as the only one to win an NBA Championship, the Spurs hold a special place in league history.

In the Beginning

The Dallas Chaparrals became the Texas Chaparrals in 1970, and the Texas Chaparrals begat the San Antonio Spurs in 1973. That move, combined with the acquisition of George "Iceman" Gervin the following year, set the stage for some great basketball.

Gervin, a sharpshooting, smooth guard, made his presence felt almost immediately. After joining the NBA in 1976, the team averaged a league-high 115 points per game, and clinched the division title in 1978 (at a time when the team played, for some reason, in the Eastern Conference). The next year, 1979, the Spurs held a 3–1 lead over the Baltimore Bullets in the Eastern Conference Finals before the Bullets came back to win.

> **Tip-In**
>
> The second-highest scoring game in league history occurred during the 1981–1982 season when the Spurs and Bucks dueled it out before the Spurs pulled away for a 171–166 triple-overtime win. George Gervin scored 50 points in that game.

The Spurs were a typical team for the era: a high-scoring unit that played poor defense but were fun to watch. The team nevertheless was a division leader for five years, a streak that ran dry in 1984. For the next five years, the Spurs were a decidedly poor basketball team.

Saved by The Admiral

In 1987, San Antonio won the NBA Draft Lottery and used the pick to select 7' center David Robinson. However, as "The Admiral" was still in the Navy, the team would have to wait two years before seeing him in a Spurs uniform.

For the 1988–89 season, the team hired coach, Larry Brown. With the new coach, rookie Sean Elliott, and Robinson finally on board, the patience of the franchise paid off as the Spurs went from worst to first in one season, winning the Midwest Division.

By the 1994–95 season, the team won 62 games, Robinson was the league MVP, and the Spurs made it to the conference finals. Yet as good as this team was, they weren't quite championship caliber.

The Final Piece

Although injuries decimated the club in 1996–97, (David Robinson missed all but six regular-season games due to an injury) it was all worth it when the Spurs won the NBA Draft Lottery again and selected Tim Duncan out of Wake Forest.

Duncan led a resurgence in Spurs basketball, and the team captured the NBA Championship in 1999, auguring well for future success.

Technical Foul

Sean Elliott averaged almost 34 minutes during the Spurs' championship run. That stat is all the more remarkable when you consider that after the team won the title, Elliott revealed that he needed a kidney transplant. His brother donated a kidney, the surgery was held on August 16, 1999, and maybe most remarkable of all, Sean Elliott returned to play in the NBA again.

San Antonio selected Tim Duncan with the first overall draft pick in 1997.

Utah Jazz

On March 7, 1974, the New Orleans Jazz joined the NBA. In the team's first move, it traded for Pete Maravich, one of the most exciting players to ever play the game. Maravich went to college at LSU and set the all-time collegiate scoring record while playing there, which still stands to this day.

Pistol Pete was unlike anything anyone had ever seen on the court, with behind-the-back, through-the-legs passes and amazing, never-before-seen shots the norm. Not only a consummate showman, Maravich was also, simply, a great basketball player. Yet even with Maravich leading the way, the Jazz throughout the '70s were a pretty bad basketball team.

In 1979, the team relocated to Salt Lake City, Utah, and became the Utah Jazz. Yet the team would soon strike just the right note, bringing in two players who would define the franchise.

Stockton to Malone

In 1983, the team began its turnaround. Rookie Thurl Bailey was drafted and Adrian Dantley was acquired via trade, 7' 4" Mark Eaton was on board, and new coach Frank Layden was hired.

Inside Stuff

Mark Eaton was a mechanic before a coach persuaded the 7' 4" man to try out for basketball. He did, and then went on to have a solid, if unspectacular, career at UCLA. He was drafted in the fourth round (back when there were four rounds) of the 1982 draft.

Eaton had an excellent NBA career, was the two-time NBA Defensive Player of the Year, made the All-Star team once, and had his number retired by the Jazz, along with Frank Layden, Darrell Griffith, and Pete Maravich.

In 1984, with only the 16th pick in the draft, the Jazz selected a little-known point guard out of Gonzaga named John Stockton. What no one knew was that Stockton would go on to become one of the greatest guards in NBA history, would become the all-time NBA assists steals leader, and would form half of a dynamic duo that would make the team a contender for the next 20 years.

Tip-In

ears later, after John
ockton became *John
ckton*, Frank Layden
pped about the 1984
, "I wasn't sure if we
hn Stockton from
r John Gonzaga from

The next year, the Jazz selected the other half of this potent pair, somehow getting Karl Malone from tiny Louisiana Tech with the 13th pick. Before it's all said and done, Malone may become the most prolific scorer in NBA history, passing even Kareem Abdul-Jabbar (38,387 points).

Stockton and Malone played together for almost 20 years. In all of that time, neither missed but a handful of games, and together, almost single-handedly, they made Utah into a championship-caliber team.

Malone and Stockton: The venerable duo.

But more important than their longevity or their durability is their basketball prowess. Their pick and roll and team effort is a joy to watch. Stockton had a killer instinct and was the ultimate team player, getting the ball to "The Mailman," Karl Malone (he delivers!), at just the right place, at just the right time. Malone could *finish* like few others in the NBA, and so, together, these two made a great pair.

In the 1988-89 season, eight-year coach Frank Layden turned over the reins of the team to former Chicago Bull All-Star Jerry Sloan and became team president. Sloan and the Jazz won 51 games that year, and were poised to make an impact for the next decade.

Hoopology

On a fast break, you have to get the ball in the hole. The highest percentage way to do that is to dunk, but a layup will work just fine, too. Either way, the key is to **finish** the play and get the basket.

Close, but No Cigar

By 1993, the Jazz made it to the conference finals, riding the backs of Stockton and Malone, but had little else; the famous pair weren't enough. However, the team soon added Jeff Hornacek and Bryon Russell, and by 1997, they made it to the NBA Finals, only to meet the Chicago Bulls and lose in six.

The Jazz made it back to the NBA Finals again the next year, only to meet Michael and the Bulls again, and only to lose in six again.

Although they haven't won the championship that many predicted and many more hoped for, John Stockton and Karl Malone are two for the ages, and if anyone "deserves" a championship, these guys and their coach do.

The Least You Need to Know

- ◆ The Houston Rockets and San Antonio Spurs won NBA Championships in the 1990s while the Utah Jazz made it to the NBA Finals back-to-back seasons.

- ◆ The Denver Nuggets, Memphis Grizzlies, and Minnesota Timberwolves have some exciting young players.

- ◆ The Dallas Mavericks are poised for a break through.

Chapter 10

Pacific Division

In This Chapter

- ◆ Golden State Warriors
- ◆ Los Angeles Clippers
- ◆ Los Angeles Lakers
- ◆ Phoenix Suns
- ◆ Portland Trail Blazers
- ◆ Seattle SuperSonics
- ◆ Sacramento Kings

Over the past few years, the Pacific Division has become the strongest one in the league, with the Lakers and Kings running the show. Yet that, too, won't last. As teams rise and fall, so do divisions. The East will surely rise again, but those in the West should enjoy their heyday while they have it.

Golden State Warriors

The Warriors are among the oldest teams in the league, as the Philadelphia Warriors were one of 11 charter members of the old Basketball Association of America in 1946–47. From the beginning of the NBA in the 1946 season, and throughout the '50s, the Warriors produced on and off winning seasons.

Inside Stuff

In his first seven seasons in the NBA, Wilt averaged:

- 1959–60: 37.6 ppg.
- 1960–61: 38.4 ppg.
- 1961–62: 50.4 ppg.
- 1962–63: 44.8 ppg.
- 1963–64: 36.9 ppg.
- 1964–65: 34.7 ppg.
- 1965–66: 33.5 ppg.

The franchise improved dramatically when, in 1959, Wilt Chamberlain came to play (having been drafted four years earlier.) Instantly, the Warriors became one of the best teams in the league.

In 1962, the Warriors moved west to San Francisco. Although they traded Wilt in 1965, things for the team weren't so bad since they drafted Rick Barry that same year, a player who would also become one of the league's great scorers. Although Barry jumped to the new ABA in 1967 (a major coup for the new league), five years later Barry rejoined the Warriors and helped lead them to the Promised Land.

That Special Season

The 1974–75 season was certainly one of the great ones in Golden State Warriors basketball history. Normally, a team is put together methodically, allowed to play together for a few years, and gel if the management thinks the team has championship stuff. The 1974–75 Warriors turned this conventional wisdom on its head.

That season, the Warrior front office essentially gutted the team and started over, keeping only Rick Barry. Coach Al Attles used this change to his advantage by creating a system that used Barry as the focus of a team game. Utilizing as many as 10 players a night, Attles's system was perfect for the new team, and, surprisingly, they won the Pacific Division that year.

Part of the team's success was due to the play of three rookies on the team. Attles recalled:

> "I think that the key to that season was that our three rookies, Jamaal Wilkes, Phil Smith and Frank Kendrick all played much better than expected. The rookies were really the catalyst that got us going."

Even though the team had the best record and had won its division, it was still considered an underdog in the Western Conference Finals against the Bulls, which, according to Attles, "always kind of amazed me." The Warriors went down to the Bulls three games to two, but were able to pull out a dramatic Game 7 victory, 83–79.

In the NBA Championship of 1975, the Warriors faced a tough Washington Bullets team that boasted two the leagues top big men, Elvin Hayes and Wes Unseld. Yet even so, this new team, this team that didn't need three years to "gel," ended up sweeping the Bullets and claimed the title of champion.

Inside Stuff

[The 1974–75 Warriors] team was very resilient. They believed in themselves and they believed in each other. We found a way to ...get back home [in the conference finals], and the next thing you know we are down 16 points in the first half at home in Game 7. But we found a way to pull it out.

I think every coach should have the opportunity to go through a situation with a team like that because you could see there was something about them—you could see it in their eyes—that they never believed they were out of games."

—Al Attles

Run TMC

The next decade or so saw the decline of fortunes of the Warrior franchise. Although the Warriors posted the league's best record the season after they won the title, they didn't make it back to the finals and things began to dip thereafter.

The Warriors went nine seasons without making the postseason. Then, in 1987, the team's fortunes started to change when Don Nelson was hired to be the team's GM. Nelson is not only an innovative coach, he knows basketball talent when he sees it, and he was able to put together an exciting team in Oakland. In 1988, Nelson also became the head coach.

Forward Chris Mullin was already on board when Nelson arrived, but Nellie was able to team him up with guards Mitch Richmond and Tim Hardaway. This potent trio, dubbed "Run TMC" (for Tim, Mitch, and Chris) played a fast-breaking style of ball that was great to watch.

Don Nelson is always looking for a "big man" to anchor his teams, and the early '90s in the Bay Area was no exception. Mullin, Hardaway, and Richmond were great, but they needed a power forward if they were to get to the next level.

On draft day in 1994, it seemed as if Nellie finally got his man. That day, he traded the No. 1 pick, Penny Hardaway, and three future first-round picks to Orlando in exchange for Chris Webber.

Although Webber is undeniably a rare talent, he and Nelson had their differences, and the team traded him to the Washington Bullets the next year. The 1993–94 season was the last one the team made the playoffs before experiencing a long post-season drought.

These days, things are looking up as the Warriors have a stable of young talent like Antawn Jamison, Jason Richardson, and Mike Dunleavy ready to break out.

Los Angeles Clippers

Not every team can be the Lakers, and the Clippers have the unfortunate experience of having to be compared to their cross-town rivals, one of the league's most successful franchise. No, the Clips have not won an NBA Championship, and nope, they haven't even come close. But that doesn't mean the franchise is not without its share of highlights, however.

The Buffalo Braves joined the NBA in 1970. The team later moved to San Diego and became the Clippers, and later still, moved to Los Angeles.

- The team has yet to retire a single player number.

- The team has played in eight different arenas.

- In its first 25 seasons, the Clippers played at or above *.500* ball six times.

Yet, even though winning hasn't been part of the Clippers' history, it doesn't mean that the team hasn't seen its share of great players:

Bob McAdoo: In 1972–73, the Buffalo Braves had a player who would go on to be one of the best scorers and exciting showmen in NBA history—Bob McAdoo. The NBA Rookie of the Year in 1973, McAdoo averaged 18 points per game. For the next three years in a row, McAdoo led the league in scoring, averaging 30, 34, and 31 points per game.

> **Hoopology**
>
> **.500 ball** means that a team is winning as many games as it is losing. In a typical 82-game season then, a .500 team won 41 games and lost 41 games. It's nothing to brag about.

Bill Walton: The big redhead joined the Clips in 1979. Problematically, and typically for the Clippers, the oft-injured Walton was *very* oft injured during the years that he was supposed to be playing for the Clippers. During the four seasons before the 1982–83 season, Walton's troublesome feet limited him to only 14 *total* games.

Danny Manning: The Clippers won the 1988 Draft Lottery and used the first pick that year to select 6' 10" Danny Manning out of Kansas. But (shades of Walton), Manning got hurt 26 games in his rookie season, tearing his ACL. Although he came back from this devastating injury and went on to have a fine NBA career, Manning was never quite the player he could have been after that injury (and subsequent similar injuries). Manning was traded in 1994.

Elton Brand: A trade in 2002 brought the power forward west from Chicago. With Brand anchoring a stable of young, talented players, the present and future are bright in L.A.

Tip-In _____

Later in his career, Bob McAdoo became an essential part of the Lakers' success, helping the Clippers' rival win NBA Championships in 1982 and 1985.

Los Angeles Lakers

Much of this book has been devoted to the history and success of the Los Angeles Lakers, and there certainly is no need to repeat it here.

The thing to note at this juncture is that while it is often noted that the Boston Celtics are the most successful franchise in NBA history with 16 NBA titles. But L.A. presents an interesting case.

Yes, the Celtics had a glorious run through the late '50s and '60s, winning those 11 titles, and yes, they won a few more in the '80s, but it is the Lakers who have consistently put together winning teams, as the following statistics indicate:

♦ The Minneapolis Lakers were the best team of the '50s.

♦ The Los Angeles Lakers were the second-best team in the '60s and the best team of the '80s.

♦ The Lakers are also the best team of the new millennium.

Count 'em up: The Lakers have dominated three out of the five decades the NBA has been around. It is an impressive legacy.

Elgin Baylor (baseline) and Wilt Chamberlain (far right) are part of the Lakers' rich history.

Phoenix Suns

The Suns have always been a fun, exciting, up-tempo team. The team joined the NBA in the 1968–69 season, and almost from the get-go were playoff-bound. Suns fans rightfully have high expectations for the team.

Inside Stuff

Like many expansion teams, the new Phoenix franchise held a community contest to name the team. More than 28,000 suggestions flooded in, including:

- Arizoniacs
- Bartenders
- Poobahs
- Sweethearts
- Rocks
- Prickly Pears
- Merry Men
- Dudes

In the end, GM Jerry Colangelo picked Selinda King's suggestion—the Suns. Ms. King won season tickets for a year and $1,000.

The first player ever to become a Sun was Dick Van Arsdale, selected from New York in the expansion draft. Van Arsdale also scored the first-ever basket for the franchise—a layup against Seattle. Van Arsdale, still known as "The Original Sun," remains with the team as a member of management.

After the next season, the Suns gained steam by acquiring Connie Hawkins. Hawkins, who had played two years in the ABA and another with the Globetrotters, was a legend in the making. With his huge hands and great leaping ability, "The Hawk" would swoop to the basket, scoring at will.

Hawkins and another new Sun, Paul Silas—as well as Gail Goodrich and Van Arsdale—combined to take the Suns into the playoffs after the franchise had been in existence after only two years. Although the next few years would be lean ones for the Suns, a fairytale season was just around the corner.

Do You Believe in Miracles?

By the 1975–76 season, the Suns hadn't made the playoffs in six years, and that year, it barely snuck in, making the postseason on the second-to-last game of the regular season. That team consisted of several prominent Suns, including Alvin Adams, Gar Heard, and Paul Westphal.

The Suns eliminated the Seattle SuperSonics in six games and then played the world champion Warriors in the Western Conference Finals, beating them in seven games. Somehow, this come-from-behind team had made it to the NBA Finals.

There they would meet none other than the Boston Celtics, starring Dave Cowens and John Havlicek. The series was tied 2–2 when "The Game" was played. As recounted earlier in this book, Game 5 of the 1976 NBA Finals is considered by many to be the best game in NBA history. That triple-overtime win for Boston propelled the boys in green to the championship, but not before Phoenix's "Sunderella" season was made.

Continued Success

Coach John MacLeod had been at the helm for 13 years by the 1986–87 season, far longer than most coaches last, and by the *dog days* of February, it was clear that the team needed a new direction. The team would change players and coaches over the next few years, but with a purpose. Soon, another great Suns team would emerge.

In 1988, point guards Kevin Johnson and Dan Majerle were brought to the team along with Tom Chambers. With Jeff Hornacek and Mark West already on board, the Suns once again had a playoff contender. They would make it to the conference finals two years in a row.

Hoopology

The NBA season lasts months. Training camp begins in early October and the NBA Finals is held in June. As such, the middle part of the regular season, occurring during the end of winter, is sometimes referred to as the **dog days.**

In 1992, three new faces also came on board, catapulting the team to the finals for the first time since 1976: Coach Paul Westphal, forward Charles Barkley, and guard Danny Ainge.

Although the 1993 Suns lost to Chicago in the NBA Finals in six games, it tells you everything you need to know about Suns basketball that 300,000 people jammed downtown Phoenix and braved 105 degrees heat to celebrate the team's second-place finish.

Portland Trail Blazers

The Blazers joined the league in 1970 and Portland quickly became a basketball mecca. Today, the franchise is blessed with great fans, a committed, wealthy owner, and a history of success. But it wasn't always so.

Inside Stuff

Suns.com asked Suns fans to vote on the all-time best Suns players. Here are the results:

FIRST TEAM
◆ Guard: Kevin Johnson
◆ Guard: Jason Kidd
◆ Forward: Charles Barkley
◆ Forward: Tom Chambers
◆ Center: Alvin Adams
◆ Coach: Paul Westphal

SECOND TEAM
◆ Guard: Paul Westphal
◆ Guard: Dan Majerle
◆ Forward: Connie Hawkins
◆ Forward: Walter Davis
◆ Center: Mark West
◆ Coach: Cotton Fitzsimmons

From Expansion Blues to Blazermania

The expansion Portland Trail Blazers were your usual mishmash of young talent and old pros. Rookie Geoff Petrie and veteran LeRoy Ellis formed what nucleus there was on the club. Petrie would go on to win Co-Rookie of the Year honors with Boston's Dave Cowens. The Blazers also had the Rookie of the Year the next year with forward Sidney Wicks out of UCLA.

Proving that it helps to be both lucky *and* smart in the draft, and that it can improve a team in a hurry, the Blazers struck gold yet again when they won a coin toss and selected three-time College Basketball Player of the Year Bill Walton, also out of UCLA, in 1974.

In the 1976–77 season, the Blazers were able to pick up an enforcer, 6' 9" Maurice Lucas, when the ABA folded, but ended up losing Petrie and Sidney Wicks in the process. Yet even so, the revamped team was quite good. Walton and Lucas were the All-Stars, and Coach Jack Ramsay led the way.

Ramsay and his young Blazers played well throughout the season, but really went on a roll as the playoffs drew near. Even though the Blazers had never even *reached* the playoffs before, they weren't intimidated. The team beat Chicago in the first round, then Denver, and then swept the Pacific Division Champion Lakers in four straight in the Western Conference Finals.

In the NBA Finals, the 76ers, featuring Julius Erving and George McGinnis, were clearly favored to win over the inexperienced, upstart Portland Trail Blazers, and Philly won the first two games. But Walton had an outstanding series—he was named the series MVP—and the brash, young Blazer team, only seven years out of the gate and making their first-ever appearance in the playoffs, ended up winning the NBA Championship.

Tip-In

Guard Jim Barnett scored the first points in Blazer history when he sank a free throw with 9:18 to go in the first quarter of the first game, against the Cleveland Cavaliers—also an expansion team—on October 16, 1970.

Tip-In

April 5, 1977, is a significant day in Blazer history. That was the last day that you could go up to Memorial Coliseum before a game and buy a ticket. For just about the next 20 years, every game would be sold out. Blazermania had been born.

The Playoffs Become Routine

Although Walton was named the league MVP the next year, he was injured late in the season, and the Blazers' bid to repeat fell short. The team would make it to the play-offs for the next few years, but they were never able to reach that championship level of play again—that is, until a fellow named Clyde Drexler glided into town.

In 1983, with only the 14th pick, the Blazers were able to pluck a gem out of the draft when it selected Drexler, out of the University of Houston. Drexler would become the team's all-time leader scorer and one of its most popular players.

By 1986, Drexler had made the All-Star team as the Blazers were getting better and better. In 1989, the team was sold to Microsoft co-founder Paul Allen. Allen is the kind of owner fans love, as he is never shy of paying for the talent the GM wants.

Inside Stuff

One day when Bill Walton was a boy, his dad was driving him to a basketball game. Walton, with dreams of greatness dancing in his head, turned and said to his father, "Dad, one day I am going to be named the Most Valuable player in the NBA, and when I do, I am going to give you the car that they give as an award." Mr. Walton replied, "What's the NBA?"

Many years later, Bill Walton did in fact win the MVP, and he did give the car that comes with it to his father; his dad still owns that car.

Clyde "The Glyde" Drexler was a key component to Portland's high-energy offense.

Technical Foul

In the 1984 NBA Draft, Portland had the second overall pick. The team could have chosen just about any player they wanted and decided to use that pick to select center Sam Bowie. Drafting next was Chicago. Whom did they pick? Some guy who was still on the board named Michael Jordan.

Rip City and Beyond

Blazermania had a resurgence in 1989 when, under new coach Rick Adelman, the team became one of the NBA's elite. In 1990, with Drexler, Terry Porter, Kevin Duckworth, Buck Williams, Jerome Kersey, and Cliff Robinson now on board, the Blazers once again made it to the NBA Finals. Although they lost to the "Bad Boy" Pistons, the team put the league on notice: These Blazers were for real.

Portland became known nationwide as "Rip City," a term coined by longtime Blazer announcer Bill Schonely to describe the high-octane team. The

Blazers made it to the NBA Finals again two years later, but lost again, this time to the Bulls.

The team thereafter entered into a rebuilding phase as beloved older stars made way for new ones. And even so, the Blazers have been a beacon of consistency, making the playoffs an amazing 18 years in a row by the start of the 2002–03 season.

Seattle SuperSonics

The Seattle SuperSonics have a great tradition of winning basketball. The team joined the league for the 1967–68 season, and only a decade later became one of the NBA's best teams, and not for the last time, either.

That Championship Season

The 1974–75 Sonics were the first to make it to the playoffs, having taken eight years to get there. That team, made up of Spencer Haywood, "Downtown" Freddie Brown, and Slick Watts made it to the second round before losing to eventual champion Golden State.

In the 1977–78 season, the Sonics brought in previous player and player-coach Lenny Wilkens to guide the ball club. Although the team ended up third in the Pacific that year, it upset the Lakers in the first round, Portland in the second, and Denver in the Western Conference Finals.

The Sonics suddenly found themselves in the NBA Finals against Wes Unseld and the Bullets. In a hard-fought seven-game series, the Bullets finally prevailed, but the Sonics vowed revenge.

The next year, the team won 52 games, its first season ever winning more than 50 games, and it took the Pacific Division. The Sonics again made it to the finals, only to find themselves in a rematch with the world champion Bullets. Unlike other teams that reach the finals, this Sonic team was not made up of superstars (it included Jack Sikma, Fred Brown, Dennis Johnson, and Gus Williams).

But what this team had were several very good players who synergized into one great team. Although Washington won Game 1, Seattle went on to win four straight, capturing its first and (so far) only NBA title.

Glove and Reign

The Sonics were an up and down team for most of the 1980s, until three new faces showed up who would once again make Seattle into a basketball powerhouse for the '90s:

- In 1989, Sonic GM Bob Whitsitt drafted a virtual unknown junior college player named Shawn Kemp. Kemp averaged but six points his rookie year, belying the high-impact, high-scoring, thunderous player he would become.

- In 1990, the Sonics drafted the College Basketball Player of the Year out of Oregon State, Gary Payton.

- Just after New Year's Day 1992, the team hired George Karl to be its coach. In the six full seasons that he would coach the Sonics, the team averaged 59 wins a season.

These three would take Seattle into the NBA elite, winning more games during that era than any other team in the league, save the Bulls. Together, they would have only one losing month, and the most games they lost in a row was three. This was one heck of a basketball team.

Inside Stuff

George Karl's first head coaching job was with the Montana Golden Nuggets of the CBA. After three years in the CBA, Karl moved on to the Cavaliers, the Warriors, the CBA, Spain, CBA (again), Spain (again), before joining the Sonics.

On the court, the reasons for their success were clear. Payton, nicknamed "The Glove" for his airtight defense, wasn't too shabby on the offensive end, either. He ran the club, made the big shots, hit the open man, and shut down the other team. Kemp was nicknamed "The Reign Man" for his fantastic, powerful dunks and inside presence.

In 1993, the team made it to the Western Conference Finals, but came up short against the Suns. The next two years saw the Sonics exiting the playoffs far too early for a team with this much talent.

But in the 1995–96 season, they proved their mettle, making it all the way to the finals. The problem for the Sonics, along with every other great team in the '90s, was that the Bulls were on a serious roll and simply that much better than the rest of the league. Seattle lost in six.

In the 1997–98 season, the team won the Pacific Division for the fourth time in five seasons, and became only the third team in NBA history to win 55 or more games six seasons in a row.

In time, Kemp would be traded to Cleveland, Karl would leave to coach the Bucks, and only Gary Payton would remain. But, oh, what a run they had.

Inside Stuff

Sonics.com asked Sonics fans to vote on their favorite Sonics:

- ◆ Best Rebounder: Shawn Kemp (62 percent)
- ◆ Best Nickname: The Glove (47 percent)
- ◆ Best Sixth Man: Sam Perkins (45 percent)
- ◆ Best Point Guard: Gary Payton (79 percent)
- ◆ Best Defensive Player: Gary Payton (86 percent)
- ◆ Best Dunker: Shawn Kemp (66 percent)
- ◆ Best Draft Pick: Shawn Kemp (47 percent)

Sacramento Kings

These days, the Kings are known as one of the most exciting teams in the NBA, their fans are considered maybe the best in the league, and Arco Arena where they play, probably the loudest stadium around. But it was not always this way.

Early Glory

The Sacramento Kings started out as the Rochester Royals, beginning play in 1945 as a member of the old National Basketball League. The Royals then moved on to become one of 17 charter members of the NBA in 1949.

The 1949 Rochester Royals were a great team. Not only did they win 15 games in a row at one point—and 23 in a row at home—and finish the season with a .750 winning percentage, but they also went 33–1 at home that year for a .971 winning percentage, the second highest in league history (Boston's 40–1, .976 average in 1985–86 is number one).

Tip-In

The Rochester Royals were an early powerhouse of professional basketball, winning the NBL Championship in 1945. In 1946, the Royals also broke the NBL color barrier when it signed African American Dolly King.

The franchise's best season probably was in 1950–51. Although they came in second behind the Minneapolis Lakers in the regular season, the Royals beat the Fort Wayne Pistons in round one, and then beat the Lakers in the second round. They went on to meet the New York Knicks in the 1951 NBA Finals.

After going up 3–0 in the series, the Royals somehow managed to lose three in a row, taking the NBA Finals to seven games for the first time ever. The game was tied at 75 with 40 seconds left when Bob Davies hit a pair of free throws, the Royals controlled the ensuing tip, and went on to win the first, and to date only, championship for the franchise.

Tip-In

What is the longest game in NBA history? It occurred on January 6, 1951 when Indianapolis beat the Royals, in six overtimes!

That kind of success would not be reached again for a long, long time. The advent of the 24-second clock in 1954 doomed the slow-paced Royals, and the team posted its first losing season that year.

The Vagabond Kings

In 1957, the Rochester Royals moved cities (and not for the last time), becoming the Cincinnati Royals. But the success that had been part of the Rochester days did not move with the team, and years of mediocrity followed.

The good news was that the team was able to draft probably the best player in franchise history on 1960 with Oscar Robertson coming on board. The versatile, 6' 5" "Big O" could do everything: dribble, pass, score, and rebound. He was named Rookie of the Year that year.

Yet despite Robertson's greatness and new teammates Jerry Lucas and Happy Hairston, the Royals of the mid-'60s never went far in the playoffs. Oscar would play for the Royals for 10 years, until April 21, 1970, when he was traded to the Bucks (where he would win a championship with Kareem Abdul-Jabbar, then known as Lew Alcindor). In his 10 years on the team, the Big O averaged a remarkable 29.3 points, 10.3 assists, and 8.5 rebounds.

In 1972, the team moved again, this time to Kansas City. Because Kansas City already had a baseball team named the Royals, the team was reborn as the Kansas City-Omaha Kings (later to be just the Kansas City Kings). But the name or place didn't matter as the '70s were just about the same for the franchise, with a few stars and a modicum of playoff success; nothing special.

Your Sacramento Kings

Greg Luckenbill was a Sacramento developer with a vision. In 1983, for $10.5 million, he and his group of investors bought the Kings, and he moved the franchise again in

1985, this time to Sacramento, California. While he had hoped that the team would be successful there, he never anticipated that Sacramento was starving for big-league sports and that Sacramento Kings fans would develop an almost unnatural bond with the team.

Although the Kings made it to the playoffs in 1985–86, the next decade would be the nadir for the once-proud franchise. The team was pathetic, changing coaches and players often, and with no change in the results. Bill Russell proved that he couldn't coach the team, but neither could Jerry Reynolds, Phil Johnson, or Gary St. Jean.

> ### Inside Stuff
>
> Luckenbill was a visionary in another way as well. When he sold the naming rights for the Kings' new arena to the Atlantic Richfield Co., such a transaction had never occurred before. ARCO Arena was the first-ever sports facility named for a business for money.

Chris Webber helped revive the fortunes of the Kings.

Things finally began to change when Geoff Petrie was hired to be the vice president of basketball operations. Petrie, of Portland Trail Blazer fame, was a sharp evaluator of basketball talent and a shrewd negotiator. Among other moves that transformed the once sad-sack Kings into an NBA powerhouse, Petrie …

- ◆ Drafted unheralded Brian Grant.
- ◆ Drafted Jason Williams, and later traded him for Mike Bibby.

◆ Drafted an unknown to U.S. fans, Peja Stojakovic.

◆ Traded an aging Mitch Richmond for Chris Webber.

◆ Signed Vlade Divac as a free agent.

The moves earned Petrie a nod as the NBA's Executive of the Year in 1999 and 2001, and turned the Kings into legitimate division rivals for Shaq and the Los Angeles Lakers.

The Least You Need to Know

◆ The Los Angeles Lakers, Portland Trail Blazers, and Seattle SuperSonics have a history of winning.

◆ The L.A. Clippers and Sacramento Kings are exciting young teams.

◆ The Phoenix Suns and Golden State Warriors are teams to watch.

Part 3

The Greatest Players Ever

Many kids dream of becoming NBA superstars, but only a few have what it takes to realize that goal. In this part, you'll meet the best hoopsters who ever played the game, and find out what made them so great. Guards like Allen Iverson, Magic Johnson, and Michael Jordan. Forwards like Tim Duncan, Karl Malone, and Larry Bird. Centers like Shaquille O'Neal, David Robinson, and Kareem Abdul-Jabbar.

Chapter 11

Great Point Guards

In This Chapter

- ◆ A new generation of playmakers
- ◆ Point guards from the '70s and '80s
- ◆ The pioneer playmakers

Point guard is one of the most critical of positions in the NBA. The point guard is the guy who leads the team and directs the offense. He's the one who sets up the play and sets the tempo.

From Magic Johnson to John Stockton to Bob Cousy and beyond, the league has seen its share of amazing point guards.

Best of the New Generation

It's easy to wax poetic about great point guards from years gone by, but in 10 years, hoopaholics will be waxing poetic about the guys who are playing right now. These guys got game.

Jason Kidd

If you were looking to start a new franchise right now and had to pick one player to build it around, Kidd might be your man.

The versatile 6' 4" guard out of the University of California has uncommon court vision and basketball smarts. He can hit the open man or make the open shot. He's not afraid to have the ball in his hands when the game is on the line, and as evidenced by his ever-increasing ability to put the ball in the basket, is always honing his skills.

Inside Stuff

Jason Kidd is only the third player ever in the history of the league to get 700 assists and 500 rebounds in the same season (he's done it twice). Magic Johnson and Oscar Robertson each did it six times.

Kidd was selected with the second overall pick in the 1994 NBA Draft by the Dallas Mavericks, and it was a smart pick. With Kidd at the helm, the Mavs won 23 more games than the year before, a remarkable turnaround. Kidd was named co-Rookie of the Year with Grant Hill.

Jason Kidd's all-around play has made him one of the NBA's best.

By 1996, Kidd made the All-Star team, and became a fixture at the game thereafter. He was on the All-Defensive First Team in 1999, and became a fixture there, too. With his all-around great game, Kidd will surely go down as one of the best ever.

The Answer

Is Allen Iverson a point guard or a shooting guard? Does it matter? Even he says he's not sure. But one thing is for certain: He is definitely one of the most exciting players in the game today, if not *the* most exciting.

Iverson's 100 mph manic mode, his fearless forays to the basket, and his willingness to shoot the ball when it matters most have endeared him to NBA fans from coast to coast. Allen Iverson loves to play basketball, and he plays it with a reckless abandon that is heartening.

Drafted by the Philadelphia 76ers, "The Answer" was the first pick in the 1996 NBA Draft, and he quickly proved why in his first year, winning NBA Rookie of the Year honors.

- ◆ He was the MVP of the All-Star Rookie Game.

- ◆ He broke Wilt Chamberlain's rookie record by scoring more than 40 points five games in a row (Chamberlain did it in only three).

- ◆ On April 12, he scored 50 points. He and Michael Jordan were the only two players to score at least 50 points in a game that season.

Hoopology

The starting lineup for the NBA All-Star Game is voted on by the fans. The top vote getters in the East and West, for each of the five starting positions, start the game—they are the **All-Star starters.** The rest of the squad is picked by the coaches.

Iverson was All-NBA First Team in 1999 and 2001, and an *All-Star starter* in 2000, 2001, and 2002. Maybe more importantly, in the 2000–01 season he led his team to the NBA Finals, garnering the league MVP trophy that year as well. (And at 6 feet even, he is also the shortest player to ever win the award.) Simply put, A.I. is one of the most talented, explosive players in the game today.

The Glove

Venerable Gary Payton has been so good for so long that it's almost easy to forget how good he actually is. Almost. Payton's consistency is only one of the things that distinguishes him as a player. Consider his airtight defense. Or his leadership. Or his big-game mindset. No matter what basketball characteristic you're looking for, you'll likely find that Payton has it.

The 1996 Defensive Player of the Year and eight-time All-Star (and counting), Payton has led his Sonic teammates through the glory years with George Karl and Shawn Kemp and has been a mentor to new players during a rebuilding phase.

In the meantime, he was a member of the third *Dream Team* in 1996 and a member of the U.S. Olympic team in 2000.

Hoopology

In 1992, the greatest basketball team of all time represented the United States in the Barcelona Olympics. That was the first year that professional basketball players could represent their country, and USA basketball wasted no time in putting together its **Dream Team.**

That first Dream Team team consisted of Michael Jordan, Magic Johnson, Larry Bird, Patrick Ewing, Charles Barkley, Scottie Pippen, John Stockton, David Robinson, Karl Malone, Clyde Drexler, Chris Mullin, and Christian Laettner and was coached by Chuck Daly.

They call Gary Payton "The Glove" for a reason.

John Stockton

If there is one player who is more consistent than Payton, it would have to be John Stockton. Stockton helped transform the Utah Jazz into a consistent winner, was a member of the original *Dream Team* (along with teammate Karl Malone), and was again a gold medalist at the 1996 Olympics. He has played in two NBA Finals, although he has yet to win the ultimate prize.

Stockton was named one of the 50 Greatest Players in NBA History by the league when it celebrated its 50th anniversary in 1996. The reasons are self-evident: He is flat-out one of the best ever. He led the league in assists an amazing nine years in a row, and is the all-time NBA career leader not only in assists, but steals, too!

All of this is all the more remarkable considering that John Stockton is only 6' 1", 175 pounds, and has played in 98 percent of all possible games over the course of his career, 13 seasons of which he never missed a single game.

Maybe the best thing about watching John Stockton play basketball is his sound, fundamental approach to the game. He isn't flashy but he gets big-time results. John Stockton continues to defy the odds, can the jumper, make the pass, and win the game.

Best of the '70s and '80s

Each era has its own stars, and the recent past is no exception.

Nate "Tiny" Archibald

Tiny Archibald, a six-time All-Star and MVP of the 1981 All-Star Game accomplished something as a member of the Kings in 1973–74 that no player has ever matched. That season, the short Archibald (6' 1") led the NBA in both scoring *and* assists: 34 points a game and 11.4 assists. It is a feat that has never been duplicated.

Lightning quick, Tiny was able to use his speed to get around and past larger, slower players, and in so doing, he paved the way for the likes of Spud Webb, Muggsy Bogues, and Allen Iverson. His pinpoint passes and exceptional shooting range made him impossible to defend and proved that there still was a place for the little man in basketball, at a time when it had become increasingly dominated by big men.

Archibald was named one of the 50 Greatest Players in NBA History and is also a member of the Basketball Hall of Fame. In 1981, he was the quarterback of the world champion Boston Celtics, a perfect bookmark to an impressive career.

Tip-In

"Coming down the stretch, especially with the game on the line, he's the guy I want on the floor, with the ball in his hands."

—Utah Jazz owner Larry Miller, on John Stockton

Inside Stuff

John Stockton was drafted out of Gonzaga with the 16th pick. During his first three seasons with the Jazz, he split the point guard position with Rickey Green. That Stockton was not a full-time starter until his fourth NBA season makes his accomplishments as the all-time assists and steals leader that much more impressive.

Dave Bing

Dave Bing of the Detroit Pistons was enshrined into the Basketball Hall of Fame in 1990, and it's easy to see why. Bing was a fundamentally sound player who always seemed to make the right play, whether it was scoring, passing, or defending.

The Rookie of the Year in 1966, seven-time All-Star, and All-Star MVP (1976) while a member of the Washington Bullets, Bing was not only the gas that fueled the Pistons, he was the team's sparkplug as well. His feathery shot won many a game for the team.

> **Tip-In**
>
> After he retired, Dave Bing founded Bing Steel. In 1984, he was named the National Small Business Person of the Year, as well as the National Minority Supplier of the Year. He now has three companies.

Walt Frazier

Walt "Clyde" Frazier was named to the NBA All-Defensive First Team seven times, was a seven-time All-Star (and one-time All-Star MVP), won two NBA Championships, was named one of the 50 Greatest Players in NBA History, and is also enshrined in the basketball Hall of Fame.

Frazier not only fashioned the Knicks' offense (he led the team in assists for 10 straight years) and was a consistent scoring threat (he led the team in scoring five times), but he was also a defensive specialist. That he had smooth moves and great style only made him sweeter to watch.

Magic Johnson

Where do we begin? Magic Johnson is one of the best point guards and one of the greatest players ever to play the game. He combined showmanship with enthusiasm, fundamentals with competitiveness, leadership with teamwork, joy with sorrow, and offense with defense. Combined, it made an awesome basketball package.

Consider his many accomplishments:

> **Inside Stuff**
>
> Beginning in 2001, the Pro Basketball Writers Association started to give out an annual award to recognize the one NBA player who best performed at an All-Star level on the court, with the media, and in the community. The name of the award? The Magic Johnson Award.

- Five NBA Championships
- Three NBA Finals MVPs
- Nine-time All-NBA First Team
- Twelve-time All-Star, two-time All-Star MVP
- Hall of Fame Inductee (2002)

Because of his infectious grin and obvious love of the game, Magic made the NBA cool again. That the NBA was resurrected by Magic and Larry Bird has been recounted many times; yet even so, it shouldn't be forgotten.

> ### Inside Stuff
>
> In 2002, *Fortune Magazine* named Magic Johnson as the 33rd most powerful black executive in the United States. Magic's 10-year-old company, Johnson Development Corp., is made up of mostly inner-city enterprises: restaurants, movie theaters, athletic clubs, and shopping malls. The most gratifying part of his business success, says Magic, is "creating black presidents, vice presidents, general managers, managers. That has been the best part."

Earl Monroe

Vernon Earl Monroe was one of those players, like Pete Maravich, Bob Cousy, or Magic Johnson, who really needs to be seen to be appreciated. His spinning, twisting, behind-the-back moves were so unique, so exciting, so fun to watch, that words simply don't do him justice.

Earl the Pearl.

The 1967 NBA Rookie of the Year made an immediate impact on the league. He and teammate Wes Unseld led a resurgent Baltimore Bullets team, and in the process,

Monroe became something of a cult hero. People loved to watch him play, and he didn't disappoint. As such, aside from "Earl the Pearl" and "Thomas Edison," it may be that his other nickname best personifies how crowds felt about him: "Black Jesus," for the many miracles he performed on court.

> **Inside Stuff**
>
> In high school, Monroe's team-mates nicknamed him "Thomas Edison" because he invented so many moves on the court.

According to Monroe's teammate from his Knicks days, Walt Frazier, "When we used to play him with the Bullets, the crowd would be in a frenzy. He didn't know what he was going to do, so how could I? He had the spin move … Swirling dervish! He's throwing up stuff from behind his back, and people are screaming 'Earl, Earl, best in the World!'"

Earl Monroe is a reminder that the NBA is graced with the most athletic, stylish, creative athletes in the world, and when given the chance, these players can change the game.

His number 15 jersey was retired by the New York Knicks in 1986, Monroe joined the Hall of Fame in 1990, and he was named one of the 50 Greatest Players in NBA History in 1996.

Zeke

Isiah Thomas is one of the best small men to ever play in the NBA. As a member of the 1981 Indiana Hoosiers, Thomas led the team to a national championship, and that same grit, determination, playmaking ability, and confidence allowed him to do the same thing in the NBA.

As a member of the NBA Champion Detroit Pistons, Thomas led a potent attack. With his ability both to hit the open man and make the big shot, he was the undisputed leader of those great Pistons teams.

> **Inside Stuff**
>
> After he retired from the game, Thomas bought into the expansion Toronto Raptors and became vice president of basketball operations. He then went on to coach the Indiana Pacers after Larry Bird vacated the job.

His accomplishments speak for themselves. Aside from the championships, Thomas …

- Was 1982 NBA All-Rookie First Team selection.

- Was a 12-time NBA All-Star (and two-time MVP).

- Was the MVP of the 1990 NBA Finals.

- Ranks fifth all time assists and collected more than 9,000 steals.

- Was named one of the 50 Greatest Players in NBA History.

Two of the best ever: Oscar Robertson (#1) and Jerry West (#44).

Pioneers

Early showmen and fundamentally sound playmakers showcased the possibilities of the point guard position and league in general in its early years.

Bob Cousy

Cousy was the first razzle-dazzle point guard in the NBA, and it's not a stretch to say that the "Houdini of the Hardwood" is one of the top five playmakers of all time. With his exceptional peripheral vision and array of behind-the-back passes, Cousy was the quarterback of those amazing Celtic teams in the '60s.

Cousy and Bill Russell are the earliest, and maybe best, example of why it is so critical to have a great point guard and center if you have championship aspirations. With Cousy leading the attack, and Russell in the middle covering

---

Inside Stuff

"Cousy was never a good defensive player. With Russell, he never had to worry about guarding anyone, and he never did. If a man drove by Cousy, he'd just run down to the other end of the court knowing that Russell would get the rebound and throw one of those great outlet passes for him."

—Former Minneapolis Laker standout point guard Slater Martin in *Tall Tales*

everyone's back, the two made everyone around them better, and with the Celtics, that was pretty impressive.

Not only did Cousy have a knack for being able to find the open man, but he was able to get the ball to that teammate with a little flair, making him a crowd favorite. According to teammate Tom Heinsohn, "Cooz was the best playmaking guard that ever played the game. Once that ball reached his hands, the rest of us just took off, never bothering to look back. We didn't have to, he'd find us. When you got into a position to score, the ball would be there."

Cousy was named one of the 50 Greatest Players in NBA History and is a member of the Basketball Hall of Fame.

Gail Goodrich

On a team considered by many to be the best ever—the 1971–72 Los Angeles Lakers—and one dominated by two of the greatest scorers of all time—Wilt Chamberlain and Jerry West—it was Gail Goodrich who ran the show and was the high scorer. Goodrich helped his team win a championship that year, but it wasn't the first time he did so.

In three years at UCLA under legendary coach John Wooden, Goodrich's team went 78–11, and the team won the National Championship in 1964 and 1965. By the time he was done, Goodrich was UCLA's all-time leading scorer, and was named College Basketball Co-Player of the Year in 1965.

He went on to play 14 years in the NBA (mostly with the Lakers), was a five-time All-Star, and was enshrined into the Hall of Fame in 1996.

Hal Greer

Hal Greer is one of those rare players who played his entire career with one team—the Syracuse Nationals/Philadelphia 76ers. Greer was an all-around superb player, and was able not only to lead the attack or get the rebound, but to make the shot as well. Greer remains the 76ers all-time leading scorer.

A 10-time All-Star, and All-Star MVP in 1968, Greer was also named one of the 50 Greatest Players in NBA History and is a member of the Hall of Fame.

Technical Foul

Hal Greer also has the dubious distinction of making one of the most infamous passes in NBA history. In the seventh game of the 1965 NBA Eastern Division Finals, the Sixers had the ball with five seconds left, down by one. Greer was taking the ball out, and was just about out of time to get the pass in, when he lobbed the ball toward Chet Walker.

According to John Havlicek in *Tall Tales*, here's what happened next: "I realized that Greer's pass was going to be a little short. I got a great jump on it [and was] able to tip the pass away from Walker and the ball went right to Sam Jones, who dribbled it a few times, then threw the ball back to me and the game was over." As Boston announcer Johnny Most immortalized the moment, "Havlicek stole the ball! Havlicek stole the ball!"

The Big O

None other than Red Auerbach says that Oscar Robertson is the best player to ever play the game—better than Auerbach's beloved Bill Russell, better than Wilt, better than Kobe, better than Magic, better than MJ. Oscar was an all-around complete, great player.

The Big O was unlike most other point guards of his era. Yes, he could pass, but just as easily, he could score at will or rebound with the best of them. At 6' 5", he was tall for a point guard in the '60s, much like Magic Johnson was tall for a point guard ... in any era!

Robertson was a three-time College Player of the Year at Cincinnati, and he set 14 different NCAA record in the process, averaging 33.8 points per game during his college career.

His NBA accomplishments include the following:

◆ He was a three-time NBA All-Star MVP (1961, 1964, 1969).

◆ He was the Rookie of the Year (beating out Jerry West and Lenny Wilkens in 1960-61).

◆ He averaged a triple double one season (1961–62).

◆ When he retired he was the all-time NBA leader in assists and free throws made.

◆ He was named one of the 50 Greatest Players in NBA History and is in the Hall of Fame.

Inside Stuff

"When I played for the Cincinnati Royals and Oscar was a freshman at the University of Cincinnati, we had already heard about him. [One day] Oscar was shooting around in a gym. Jack Twyman and I were there. Twyman was an NBA All-Star, a future Hall of Famer. He said to me, "I'm going to teach that kid a lesson. So Jack challenged Oscar to a 1-on-1 game. Oscar won 21–0. That's how great Oscar was."

—Wayne Embry in *Tall Tales*

Tip-In

The only two people to be enshrined in the Basketball Hall of Fame as both a player and a coach are John Wooden and Lenny Wilkens.

Lenny Wilkens

These days, people recognize Lenny Wilkens as one of the great coaches in the game (he is the winningest coach in NBA history). That just goes to show you how great Wilkins actually is, considering he is also one of the greatest players to ever play the game.

Wilkens was always an intelligent player, able to beat opponents with his head as much as his skill. A nine-time All-Star and 15-year veteran of the game, Wilkins is considered one of the best pure playmakers ever to grace the court.

The Least You Need to Know

♦ A new generation of playmakers make the game exciting to watch.

♦ Point guards from the '70s and '80s brought a creative flair and special "Magic" to the hardwood.

♦ The pioneer point guards paved the way for today's superstars.

12

Great Shooting Guards

In This Chapter

- ◆ A new generation of explosive scorers
- ◆ Their predecessors who paved the way
- ◆ Great shooting as an NBA tradition

The shooting guard, also known as the 2-guard or off guard, has one main job: Get the ball in the basket. The point guard distributes the ball, and the off guard is the guy he often distributes it to.

Shooting three-pointers, lofting fadeaway jumpers, slashing to the basket, or finishing the fast break—it doesn't matter how they do it, as long as they get the ball in the basket.

New Kids on the Block

NBA basketball is always evolving. There was a time when play slowed to a standstill and players shot a two-handed *set shot*. Later, the game became quicker, and the shooters began to jump when shooting the ball. These days, high-flying, in-your-face scorers are all the rage. Who knows what will come next?

Kobe Bryant

For years, NBA watchers have wondered, "Who will be the next Jordan?" Michael Jordan had so dominated the game, and the consciousness of NBA fans, that everyone was anxious to see who might be able to actually fill those large shoes.

While there will never be another MJ, if anyone comes close, it will be Kobe Bryant. In fact, Bryant's air attack, ability to consistently can the game-winning shot, and incredible athleticism may prompt people down the road to ask, "Who will be the next Kobe?"

Tip-In

"I enjoy the pressure of being considered the next Jordan. I like that situation—the one I've wished to live since I was a child. But, obviously, it's pretty soon to start talking in those terms. I just want to win as many rings as possible."

—Kobe Bryant

Kobe Bryant thrills fans with his acrobatic style of play.

Kobe Bryant is a rare athlete. His deadly shooter's touch, intense desire to be the best, natural ability, cockiness, and grace under pressure make him maybe the best player in the game today.

Yes, it helps to be playing for the Los Angeles Lakers under Coach Phil Jackson and with Shaq, but Kobe's greatness goes beyond that. Like all the great ones, Kobe gets better with age, due in large measure to his commitment to the game. "I think you should never quit working on any aspect of the game because you can always make some progress," he says.

If Kobe Bryant vows to continue to work on his already impressive game, then the basketball is in good hands.

> **Hoopology** ——————————————————————
>
> Back in the day, at the dawn of the NBA, most outside shooters would plant their feet, grab the ball on either side, and let fly something called a **set shot.** By 1950, the jump shot had started to displace the set shot.

Vinsanity

Vince Carter is that new breed of NBA athlete. Bigger, stronger, more agile, and more of a leaper than his earlier counterparts, Vince is a joy to watch. Whether he is flying to the basket to dunk the ball or nailing the jumper from behind the arc, he somehow always finds a way to score and thrill the fans.

Like Michael Jordan, Carter came out of that University of North Carolina system that stresses teamwork over individuality. As such, no one really knew how good Vince was, nor how great he would be in the NBA, when he was available in the 1998 draft.

So that year, Gary St. Jean of the Golden State Warriors selected Vince with the fifth pick and then traded him to the Toronto Raptors for sixth-pick Antawn Jamison—Carter's roommate at North Carolina—and cash. While Jamison is an excellent player in his own right, he is no Vince Carter.

Vince Carter won Rookie of the Year honors in 1999, getting an amazing 96 percent of the vote. He also won the 2000 NBA.com Slam Dunk Contest. As former New York Knicks coach Jeff Van Gundy says about Vince Carter, "If he's driven, he'll be one of the greats in this league for a long time and perhaps one of the greatest of all time."

> **Tip-In** ——————————————
>
> "What was my favorite part? Watching Vince dunk, of course. I've never seen anybody who dunks like that."
>
> —Shaquille O'Neal on the 2000 All-Star Weekend

Clyde the Glide

Clyde Drexler led the Portland Trail Blazers throughout the late '80s and '90s and became one of the most beloved Blazers of all time. It's easy to see why. He not only had physical gifts and determination; he had class, too. Clyde is everything an athlete should be: Great at what he does, while at the same time appreciative, gracious, and respectful.

He was also, flat-out, a great basketball player. Take a look at some of his accomplishments:

- He is 17th in NBA history with 22,195 points.

- He is fourth in steals with 2,207.

- He was a 10-time All-Star and earned All-NBA honors five times.

- He was a member of the gold-medal Dream Team at the 1992 Summer Olympics in Barcelona.

- He participated in the playoffs every year he played.

- His NBA Finals scoring average of 24.5 points per game is tenth best in NBA history.

- He won an NBA Championship in 1995 with Houston.

> **Inside Stuff**
>
> Drexler is Mr. Portland. He is the Blazers all-time leader in scoring, games played, minutes played, field goals made, field goals attempted, free throws made, free throws attempted, total rebounds, offensive rebounds, and steals.

In his last season, his fifteenth, Drexler became only the third player ever to score 20,000 points, pull down 6,000 rebounds, and pass for 6,000 assists in his career. The other two were John Havlicek and Oscar Robertson.

Clyde was named one of the 50 Greatest Players in NBA History in 1996.

Michael Jordan

Many consider Michael Jordan the greatest player to ever play the game. His ability to excel at every aspect of the game, both mentally and physically, is what sets him apart. Need a game-winning shot? MJ's your man. Need 50 points? Air Jordan's the guy. Want a spectacular dunk, a turnaround jumper, a steal, a defensive stop, a great pass, a timely rebound, or a three-pointer at the buzzer? Michael's the one.

Indeed, Jordan led the league in scoring for seven straight years (10 total), a feat only matched by the Big Dipper, Wilt Chamberlain; but just as importantly, he has been the Defensive Player of the Year and a nine-time All-Defensive First Team selection. And let's not forget those six championships.

MJ: His Airness.

The interesting thing about MJ the player is that he has adapted and changed his game over the years—something few players are able to do. Whereas he began as a slasher, he ended up being an outside shooter. Although he started out as a great individual performer, he became the ultimate team player, pushing everyone in the same direction. The offensive genius became a defensive specialist.

Inside Stuff

Jordan's NBA All-Star stats:

- Thirteen appearances, starting 10 times
- The first player ever to receive more than 2 million votes
- First player ever to record a triple double (1997: 14 points, 11 rebounds, and 11 assists)
- Scored 40 points in the 1988 All-Star Game
- MVP twice (1988, 1996)
- Named an All-Star starter again in 2002 after coming out of retirement

According to Phil Jackson, "When he first came into the league in 1984, he was primarily a penetrator. His outside shooting wasn't up to pro standards. So he put in his gym time in the off-season, shooting hundreds of shots each day. Eventually, he became a deadly three-point shooter." By the same token, Jackson notes, "Playing outstanding defense didn't come automatically to him either."

This intense need to compete, to be the best, is the fuel that fires the engine. According to teammate Steve Kerr, "Every practice, every shooting drill was just a huge competition. It set the tone for our season."

Ultimately, Jordan became a global cultural icon. Yet he even was able to make that look easy, handling the lack of privacy and extreme adulation with grace and class.

And, as Jordan grew in popularity, so did the NBA. It became a symbiotic, mutually beneficial relationship. Jordan, the new ambassador for the league, helped the NBA grow to unprecedented heights every time he hit the game-winning shot, stole the ball, swooped in for a dunk, scored 60 points, or won another championship.

Many years from now, there will be those who will get to say "I saw Michael Jordan play in person. He was the best ever." And indeed, those who were fortunate enough to see him in his prime, who saw MJ shrug his shoulders, or who saw him score at will, or shake off Bryon Russell for the game-winning shot in the 1998 NBA Finals, will know that it was a rare treat, a privilege.

T-Mac

Tracy McGrady was the ninth overall selection in the 1997 NBA Draft—not bad for an 18-year-old high school kid. Like his cousin Vince Carter, the Toronto Raptors drafted T-Mac. And like "Air Canada," McGrady is an amazingly athletic player. McGrady is almost unstoppable one-on-one, he has the ability to either *take the ball to the rack* or hit the outside jumper, he can hit the three or block the shot, and he averages about five assists per game.

Hoopology

When a player drives to the basket, it is also called **taking the ball to the rack.**

McGrady is a scary player because his game has improved every year he has been in the league. While he started out as most direct-from-high-school players do—on the bench with a lot to learn—he learned awfully fast.

In the 2000–2001 season, he joined the Orlando Magic and immediately began to flex his muscles. With teammate Grant Hill injured for the year, the burden was upon McGrady to carry the team, and carry the team he did, winning Most Improved Player that year. The next year, he was named All-NBA First Team.

Emerging as one of the game's next great players, Tracy McGrady is one to watch.

Reggie Miller

Reggie Miller was drafted out of UCLA in 1987 by the Indiana Pacers and went on to become the most prolific three point shooter in the history of the NBA, making his 2,000 three-point field goal in 2002. He is deadly from beyond the arc.

While Miller's uncanny long-range shooting is impressive enough, what really distinguishes him is his killer instinct. Reggie Miller is a big-game player who seems to do his best when an important game is on the line.

> ### Inside Stuff
>
> Miller comes from good basketball stock. His sister Cheryl was a three-time College Player of Year (1984–86). She led USC to the Women's NCAA title and led the U.S. Olympic team to the gold medal in 1984. She went on to coach USC to 44–14 record before joining Turner Sports as an NBA reporter. She also coached the WNBA's Phoenix Mercury for four years.

'70s and '80s

Shooting guard has always been a glamour position. Given the green light to shoot the ball, off guards are great scorers.

George Gervin

The "Iceman" has that nickname for a reason: George Gervin was a cool character, had a smooth game, and he had ice in his veins. He was unflappable. Although skinny by today's NBA standards, Gervin was simply a great shooter. He could finger roll better than anyone, and had a graceful, deadly jumper.

How well did this guy shoot the ball?

- He is one of only three players in NBA history to win four or more scoring titles, doing so in 1978, 1979, 1980, and 1982.

- He is one of only seven players to score at least 2,000 points six seasons in a row.

- His combined ABA and NBA career point total of 26,595 is eighth best in basketball history.

- His career scoring average of 26.2 is sixth best in NBA history.

> ### Inside Stuff
>
> Kareem Abdul-Jabbar played in 19 All-Star Games, the most mid-season classics played by anyone.

Gervin played two years for the Virginia Squires in the ABA before joining the NBA and playing for the San Antonio Spurs for 11 seasons. He led the Spurs to five division titles and was a nine-time All-Star.

Pistol Pete

Pete Maravich is arguably the most exciting player to ever play in the NBA. The Pistol had an array of dazzling offensive moves that made him unlike any other player, ever.

Consider first his passing ability. Maravich, an adept showman, could pass through his own legs (or those of his opponent), behind the back, over his shoulder, or in almost any other wild combination that you have never seen. And the passes were on the money, too.

Sure, some called it "hot-dogging," and maybe it was. But NBA basketball isn't only about winning and losing. It's also entertainment, and Maravich knew that.

Pistol Pete was one of a kind.

Yet Pete didn't just make the amazing pass to show off; he was an artist, the basketball court was his canvas, and the ball was his brush. He did things no one else did because that was who he was. As he once said, "If I have a choice whether to do the show or throw a straight pass, and we're going to get the basket either way, I'm going to do the show."

His shooting ability was no less dynamic. He could hit the deep shot, take it to the rack (while sometimes passing to himself), or throw up any number of other combinations that somehow went in. With his floppy hair and trademark floppier socks, Maravich was great fun to watch.

Maravich's college career is the stuff of legend. Playing for his father, Press Maravich, the coach at Louisiana State University, Pistol Pete was given a green light to score, so score he did. In three years, he averaged an amazing 44.2 points per game, led the nation in scoring all three years, and set an NCAA record by scoring 50 points or more 28 times.

Moreover, Pete ...

- ◆ Has the NCAA record for highest overall per-game average at 44.2.

- ◆ Has the NCAA record for most field goals made and attempted.

- ◆ Has the NCAA record for most free throws made and attempted.

- ◆ Has the NCAA record for the highest per-game average in a season (44.5 in 1970).

> **Inside Stuff**
>
> As a kid, Pete would practice four to five hours a day, and in the process, developed an amazing array of moves, surprising even his father. "I gave him the fundamentals," said Press, "but the between-the-legs, behind-the-back, blind stuff Pete does, I never even thought of that."

> **Tip-In**
>
> On January 5, 1988, while playing three-on-three basketball in Pasadena, California, Pete Maravich had a massive heart attack and died. He was 40 years old.

Drafted third by the Atlanta Hawks in 1970, Maravich took his show to the NBA and delighted crowds there as well. His no-look passes and 25-foot shots endeared him to many fans. Pete scored a career-high 68 points against the Knicks in 1977, and averaged 24.2 points for his career.

Pete Maravich was named one of the 50 Greatest Players in NBA History and is in the Basketball Hall of Fame.

Getting the Ball Rolling

While the players of today may be flashier and stronger than their earlier counterparts, the pioneer shooting guards laid the foundation of great play and great moves for others to follow.

Paul Arizin

Although Paul Arizin isn't a name that you have likely heard of, it is one you should remember. Arizin arrived on the NBA scene when the league was in its infancy and immediately became one of the game's top scorers.

With a jump shot so perfect that it was often described as a Rembrandt or Renoir, Arizin led the Philadelphia Warriors to the 1956 NBA Title, and retired as the third-leading scorer in league history (today he stands around number 80).

Arizin's story is all the more remarkable considering he never played basketball in high school. He went to Villanova, and didn't make that team until he was a sophomore. A year later, he scored 85 points in one game, led the nation in scoring by the time he was a senior, and was named the College Basketball Player of the Year.

Arizin is in the Hall of Fame and was named one of the 50 Greatest Players in NBA History.

Sam Jones

Which player has the most championship rings, besides Bill Russell? The answer: Sam Jones. Jones was the off guard for the Boston Celtics throughout their championship run in the '60s. He was a prolific scorer, with a wide array of moves. When the Celtics needed a bucket, they usually turned to the reliable Jones.

Sam Jones: Championship guard.

When fans today see Tim Duncan hit that bank shot of his, it is often called "old school." Well, if that's so, then Sam Jones was the schoolmaster. Jones knew that the backboard was his friend.

> **Tip-In**
>
> Red Auerbach had a keen eye for basketball talent. Sam Jones was a relatively unknown player, playing at the all-black North Carolina Central College. He was not an All-American and wasn't on the NBA radar when Auerbach selected him in the first round of the NBA draft. Sam Jones ended up becoming one of the 50 Greatest Players in NBA History.

Bill Sharman

Bill Sharman is one of only 10 players in the history of the NBA to have won championships as both a player and a coach. Often called a "pure shooter," Sharman, like Sam Jones, played off guard for those great Celtic teams. In his 10 seasons with the Celtics, Sharman was All-NBA seven times, was in eight All-Star games, and was the MVP of the 1955 game.

Bill Sharman is also one of the all-time great free-throw shooters in NBA history, hitting them at roughly an 88 percent clip—sixth-best on the all-time list.

> **Tip-In**
>
> Bill Sharman is also one of the best coaches in basketball history. He won championships in 1962 with the ABL's Cleveland Pipers, the 1971 ABA Utah Stars, and the 1972 Los Angeles Lakers (with that amazing 33-in-a-row winning streak), making him the first coach to ever win championships in three different leagues.

Jerry West

If general managers made it into the Hall of Fame, Jerry West would be the first player ever inducted as both a player and a GM; but as things stand, we must be satisfied with honoring his playing prowess.

Jerry West is arguably the second-best off guard of all time (see MJ, discussed previously). His beautiful jump shot, great defense, and ability to hit the game-winner at the buzzer made him a joy to watch. Indeed, that last trait has earned him the nickname "Mr. Clutch."

He was also a winner. He led the Lakers to the NBA Finals nine times (winning it once), made All-NBA First Team 10 times, All-Defensive First Team four times, was a 14-time All-Star, and was the All-Star MVP once and the NBA Finals MVP once.

Tip-In

Although he won only one championship as a player, Jerry West won five as an executive.

West was a driven player, never content to be second best, yet forced there by the Celtics many, many times. Even so, he always pushed himself and his teammates ever harder, which seems to be a trait common to the great ones. Says former teammate Tommy Hawkins, "If you didn't come into the game breathing fire every night, Jerry couldn't understand."

The Least You Need to Know

◆ From Kobe Bryant to Vince Carter, great scorers are plentiful in today's NBA.

◆ Pete Maravich and George Gervin paved the way for today's off guards.

◆ And Jerry West, Bill Sharman, and Co. paved the way for guys like Maravich and Gervin.

Great Small Forwards

In This Chapter

- ◆ Today's not-so-small small forwards
- ◆ The fantastic 3's
- ◆ The guys who invented the position

Small forward is a bit of a misnomer; there is nothing small about these guys. However, when compared to their counterpart position, power forward, they might seem a bit "smaller" in comparison. Either way, small forwards are usually a graceful blend of skill and power. Their job is to score and rebound when possible.

Best of the New Breed

Taking what they saw older players do and transforming those moves into to-day's more powerful game, the new small forward has reinvented the position.

Shareef Abdur-Rahim

Abdur-Rahim is one of the most overlooked, underrated players in the game today. He was drafted out of the University of California after only one year of play by the then–Vancouver Grizzlies (with the third overall pick), which didn't give people much of a chance to find out about him as an NCAA star.

But once fans see him play, they quickly figure out that this guy's got game. Consider the following:

Tip-In

After his first and only year at UCLA, Abdur-Rahim was named the PAC-10 Player of the Year, becoming the first freshman in PAC-10 history to win Player of the Year honors.

♦ His second year in the league, 1997–98, Abdur-Rahim averaged 22.3 points per game, sixth best in the NBA.

♦ He scored the 5,000th point of his NBA career on December 23, 1999, becoming the second-youngest player ever to do so.

♦ He was selected to play on the U.S. Olympic team in 2000.

An exciting player, one full of potential, Shareef Abdur-Rahim is sure to shine in the years to come.

Kevin Garnett

If you need proof that small forwards aren't so small anymore, KG is Exhibit No. 1. The 7-foot-tall Garnett once remarked that he wanted to be known as being "six-foot-twelve" because he knew that if he said he was 7 feet tall, he would likely be forced to play center in the NBA, a position that is contrary to his fluid, graceful abilities.

Inside Stuff

Kevin Garnett was a basketball prodigy. He attended high school for three years in South Carolina and was named "Mr. Basketball" in the state after only his junior year. For his senior year, he enrolled in Farragut Academy in Chicago, and was "Mr. Basketball" in Illinois, too.

In 1995, he was named the High School Player of the Year by *USA Today* and was selected to the *Parade* magazine First Team after leading Farragut to a 28–2 mark. That year, he averaged 25.2 points, 17.9 rebounds, 6.7 assists, and 6.5 blocks per game, and shot an astounding .666 from the field. That year, too, Garnett was named the Most Outstanding Player at the McDonald's All-America Game.

The Minnesota Timberwolves selected Garnett out of high school with the fifth pick in the 1995 NBA Draft, hence his nickname, "The Kid." It didn't take long for people to see that he should have been the first pick. As Garnett has matured as a player over the past few years, it is also evident that he has become one of the top five players in the game today.

By 2002, Garnett had become a two-time All-NBA First Team selection, and a three-time All-NBA Defensive First Team selection. He played in his first All-Star Game in 1997, and was selected to start the game in 1998, 1999, 2000, 2001, and 2002. And he's only in his mid '20s.

Grant Hill

Because he was sidelined for the better part of two years after joining the Orlando Magic with a foot injury, it's easy to forget just how well Grant Hill can play basketball. Hill is one of those all-around players in the game, able to shoot, pass, rebound, and defend equally well. As such, he led the NBA in triple doubles for three seasons in a row.

Grant Hill: One of the game's most well-rounded players.

Hill is a product of Duke University, where he learned to play ball the right way. He was a First-Team All-American in 1994, was the Atlantic Coast Conference Player of the Year, and led his Blue Devils to three Final Four appearances, winning two NCAA Championships in the process.

Hill was selected by the Detroit Pistons with the third overall pick in the 1994 draft, and shared Co-Rookie of the Year honors with Jason Kidd. That year, 1995, he became the first rookie ever to lead the league in All-Star voting, and for good measure he did it again the next year, too.

Tip-In

Grant Hill's father is Calvin Hill, the former running back of the Dallas Cowboys.

Inside Stuff

As a rookie, Paul Pierce led the Celtics in three-pointers, three-pointers attempted, three-pointer percentage, and steals. In 2001–02, he was the first Celtic to score 2,000 points in a single season since Larry Bird did so in 1987–88.

Paul Pierce

When Paul Pierce dropped to the 10th spot in the 1998 draft, the Boston Celtics couldn't believe their luck. Pierce had been projected to go much higher in the draft, and considering the kind of player he has become, he undoubtedly should have.

Pierce is a high-octane scorer with a variety of moves, both inside and outside. As a rookie, he averaged 16.5 points per game, and that scoring average has increased every year he has been in the league. Equally comfortable dunking the ball or pulling up for the three, Piece has become one of the best young forwards in the game.

Paul Pierce takes it to the hoop.

Scottie Pippen

Some people make the mistake of dismissing Scottie Pippen as Michael Jordan's side-kick on the Chicago Bulls, but by doing so, they are overlooking what a special player Pippen really is. While it's true that Pippen has never won a championship without MJ, it's equally true that Jordan never won one without Scottie.

Scottie Pippen was named one of the 50 Greatest Players in NBA History, and it's easy to see why. With his lanky body and long arms, he could defend almost anyone, and in the process, became an eight-time All-Defense First Teamer. A smart player, excellent ball handler, and good shooter, Pippen has the all-around sort of game that coaches love.

According to opponent Glen Rice, "Guarding Scottie Pippen is what us small forwards like to call 'Mission Impossible.' If you guard him tight he's gonna break your ankles, if you guard him loose he's gonna drain three after three over you. Scottie's just got to many moves." Nick Van Excel once called Pippen "the best all-around player in the game."

His accomplishments speak for themselves:

◆ Six NBA Championships

◆ Three-time All-NBA First Team

◆ Original Dream Team member

◆ Seven-time All-Star; All-Star Game MVP in 1994

Inside Stuff

As you get older the mental part of this game gets easier for you. It's easier for you to get up because you don't sleep as much when you're older. The physical part of it involves the nagging pains, the injuries don't heal up as fast, and the aches last a little bit longer. Those are the things that, as you get older, keep reminding you that you are getting older as a player.

—Scottie Pippen in *Rip City* Magazine

Peja Stojakovic

You're going to hear more about Predrag "Peja" Stojakovic in the future. With one of the sweetest shots this side of Larry Bird, Peja won the Three-Point Shootout in 2002 in Philadelphia. His ability to hit the three or take the ball to the hoop makes him very difficult to defend, and the league has begun to take notice, making him an All-Star for the first time in 2002.

Stojakovic's route to the NBA was certainly a circuitous one. He grew up in Belgrade, Yugoslavia, but immigrated while still a teen in the 1990s to Greece, both to escape the violence of his homeland as well as to continue his basketball education.

When he was only 16 years old, in 1993, he joined the Greek League and immediately became a star. By 1996, he had caught the attention of Geoff Petrie of the Sacramento Kings, and Petrie used the four-teenth overall pick of the draft that year on Stoja-kovic.

But Stojakovic wasn't ready to leave Europe, and he was under contract with his Greek team through the 1997–98 season, where he was named the MVP of the league. So, although he was an NBA rookie when he finally joined the Kings in 1998, he had already been playing professional basketball for several years at the ripe old age of 22.

> **Technical Foul**
>
> European basketball and NBA basketball are played very differently. Euro ball is more wide open, it's far less physical, defenses are not as intense, and the rules are different.
>
> Accordingly, it takes a few years for most European players to understand the differences, learn to play the American way, play better defense, and shine as brightly as they did in their country.

As with most European players who come to the United States to play, it took awhile for Peja to adapt his game and learn NBA basketball; but once he did, boy, did he. The league now knows who this kid from Yugoslavia is.

Best of the '70s and '80s

Small forwards from the old ABA days, and from the NBA's Golden Age of the '80s, were no less skillful than their counterparts today.

> **Inside Stuff**
>
> In 1978, at age 35, Bill Bradley was elected to the United States Senate from New Jersey. He was reelected in 1984 and again in 1990. In 1996, Bradley decided not to seek reelection, although he vowed to stay in "public life." True to his word, Dollar Bill ran for president in 2000, losing to Al Gore in the Democratic primaries.

Bill Bradley

"Dollar Bill" Bradley was both a great college and pro player. A highly recruited high school player (no doubt in part to a couple of 50-point games), Bradley entered Princeton, where …

- He was a three-time All-American.

- His team won the Ivy League Championship three years in a row.

- He was the 1965 College Basketball Player of the Year.

Captain of the 1964 U.S. Olympic team, Bradley was also offered a Rhodes Scholarship, and so, rather than immediately joining the NBA, chose to study at Oxford.

Upon completion of his studies, Bradley joined the New York Knicks. A solid, fundamental, smart basketball player, Bradley helped New York win NBA Championships in 1970 and 1973.

Rick Barry

Rick Barry's is the tale of two players. On the court he was aggressive, hard-nosed, determined, and intense. He was a terrific scorer, with a wide variety of moves, both inside and outside the lane.

But when he got to the free-throw line, he looked, well, anything but intense. Barry is one of the last players to shoot a free throw underhanded, as they used to in the early days of basketball. But there was a method to his madness. Rick Barry is the second-best free-throw shooter of all time, hitting just shy of 90 percent.

Barry was an all-around terrific player, one who has many accomplishments of which to be proud, including …

- 1966 Rookie of the Year with the (then) San Francisco Warriors.

- 1967 NBA All-Star MVP.

- Eight Time NBA All-Star/Four Time ABA All-Star.

- Five Time All-NBA/Four Time ABA First Teams.

- The only player in history to lead the NCAA, ABA, and NBA in scoring.

- 1975 NBA Finals series MVP with the Warriors.

- Named one of the 50 Greatest Players in NBA History and a member of the Basketball Hall of Fame.

Larry Legend

Larry Bird was not the best athlete on the court; he wasn't a leaper, he wasn't all that strong, and he had slow foot speed. Yet throughout the '80s he was the very best at his position, and indeed one of the very best ever.

What he lacked in natural athletic ability he more than made up for in hard work, court savvy, and killer instincts. He knew when to shoot, when to pass, and where the ball and other players were going. Gutsy under pressure, Larry Legend had an

Tip-In

The 1979 NCAA Championship game between Bird, Magic, and their respective teams remains the highest-rated NCAA Championship contest of all time.

amazing outside shot that had a knack for going in the hole when his team needed a basket most.

The "Hick from French Lick" (as he is sometimes called) was also a winner. He led his 33–0 Indiana State team into the 1979 NCAA Championship game (where they lost to Magic and his Michigan State team), and then led his Boston Celtics to the NBA Finals five times, winning it three times (1981, 1984, and 1986).

Larry Bird could do it all.

Bird was a 12-time NBA All-Star, and was the MVP of the 1982 game. The NBA Rookie of the Year for 1980 (beating out Magic), Bird held or shared 27 different Celtic records when he retired in 1992, his team had won Atlantic Division Titles 10 times, and they won more than 50 games 12 times as well.

Alex English

Alex English scored more points during the decade of the '80s than any other player. The leader of the Denver Nuggets during that decade, English led the team to nine playoff appearances, two Midwest Division Titles, and the Western Conference Finals (in 1985).

With one of the smoothest shots you ever saw, unstoppable at times, English was the first player in NBA history to score more than 2,000 points for eight seasons in a row, winning the scoring title in 1983. English also won the NBA's *J. Walter Kennedy Citizenship Award* in 1988.

Hoopology

The **J. Walter Kennedy Citizenship Award** has been presented annually since 1975 by the Professional Basketball Writer's Association. The award is named for the second commissioner of the NBA and is given to an NBA player or coach for excellence in community service.

Julius Erving

Even the most casual NBA fan has seen that incredible footage of Dr. J swooping in on one side of the basket, hanging, and then coming out the other side for a reverse layup against the Los Angeles Lakers. The shot happened this way:

During Game 4 of the 1980 NBA Finals, Dr. J headed to the basket along the right baseline past defender Mark Landsberger. Intending to make a lay-up, Erving found his path blocked by 7' 2" Kareem Abdul-Jabbar. Erving lept, floated past Kareem, kept going, went under the basket to the other side of the hoop and put in a reverse layup. Said Magic Johnson after the game, "I thought, 'What should we do? Should we take the ball out or should we ask him to do it again?'"

What most people don't know is that shot came late in the Doctor's career, when he wasn't as amazing or athletic as he was when he was younger.

Actually, the good Doctor used to make those sorts of moves on a nightly basis, but very few people ever really saw what he did. Erving played in the ABA for his first five seasons, and ABA games were not often televised. *SportsCenter* was nonexistent, and 24-hour cable hadn't been invented. So Dr. J's greatest moves will live on only for those who actually saw them, the lucky few.

As former NBA player and coach Kevin Loughery put it in *Loose Balls* by Terry Pluto:

> When Julius came to the Nets from Virginia, the word was out that he could do things that had never been done before on the court. I was in the NBA so I hadn't seen him with Virginia. You hear things about a guy and you say, "Yeah, right." Hey, I had been watching the world's greatest players in the NBA, so I had some real doubts about Julius.

In the first game I coached Doc with the Nets, he had the ball ... and the clock was running down. Doc drove the baseline and found himself under the basket with ... two big guys going for the block. Somehow, Doc floated between [them] and then almost tore down the rim with a slam.

To that point in my life, that was the greatest dunk I had ever seen, and Doc did it in the first half of my first game with him. After that, there were a lot of "greatest dunks."

And Rod Thorn of the Nets recalls the time that "Julius brought the ball down on a fast break and Teddy McClain was between Doc and the basket. Teddy crouched a bit in the standard defensive stance. Doc just took off, *high jumped over Teddy*, and then dunked. I can still see McClain looking up and watching Julius fly over him."

His huge hands, leaping ability, charisma, and flash made Julius Erving both a crowd favorite, as well as one of the greatest of all time, as evidenced by these stats:

- One Time NBA MVP/Two Time ABA MVP
- One NBA title/Two ABA titles
- Eleven Time NBA/Five Time ABA All-Star
- Five Time All-NBA First Team/Four Time All-ABA First Team

The one and only Dr. J.

James Worthy

On a team dominated by Magic Johnson and Kareem Abdul-Jabbar, James Worthy was the steady third wheel. Known for his explosive drives to the basket and being one of the best "finishers" in the game, Worthy could score and rebound with grace and apparent ease.

Worthy helped the Lakers win championships in 1985, '87, and '88, and was named one of the 50 Greatest Players in NBA History. So what does "Big Game James" consider his greatest accomplishment? Says Worthy:

> "In 1985, beating the Boston Celtics. They had dominated professional basketball since its existence almost, and more importantly, they had dominated the Lakers in particular. So we felt there was a lot of history on our backs.
>
> We represented all the guys from past years—Elgin Baylor, Jerry West, Wilt Chamberlain—all the guys that were defeated in those years—Happy Hairston—all those guys. We had them on our shoulders. And [the Celtics] beat us in 1984, which made it even more devastating because the dominance continued on into the '80s, into a new era. So to beat them, in Boston, on the parquet floor in 1985, was a major highlight."

Forefathers

Before Dr. J swooped, before Rick Barry drove, a few guys showed what could be done.

Elgin Baylor

It is often said that Julius Erving's above-the-rim play paved the way for Michael Jordan and the modern game. While true, it is equally true that Elgin Baylor paved the way for the Doctor.

Baylor was the first player ever to hang in midair and do something creative, not just shoot a jump shot or make a layup. As one reporter put it about Elgin, "He never broke the law of gravity, but he's awfully slow about obeying it."

He was a highly creative offensive player who had no one to emulate; he was the original. No less an authority than Chick Hearn said that Elgin "may have been the greatest player ever." Says Baylor in *Tall Tales*, "I did things that were spontaneous. I had the ball, I reacted to the defense."

Hearn was a bit less humble: "I had never seen a player like this—all his high-flying moves and how he used reverse english on the ball to make a lay-up from unbelievable angles. He would hang in air so long that you'd worry that he'd get hurt when he came down. A lot of moves people say were invented by Michael Jordan or Julius Erving, I saw Elgin do first."

> **Tip-In**
>
> Elgin Baylor was an 11-time All-Star, and co-MVP of the game in 1959. He holds the record for most points in a finals' game (61), and when he retired, he was the third-leading scorer in NBA history. (Today, the top five scorers of all time are Kareem Abdul-Jabbar, Karl Malone, Wilt Chamberlain, Michael Jordan, and Moses Malone.)

Drafted in 1958 by the Minneapolis Lakers, he was the Rookie of the Year that year, and was also named All-NBA First Team as a rookie (he would be All-NBA 10 times). In 1960, the Lakers moved from Minneapolis to Los Angeles, and Baylor took to the sun well. Averaging 34.8 points per game and 19.8 rebounds per game, he also scored 71 points one special night.

Although Baylor played in six NBA Finals, he retired at the beginning of the 1972 season, the year when the Lakers finally won it all. That omission does little to obscure the fact that fans today can thank this Hall of Famer, one of the 50 Greatest Players in NBA History, for showing what the NBA could become.

The Kangaroo Kid

Billy Cunningham was a high-scoring, high-jumping forward for the Philadelphia 76ers. With great desire and a leaping ability to match, Billy the Kid helped the Sixers win the title in 1967 as a *sixth man* (and he helped them do it again in 1983 as the coach of the team).

Cunningham jumped to the rival ABA in 1972, where he averaged 24.1 points per game and 12 rebounds per game, earning him MVP honors. He rejoined the Sixers in 1974, but he blew out his knee a year and a half later and had to retire at the age of 32.

He had been on three All-NBA First Teams, was an All-Star four times, had his number retired by the 76ers, made it to the Hall of Fame, and was named one of the 50 Greatest Players in NBA History.

John Havlicek

While not nearly as flashy as Baylor, Hondo Havlicek was no less important to the development of the league. The greatest *sixth man* in NBA history, Havlicek was a steady, sturdy all-around player who could shoot, pass, dribble, defend, and rebound.

One of the things that made Havlicek a great sixth man was that he was willing to whatever it was his coach wanted. Says Hondo in *Tall Tales*, "No matter what Red said, I'd say, 'You've got it.' I didn't care if he wanted me to press from endline to endline."

Eventually, as the Boston Celtics aged and Havlicek improved, he became too valuable to keep on the bench and became a star in his own right. Helping the Celtics win eight championships, and being named the MVP of the 1974 Finals, Havlicek was All-NBA First Team four times and All-Defensive First Team five times, was elected to the Hall of Fame, and was named one of the 50 Greatest Players in NBA History.

Hoopology

The **sixth man** was one of Red Auerbach's great inventions. While the five best players on the team usually start the game, Red realized that another great player waiting on the bench was necessary—a player who could give the team a boost about 10 minutes into the game and ignite the team. The first was Boston's Frank Ramsey.

The Least You Need to Know

◆ Today's small forwards owe much to the guys who came before them.

◆ Julius Erving was fantastic to behold.

◆ The early small forwards like Baylor and Havlicek started it all.

Chapter 14

Great Power Forwards

In This Chapter

- ◆ A new breed of power forward
- ◆ Power forwards from the '70s and '80s who left their mark
- ◆ The original power forwards

The power forward, or 4 position, is probably the roughest, most physical position in the NBA today. The power forward is expected to box out the opponent, crash the boards, rebound, tip it in, score, and defend.

Putting the Power in Power Forward

Today's power forwards are stronger and altogether more muscular than their earlier counterparts.

Tim Duncan

"Old school" is a phrase sometimes associated with Tim Duncan, and it's easy to see why. With his deft, feathery touch and off-the-glass shots, his obvious work ethic, and down-to-earth style of play, Duncan is surely reminiscent of the player of yore.

Duncan played four full years at Wake Forest, where he was named College Basketball Player of the Year as a senior. In 1997, he was taken with the first overall pick by the San Antonio Spurs. That year, Duncan led the league in double doubles, was the only rookie selected to the NBA All-Star Game, and ran away with NBA Rookie of the Year honors, garnering 113 out of a possible 116 votes.

Inside Stuff

Tim Duncan grew up on the Caribbean island of St. Croix. His older sister Tricia was in the 1988 Olympics, and it was Tim's first ambition in life to follow in her footsteps and be an Olympic swimmer.

However, in 1989, Hurricane Hugo hit the tiny island and destroyed every swimming pool in the country, and Duncan's Olympic hopes as well. As such, he turned to basketball, playing for the first time in ninth grade.

In 1992, a Wake Forest graduate and NBA rookie named Chris King was visiting St. Croix on a goodwill mission when he saw the 16-year-old Duncan play. King immediately called his college coach, urging him to come down and scout this amazing young player. Dave Odom listened, came to St. Croix, and in 1993 convinced Duncan to attend Wake Forest.

Duncan has developed into an all-around great player, with the ability to shoot, rebound, pass, and defend equally well. And by the 1998–99 season, his impact was so strong that he, along with teammate David Robinson, led the Spurs to the NBA championship. The MVP of the entire league in 2002, Duncan is sure to be one of the all-time greats before his career is over.

Mailman

Karl Malone has a good chance of passing Kareem Abdul-Jabbar as the all-time leading scorer in NBA history. And he will do so, not because he is an offensive machine like Wilt, Michael, or Kareem were, but rather because he is one of the steadiest, sturdiest, most consistent players ever.

Malone has a workman-like reputation for a reason—he works hard, is committed, and rarely misses a game. Indeed, in the first 16 years of his career, he missed but six games. That kind of dedication is admirable.

Malone was drafted by the Utah Jazz in 1985, and he, along with John Stockton, transformed the once-dormant franchise. Their patented pick-and-roll play, which they have learned to execute to perfection, has stymied opponents for nearly 20 years. Even when they know it's coming, there is little other teams can do to stop this picture-perfect play.

Karl Malone holds the distinction of being the strongest player in the game today (save for maybe Shaq). This allows him to rebound efficiently and defend well, all while maintaining a sweet outside shot. He has set a new standard for the power forward position.

Dirk Nowitzki

In 1998, when Dallas Mavericks GM Don Nelson traded for the draft rights to Dirk Nowitzki, few had ever heard of the German-born player. Nowitzki had played on the 1996 German National Junior Team, the European Junior Select team, the World Junior Team, and the 1996 German Under-22 National Team. Nelson knew that the kid had the potential to be great, boldly predicting that Nowitzki would become a star in the NBA. He was right.

Maybe the best international player to ever play in the league, Nowitzki is a fluid 7-footer who shoots like Larry Bird, can put the ball on the floor, and is able to hit the three. His versatile game and large body make him hard to defend, and once he learned NBA basketball, it became that much harder for the opposition.

By the 2000–01 season, he was already an All-NBA Third Team member; he made the Second Team in 2001–02, and the NBA All-Star team that year as well. He figures to be a fixture there for some time to come.

Two of the best European players in the game today: Peja Stojakovic and Dirk Nowitzki.

C-Webb

Chris Webber of the Sacramento Kings has always been an intriguing player. As a youth in Detroit he was already labeled a "can't-miss" prospect, and he solidified that reputation at the University of Michigan.

Drafted in 1993 by the Orlando Magic and immediately traded to the Golden State Warriors, Webber earned NBA Rookie of the Year honors. A *player* with an array of moves around the basket, exceptional hands, and an especially soft jump hook, Webber has also developed a consistent 15-foot jump shot to keep defenders on their heels. When you combine these skills with his big paws and exceptional passing ability, you can see why he has always been such a coveted player.

After winning top rookie honors in Golden State, Webber was traded to the Washington Bullets, now known as the Wizards, where he teamed up with his old college chum, Juwan Howard. Together, these two were supposed to bring about a revival in Wizard basketball—a revival that never really happened, although the team did make the NBA playoffs in 1997. Webber was eventually traded to the Sacramento Kings.

Webber's arrival, along with that of Vlade Divac and Jason Williams, signaled a turn-around for the franchise, and before long, the Kings were making some noise in the competitive Western Conference. In the 2002 NBA Playoffs, the Kings went toe-to-toe with the two-time defending NBA Champion Los Angeles Lakers in the Western Conference Finals. The series went to a thrilling Game 7, which the Kings lost in overtime. Webber and his new point guard, Mike Bibby, just fell short of advancing to the NBA Finals.

The previous summer, Webber signed a multiyear contract extension with the Kings, something many basketball insiders thought wouldn't happen. But with his career back on track, his team winning, and fans that adore him, Chris Webber knew a good thing when he saw it. As he says, being traded to Sacramento was a blessing in disguise.

Power Forwards from the Golden Era and Beyond

The '70s and '80s were a time when the NBA was blessed with some of the best forwards ever to play the game.

Sir Charles

Although Charles Barkley was usually a good four or five inches shorter than his counterparts on the hardwood, what he lacked in height he more than made up for in strength, grit, and confidence. At 6' 6" (some say he was really 6' 4"), Barkley was short for a power forward, but that didn't stop him from leading the league in rebounding in 1986–87.

Barkley was simply a monster on the court, boxing out bigger guys, scoring almost at will, and making big play after big play. That he was at times outrageous made him all the more fun. In an era where athletes are brands, and what they say seems almost scripted sometimes, Charles was always a welcome relief, even if what he said was sometimes extreme.

Sir Charles was an all-around play maker.

While Sir Charles certainly is entertaining to listen to, that shouldn't obscure his basketball accomplishments:

- ◆ NBA MVP (1992–93)
- ◆ Five-time All-NBA First Team, and five-time All-NBA Second Team
- ◆ An original Dream Team member (1992)
- ◆ An 11-time NBA All-Star, and MVP of the 1991 game
- ◆ Named one of the 50 Greatest Players in NBA History

Inside Stuff

The quotable Barkley:

♦ "My family got all over me [for supporting President George H. Bush] because they said Bush is only for the rich people. Then I reminded them, 'Hey, I'm rich!'"

♦ "Kids are great. That's one of the best things about our business, all the kids you get to meet. It's a shame they have to grow up to be regular people and come to the games and call you names."

♦ "I don't believe professional athletes should be role models. I believe parents should be role models .... It's not like it was when I was growing up. My mom and my grandmother told me how it was going to be. If I didn't like it, they said, 'Don't let the door hit you in the [rear end] on your way out'; parents have to take better control."

♦ "These are my new shoes. They're good shoes. They won't make you rich like me, they won't make you rebound like me, they definitely won't make you handsome like me. They'll only make you have shoes like me. That's it."

♦ "My initial response was to sue her for defamation of character, but then I realized that I had no character!"

Hoopology

In basketball parlance, a player who likes to battle it out underneath the boards, fight for rebounds, and otherwise mix it up down low is called a **banger**.

Tip-In

After his career was over, Dave DeBusschere went on to become the New York Nets general manager, commissioner of the ABA, and executive vice president of the New York Knicks.

Dave DeBusschere

In the late '60s, the New York Knicks were a very good basketball team, but it took Dave DeBusschere to push them over the top and turn them into a great one. DeBusschere was the *banging* type of forward the Knicks lacked up to that point. With him on board, the team went on to win championships in 1970 and 1973.

His individual stats weren't too shabby, either. An All-Defensive First Team member five times, a seven-time NBA All-Star, and a member of the Hall of Fame, DeBusschere was also named one of the 50 Greatest Players in NBA History.

Elvin Hayes

Although the "Big E" played center in a historic matchup against Lew Alcindor (now Kareem Abdul-Jabbar) in college, when he got to the pros, Hayes ended up as one of the great power forwards of any generation.

Inside Stuff

The January 20, 1968, game between UCLA and the University of Houston has come to be known as the college "Game of the Century." It pitted Lew Alcindor and his top-ranked UCLA Bruins, who were riding a 47-game winning streak, against the No. 2—ranked University of Houston Cougars, led by Elvin Hayes.

It was a game of many firsts. It was the first regular-season college basketball game ever to be shown on national television; it was the first game ever to be played in the Astrodome; and it was the first game ever to have more than 50,000 fans attend.

In the end, it was also the first game that UCLA would lose that year, as Hayes scored 39 points in an epic battle, with the Cougars upsetting the Bruins 71–69.

Originally drafted by the San Diego Rockets, where he continued to play center, Hayes was traded to the Baltimore Bullets in 1972, who already had Wes Unseld camped out at center. So Elvin Hayes switched positions and became a strong, tough power forward who could score in a variety of ways. It was a style Karl Malone would later exemplify.

With a great turnaround jumper and the ability to bang the boards, Hayes …

- ◆ Helped lead the Bullets to the NBA Championship in 1978.

- ◆ Retired as the fourth-leading rebounder in NBA history.

- ◆ Left as the fifth all-time leader in number of games played.

- ◆ Was elected to the Hall of Fame.

- ◆ Was named one of the 50 Greatest Players in NBA History.

Kevin McHale

Like Bird, Celtic teammate Kevin McHale did not look like a gifted athlete. Skinny, almost scrawny, McHale nevertheless was one of the great *post-up players* ever. With a wide variety of head fakes, spins, fadeaway jumpers, double and triple pumps, and up-and-under moves, McHale always seemed to find a way to score when he got the ball down low.

McHale, Bird, and Robert Parish made up arguably the greatest front line in NBA history, catapulting the Celtics to amazing success throughout the '80s. And while it is easy to wax poetic about what a great team that was, let's not, in the process, forget how great each was individually. For example, McHale ...

Hoopology

The prototypical power forward will get set up down low with his back to the basket, called "posting up." When he gets the ball, he will use a variety of moves to fake out his man and try to score. These are **post-up players**.

- ◆ Won the NBA Sixth Man of the Year award in both 1984 and 1985.

- ◆ Was a seven-time NBA All-Star.

- ◆ Had the ninth-best shooting percentage in NBA history (.554).

- ◆ Was a three-time All-Defensive First Teamer.

- ◆ Was enshrined into the Hall of Fame (1999).

- ◆ Was named one of the 50 Greatest Players in NBA History.

Godfathers of Rock and Roll

Power forwards have always been a tough lot, and the guys who invented the position were no exception.

Jerry Lucas

For a big man (6' 8"), Jerry Lucas had an excellent outside shot, with a knack for hitting not just the long jumper, but what would today be a 3-point shot. Hard-nosed and hard-working, Lucas also averaged at least 17 rebounds a game for six straight seasons.

A seven-time NBA All-Star and MVP of the All-Star Game in 1965, Lucas was also the NBA Rookie of the Year in 1964. Alongside Oscar Robertson, Lucas helped make the Cincinnati Royals of the '60s an excellent basketball team. He, too, is in the Hall of Fame and was named one of the 50 Greatest Players in NBA History.

Vern Mikkelsen

The NBA's first dynasty—the Minneapolis Lakers—had a Hall of Fame front line. Playing alongside George Mikan were Jim Pollard and Vern Mikkelsen. Mikkelsen's ability to get the rebound as well as score *in the paint* showed what a true, great big man can do.

Combining both strength and size, Mikkelsen was able to dominate the court, and opposing teams often resorted to stalling tactics to keep the ball away from him. That was but one reason why a 24-second clock needed to be introduced. Mikkelsen missed only five games throughout his career, was a six-time NBA All-Star, and is a member of the Hall of Fame.

Hoopology

The area inside the key is painted a different color than the rest of the floor. Players who can score in that area, **inside the paint**, are valuable because it's a tough zone with a lot of bodies and elbows flying around.

Bob Pettit

Bob Pettit was one of the game's first true stars, and was the premier power forward of his era. This might be surprising considering he twice didn't make his high school basketball team. But Pettit was nothing if not determined, and it was that same determination that turned him into one of the league's best. As he once said, "I was never satisfied, never totally happy with the way I played. I always felt there was room for improvement."

Starring for the St. Louis Hawks, Pettit defined the role of power forward. Says one-time teammate Lenny Wilkens, "He was a power forward who could really score. You didn't find guys like that in those days." Pettit's stats include …

- NBA Rookie of the Year for 1954–55.
- 10-time All-NBA First Team.
- First player in NBA history to score 20,000 points.
- Two-time NBA MVP.
- Hall of Fame.
- One of the 50 Greatest Players in NBA History.
- Four-time NBA All-Star Game MVP (a record).

Dolph Schayes

Schayes was a durable player (he played for 16 seasons, leading the league in minutes played twice) and a consistent scorer and rebounder. Schayes helped lead the Syracuse Nats to their only championship, and was All-NBA First or Second teamer for 12 years in a row, as well as being a 12-time All-Star. Schayes is idolized in Syracuse where he still lives.

Although he joined the league when it was but three years old, Schayes is not forgotten; he was named one of the 50 Greatest Players in NBA History in 1996.

The Least You Need to Know

- ◆ A new breed of power forward such as Karl Malone has redefined the position.
- ◆ Power forwards from the '70s and '80s like Kevin McHale and Charles Barkley are legends.
- ◆ The original superstar power forward was Bob Pettit.

Chapter 15

Great Centers

In This Chapter

- ◆ Shaq and Co. play it tough
- ◆ Kareem and Co. were great centers
- ◆ Wilt and Russell paved the way

An old saying around the league is *you can't teach height.* Finding someone 7 feet tall is one thing, but finding a 7-footer who is also coordinated, strong, swift, and agile is rare indeed. That's why teams are always looking for one, and why the big man is celebrated in NBA lore.

When you do find that special big man, you better ride that pony for as long as you can, because it will be awhile before the next good, big guy will come along.

New Breed

Today's center is bigger and stronger than his earlier counterparts. Using new strength and conditioning exercises, the center is now a specimen.

Patrick Ewing

Prior to the arrival of Patrick Ewing in New York, the proud Knicks franchise was not what it once was. But the chance to land the 7'0" Ewing, the NCAA champion, MVP, and College Basketball Player of the Year from Georgetown, brought hope to the Knicks faithful. Luckily for the Knicks, that year, 1985, happened to be the first year of the draft lottery, and New York landed the rights to draft first. They took Ewing, who went on to become the NBA's Rookie of the Year.

> **CAUTION**
>
> **Technical Foul** _____
>
> Prior to 1985, the draft was conducted in reverse order of that year's standing, so that the team with the worst record would draft first.
>
> Although the plan makes sense in theory, in practice it was perceived that by the end of the year, the teams near the bottom of the standings were, possibly, losing on purpose, or at least not trying hard to win, so that they might get the chance to draft first. To prevent this, the NBA instituted a lottery system in 1985 that *weighted* the first pick toward the worst team, but did not *guarantee* it.

Although it was fervently hoped that Ewing would bring an NBA Championship back to the Big Apple, it never materialized. Ewing and the Knicks came close, losing in seven games to Houston in the 1994 NBA Finals. Yet that small hole in an otherwise stellar career cannot diminish Ewing's impact. He brought playoff basketball back to New York on a yearly basis and led the team to the NBA Finals once.

Ewing was also a six-time All-NBA player (either First or Second team), an 11-time NBA All-Star, and an original Dream Team member, while becoming the all-time Knicks leader in points, rebounds, blocks, and steals.

Zo

Alonzo Mourning is a remarkable athlete. In 2000, the Miami Heat center was diagnosed with a rare kidney disease. Unable to play that year, Zo nevertheless vowed to return, and return he did. In the very next season, he shook off the cobwebs to average 15.7 point per game and 8.4 rebounds per game.

It's not surprising however that Mourning returned to the NBA. He is, and always has been, an exceptionally hard-working, intense competitor. As he himself told *Sports Illustrated* in 1998, "I can't change the way I play. My intensity is part of my game. It gets me up and ready to play. I've always been excited, anxious, and my emotions have been there ever since I picked up a basketball. You can't just turn that off overnight."

Drafted by the Charlotte Hornets and then later traded to Miami, Mourning seemed to find his basketball soulmate in Coach Pat Riley. The intense Riley and the intense Mourning make a formidable pair, and Miami is almost always a playoff threat. Zo is a multiple NBA All-Star and was twice named the NBA Defensive Player of the Year. However, the kidney disease returned and Mourning's career is in jeopardy.

Hakeem the Dream

There was a time when Hakeem Olajuwon was the epicenter of the NBA universe. Back in the mid-'90s, with Michael Jordan seemingly safely retired and Hakeem the Dream's Houston Rockets winning back-to-back titles, Olajuwon was considered the best player in the game, and it's easy to see why.

With his patented move, the unstoppable "Dream Shake," his ability to control the boards and game, his earnest, almost regal, bearing, and his quickness and heart, Olajuwon is what fans want a superstar to be: a gentleman, a great player, and a winner. Indeed, in the 1999–2000 season, he received the NBA's Sportsmanship Award for the Midwest Division. He is also a versatile player, as the following stats indicate:

◆ He is the all-time leader in NBA history in blocks (3,830).

◆ He is in the top 10 in points and steals.

◆ He won two NBA championships (1994 and 1995).

◆ He was the NBA MVP (1994).

It is little wonder, then, why the native Nigerian was named one of the 50 Greatest Players in NBA History.

Shaq Attack

Shaquille O'Neal is not only the most dominating big man of his generation, he just may go down as the best center of all time before it's all said and done. Considering he has Wilt Chamberlain, Bill Russell, and Kareem Abdul-Jabbar in his way, that would be an amazing thing. But it's not farfetched.

O'Neal has an amazingly rare combination of almost superhuman strength, speed, size, agility, foot speed, power, and will. He has added a beautiful array of post moves to go along with his towering dunks, and has learned to play in a team-oriented system.

With three NBA titles under his belt (and counting), Shaq is combining Wilt's strength and offense with Russell's championships and defense, and becoming an unstoppable force in the process.

Shaq powers two to the hoop.

Like Jordan before him, Shaq has become that unique sort of player who teams and coaches draft strategy around. In fact, he became so dominating that teams began to add and drop players in a vain effort to stop the 7' 1", 350-pound self-proclaimed Superman. But, as the song goes, you don't want to tug on Superman's cape. It might fire him up.

How good is Shaq? Consider that in 1996, after playing only four years in the league and before winning a single championship, he was named one of the 50 Greatest Players in NBA History. While a few looked askance at the selection then, it seems prophetic now.

Tip-In

Shaquille O'Neal also has a reputation for being a softie off the court, and a generous one to boot. For example, he gave $1 million to establish technology centers in Boys & Girls Clubs nationwide.

Said Shaq, "I am lucky enough to be in a position to help kids. I thought about building recreation facilities, and they are important, but not every kid is going to make it to the NBA. So I started thinking about how technology is such a huge part of my life, and that kids who don't understand computers are going to be at an even greater disadvantage in the next century than they are today."

When asked once how he would defend himself if he were another player, Shaq replied, "I wouldn't. I would just go home. I'd fake an injury or something."

The Admiral

Getting one franchise player, such as the San Antonio Spurs did in Tim Duncan, is a basketball blessing, but having two at the same time might be NBA nirvana. The Spurs started out down this road in the 1989–90 season when Naval Academy graduate David Robinson joined the team after two years of active duty.

Strong and smooth, articulate and intelligent, the Admiral quickly established himself as a force to be reckoned with. His sweet outside shot belied his tough inside presence, and eventually Robinson came to be considered one of the best centers ever.

The NBA Rookie of the Year, and later MVP and Defensive Player of the Year, David Robinson was also an original Dream Teamer and named one of the 50 Greatest Players in NBA History. He and Tim Duncan helped the Spurs to the NBA title in 1999.

Great Centers from the Past

There simply is no shortage of great centers in the annals of the NBA.

Kareem Abdul-Jabbar

Kareem may be the most underrated superstar in the history of the game. Now, no one doubts that Kareem and his legendary skyhook were great, but many people don't realize, or don't remember, just how great of an all-around offensive player he was.

Along with Michael Jordan and Wilt, Kareem was simply one of the top three offensive players ever, and maybe the most unstoppable of the three. Consider his remarkable achievements:

- The greatest scorer in the history of the league (38,387 points!)
- Six-time NBA MVP
- Six-time NBA champion, two-time NBA Finals MVP
- Nineteen-time NBA All-Star
- Hall of Famer
- One of the 50 Greatest Players in NBA History

Battle of the titans: Kareem Abdul-Jabbar and Patrick Ewing.

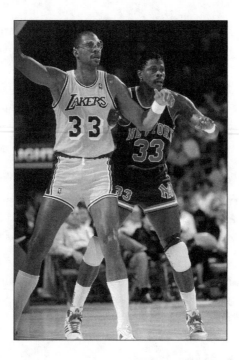

Kareem is mentioned in the same breath as Wilt, Russell, and now, Shaq, as the game's greatest centers. Abdul-Jabbar's graceful skyhook was the singular most effective shot in the history of the game.

It may also be that Kareem was too dignified, too proud, and too outspoken for some. Boycotting the 1968 Olympics because of U.S. treatment of African Americans, Abdul-Jabbar let us know early on that he was a man of intelligence and introspection. He has since penned several books, taught basketball on an Indian reservation, and continued to be one of the great jazz aficionados of the day.

But, as we recall Kareem the man, let's not forget that Kareem the player was a sight to behold. He played longer, and in more games, than almost anyone. He won championships with two different franchises. And when the game was on the line, Kareem's skyhook was the shot that the coach called, the shot the opposing coach knew was coming, and the shot that usually went in the hole anyway.

When choosing the best team of all time, you would need to strongly consider Kareem Abdul-Jabbar.

Dave Cowens

Cowens is the undiscovered Celtic. While Boston fans surely remember the short (6' 9") center who played in the '70s, many others do not. And it's too bad they don't, because Cowens was truly a remarkable center.

With a deft shooting touch and the ability to both dribble and pass well, Cowens forced the bigger centers whom he played against out of their comfort zone. Equally comfortable *shooting the J*, driving to the hoop, or passing out of the double team, Cowens and John Havlicek led the Celtics to two more titles in the '70s.

Hoopology

When a player shoots a jump shot, it is sometimes referred to as **shooting the J.**

Cowens was named NBA Co-Rookie of the Year in 1971, the MVP of the league in 1973, and played in the NBA All-Star Game in 1973, and he was inducted into the Hall of Fame in 1990. You've probably guessed what's coming next: He was also named one of the 50 Greatest Players in NBA History.

Moses Malone

Moses Malone was a monster. The all-time leader in free throws made and offensive rebounds, Malone is also the league's third-leading rebounder and fifth all-time scorer. A three-time MVP, Malone dominated games on both ends of the court.

In high school, Malone averaged 38 points per game and 19 rebounds per game, and led Petersburg High School in Virginia to 50 consecutive victories and back-to-back state championships. As such, he became the first player ever to jump straight from high school to the pros, and seemingly didn't miss a beat. He quickly became a dominant force in the ABA. When the ABA folded in 1976, the NBA finally saw what all the fuss was about.

Tip-In

"My thing was that I just loved to play the game. When I went into (professional basketball), it wasn't about the money. It was about the pride of playing against the best. Yeah, when I was the first one to go from high school to the pros, I thought it was a big thing. I figured I could always go to school if I wanted to, but I could make the money, too."

—Moses Malone

A hard-working, in-the-trenches, no-frills sort of player, Moses Malone gave it his all. His hard work paid off. Moses led the 76ers to the 1983 NBA title, earned Hall of Fame honors and a spot in the record books as one of the 50 Greatest Players in NBA History.

The Chief

Despite his stoicism on the court, Robert Parish was a tough-as-nails competitor who was all about winning. Throughout the 1980s, he, Larry Bird, and Kevin McHale made up the great Celtic frontcourt, propelling the team to three NBA championships.

Nicknamed "Chief" by Cedric Maxwell due to his resemblance to a character in *One Flew Over the Cuckoo's Nest*, Parish played the game like his more celebrated predecessor, Bill Russell. Concentrating on defense and rebounding allowed Bird and McHale to concentrate on offense.

This is not to say that he didn't have an offensive game, for he certainly did. With a sweeping hook shot that was difficult to defend, Parish added offensive punch when needed. He was durable, too; Robert Parish played a record 21 seasons in the NBA and retired when he was an amazing 43 years old.

Willis Reed

How good was Willis Reed? He played in two NBA Finals (1970 and 1973), his team (the Knicks) won both, and he was the MVP of both series. That's accomplishment enough on their own, but considering that his Game 7 performance in 1970 is the stuff of legend, you begin to see what made Willis Reed such a special player.

In that never-to-be-forgotten Game 7 against the Los Angeles Lakers, Reed hobbled onto the court with a torn thigh muscle, gutted out a couple of minutes and a couple of shots, and single-handedly helped turn the NBA into a mainstream league. It was an amazing, goose-pimply moment when Reed took to the floor, and few have ever forgotten it (see Chapter 3). As Reed says, "There isn't a day in my life that people don't remind me of that game."

> **Inside Stuff**
>
> The year 1970 was indeed magical for Willis Reed, as he became the first player ever to win the All-Star MVP, the regular-season MVP, and the NBA Finals MVP in the same year. The only other time that feat has been accomplished was in 1996, by none other than Michael Jordan.

But Willis Reed is more than one gutsy performance in one important game. He had an excellent 10-year career with the Knicks, where he was a seven-time NBA All-Star, and was the first Knick to ever have his number retired. His strength, soft touch, and toughness made him a special player. Before long, he would be inducted into the Hall of Fame and named one of the 50 Greatest Players in NBA History.

Wes Unseld

It's hard to imagine 6' 7" Wes Unseld playing center today, but then again, it is hard to imagine him playing it yesterday, too. But what Unseld gave up in inches, he more than made up for in bulk and muscle. Like Shaq and Wilt, Wes Unseld was one of the strongest men ever to play in the NBA.

Drafted second by Baltimore in 1968, Unseld is the only other player besides Chamberlain to win Rookie of the Year and league MVP in the same year; that's what an impact Unseld had on the league. He helped turn the Bullets franchise into a playoff contender, and in 1978 led the team to the championship.

For a man of his size, it says a lot that Wes Unseld remains the ninth-best rebounder in NBA history. For his contributions to the game, he, too, was inducted into the Hall of Fame and named one of the 50 Greatest Players in NBA History.

Bill Walton

It is easy in any discussion about Bill Walton to wonder what level of NBA greatness he would have achieved had he not been hurt as much as he was (Walton played in just more than half of the scheduled games over his 10-year career.)

But to focus on what might have been misses the point about Walton entirely, namely, what was. Bill Walton, despite any foot injury he ever had, was easily still one of the greatest centers to ever play the game.

The beauty of Bill Walton's game was multifold: his ability to grab the rebound when it was most needed, his soft touch around the basket, his midrange jumper, the precise passes, the quick outlets, the basketball smarts, the commitment to teamwork. Watch Walton play and you knew that you were watching basketball the way it was meant to be played.

It was Walton who led the Portland Trail Blazers to their magical championship in 1977, and it was Walton who was the key sixth man for the Celtics' title run in 1986. In between, he was the league MVP in 1978, All-NBA a few times, and then in 1986, the NBA's Sixth Man of the Year.

> **Tip-In**
>
> Before he was a pro, Walton was a college basketball legend. A three-time All-American, he was also the *Sporting News* Player of the Year for three straight years and Final Four MVP for two years. His UCLA teams won 88 games in a row.
>
> On March 26, 1973, Walton's UCLA Bruins were playing Memphis State for the national championship. That night, big Bill played maybe the finest game in collegiate basketball history. Hitting 21 of 22 shots, Walton led the Bruins to the NCAA title.

Since retiring, Walton has become a very successful broadcaster and basketball analyst. In 1991, he received the National Basketball Players' Association Oscar Robertson Leadership Award, and in 2002 he received the NBA Retired Player's Association Humanitarian Award. He has also won the Southern California Sports Broadcasters Association award for Best Television Analyst/Commentator multiple times, and in 2002 was named the lead analyst for ESPN and ABC's coverage of the NBA.

He is, needless to say, in the Hall of Fame and one of the 50 Greatest Players in NBA History. Not bad for a guy who was, according to his own admission, the most injured player in the history of the league, too.

Guys Who Set the Precedent

Center has always been the dominant position in the NBA. It was a big man's league almost from the start.

Wilt

What is left to say about Wilt Chamberlain that hasn't already been said in this book? When talking about dominating big men, Wilt is always the obvious comparison. When discussing great scorers, Wilt is the benchmark.

How about this statistic: When he joined the Lakers, Wilt became the only center ever to lead the league in assists. As center Dan Issel put it, "As I grew up, Wilt the Stilt was *the* player. Just the things he was able to do. I guess one year they told him he couldn't make as much money as he wanted because he couldn't pass the ball, so he went out and led the league in assists. Watching Wilt, you always kind of got the idea he was just playing with people. That he was on cruise control and still 10 times better than anybody else that was playing at that time."

Indeed, no matter what Wilt tried, he did with gusto, and usually was the best. Former teammate and NBA great and coaching great Billy Cunningham once said of Wilt, "The NBA record book reads like Wilt's personal diary." Indeed, as NBA Commissioner David Stern said about the Big Dipper after Wilt passed away in 1999, "We've lost a giant of a man in every sense of the word. The shadow of accomplishment he cast over our game is unlikely ever to be matched."

Inside Stuff

Interesting Wilt Chamberlain facts:

- The distance from the tip of Wilt's middle finger to his wrist was $9^1/_2$ inches.
- Scored 100 points in a single game!
- Wilt was once offered a contract to play football for the Kansas City Chiefs.
- Of the eight times that an NBA player has scored 70 or more points, Wilt gets credit for six of them.
- In college at Kansas, Wilt was undefeated in the shot put and won the Big 8 title in the high jump.
- Wilt could bench press 500 lbs.
- Wilt ran a 50-mile race when he was over 60 years old.
- *Averaged 50.4 points during the 1961-62 season.*
- Wilt *never* fouled out of a game in his NBA career.
- Wilt averaged over 48 minutes per game during the 1961–62 season. He did not play a *total* of only seven minutes during the entire season!

George Mikan

George Mikan was the first true great center in the NBA. He set the standard for what a great center should be. He was agile and strong, could shoot, rebound, and defend, and was a winner. His team won the college championship in 1945, and his Minneapolis Lakers won six championships in seven years.

Because of this success, and because he was 6' 10" George Mikan became an icon at a time when basketball icons were few and far between. Says former teammate Vern Mikkelsen, "In our time, George was Michael Jordan, Magic Johnson, and Larry Bird all rolled into one." Mikan was a tough, physical player, and one of the few to play with glasses.

The Associated Press Player of the Half Century in 1950, Mikan is also in the Hall of Fame and one of the 50 Greatest Players in NBA History.

George Mikan (far right) with fellow Laker centers Kareem and Shaq (center).

Bill Russell

Like Wilt, there isn't much more to say about Bill Russell that hasn't already been said. Russ was, first and foremost, a winner. Taking his college team, his Olympic team, and his professional team to the championship time and again, Russell could win like no other player, ever.

Tip-In

According to Philadelphia 76er stat man Harvey Pollack, Chamberlain and Russell played each other 142 times. During those contests, Wilt averaged exactly 28.7 ppg and 28.7 rpg. Russell averaged 23.7 points per game and 14.5 rebounds per game.

Wilt certainly had his way with Russell on many occasions: On January 14, 1962, playing against Russell, Wilt scored 62 points, and on six other occasions had at least 50 points against Russell. On November 24, 1960, Wilt nabbed an NBA-record 55 rebounds against Russell. When the Sixers beat the Celtics in the 1967 playoffs, Wilt averaged a triple double: 22 points, 32 rebounds, and 10 assists.

By the same token, however, during the 1960s when they were both in the league, Russell had eight championships to Wilt's one. The Celtics were considered a better, deeper team.

No, he wasn't the dominating physical presence that Wilt was, and no, he wasn't a great scorer. But could he score and dominate? You bet. The opportune block, the defensive stop, the sly hook, Russell did whatever it took to win the game.

How good was Bill Russell? In 1980, the Professional Basketball Writers Association of America named Russell as the "Greatest Player in the History of the NBA."

Bill Russell was a defensive wizard.

Nate Thurmond

If Wilt and Russell were the generals of this era, Thurmond was their second in command. A defensive specialist in the mold of Russell, Nate Thurmond is fifth all time in rebounding. Kareem once said that Thurmond was his toughest matchup.

But Thurmond was no slouch when it came to offense, either; it's just that it was on the defensive end where he made his reputation. Averaging 15 points per game for his career and was also the first player ever to rack up a *quadruple double*: 22 points, 14 rebounds, 13 assists, and 12 blocks.

Thurmond is in the Hall of Fame and was named one of the 50 Greatest Players in NBA History.

The Least You Need to Know

- Shaquille O'Neal and company have kept the center position dominant.

- Abdul-Jabbar is the "kareem" of the crop as the NBA's all-time scoring leader.

- Wilt Chamberlain and Bill Russell cast *very* large shadows.

Part 4

Rounding It Out

While players justifiably steal the show, coaches and refs play a crucial role in the most exciting professional sports league around. In this part of the book, you'll meet the best coaches ever, and see what it takes to become a referee in the NBA today. Moreover, we'll take a stab at that age-old parlor game: Which team is the best ever? Is it the Celtics of the '60s, the Lakers of the '80s, the Bulls of the '90s, the Lakers of today, or some other team? You decide.

Finally, you'll get to relive some of the best moments in NBA history—those heart-pounding, buzzer-beating shots and plays that win games in crunch time. From Jerry West's 60-foot shot to Michael Jordan's incredible game-winners, it's all here.

Chapter 16

The Best Coaches

In This Chapter

- ◆ Coaching in the NBA
- ◆ Finding a coach
- ◆ Tricks of the trade
- ◆ The top 10 coaches of all time

Coaching in the NBA has never been easy. Not only do the coaches have to deal with the pressures of the job and coaxing greatness to achieve maximum results from their players, but they are the people on the front line. When something goes wrong, they are the first to be blamed and often the ones to get fired.

So it's no wonder that the list of coaches from the NBA who tried and fizzled is long indeed. What is surprising is how many great coaches there actually are and have been, and how many different styles and strategies seem to work.

Coaching in the NBA

Coaching an NBA team is akin to being an air traffic controller. It is a high-stress occupation with a cadre of expensive assets relying on one person's judgment. In both occupations, there is a constant demand on their time and

Tip-In

"The coach should be the absolute boss, but he still should maintain an open mind."

—Red Auerbach

abilities, as competing factors vie for their attention and other factors endeavor to distract their charges. Oh, there's one more similarity: One big mistake, and you are grounded.

In fact, an NBA coach wears the hat of many different occupations; part general, part motivational speaker, part entertainment director, part therapist, and all-around leader, it is the coach who sets the tone for his team and leads the way.

Inside Stuff

At the start of the 2001–02 season, the all-time winningest coaches in NBA Playoff history were as follows:

(2002–03 head coaches in capital letters)

Coach	W	L	Pct
PHIL JACKSON	156	54	.743
PAT RILEY	155	100	.608
Red Auerbach	99	69	.589
K.C. Jones	81	57	.587
LENNY WILKENS	80	94	.460
JERRY SLOAN	77	76	.503
Chuck Daly	75	51	.595
Billy Cunningham	66	39	.629
LARRY BROWN	63	66	.488
John Kundla	60	35	.632
DON NELSON	59	71	.454
Red Holzman	58	47	.552
GEORGE KARL	57	63	.475
Dick Motta	56	70	.444
Bill Fitch	55	54	.505
RICK ADELMAN	53	50	.515
RUDY TOMJANOVICH	51	39	.567
Tom Heinsohn	47	33	.588
John Macleod	47	54	.465
Alex Hannum	45	34	.570

Succeeding in a Tough Business

Few occupations rival that of NBA coach for instability. What other profession has a daily scorecard for how you're doing and sometimes gives you less than a year to prove yourself?

Aside from the demand that you win, and win *now*, consider that an NBA coach …

◆ Travels for much of the year away from his family.

◆ Has to constantly find nonmonetary ways to motivate his players. Although money is the normal way managers motivate employees, it has little effect in the rarefied financial strata in which NBA players exist.

◆ Is publicly scrutinized, in both strategy and skill, after every game.

No, it's no easy task being an NBA coach. Rare is the coach who can judge talent, mold it, get it to buy into the system, and then have that talent execute as expected. For every Pat Riley, there are a dozen or so others left on the cutting-room floor. But when that special sort of coach does come along, magic can occur.

Witness the Los Angeles Lakers of the mid- to late '90s. That team was a study in dysfunction: Shaq and Kobe perceivably couldn't get along, players didn't know or accept their roles, a variety of coaches came and went, and great expectations were constantly unfulfilled.

A familiar scene: Red Auerbach and Bill Russell win again.

Enter Phil Jackson. In his first year coaching the team (1999–2000), Jackson was able to turn it all around, completely around. Using his patented Zen approach that combined mysticism, prodding, respect, and triangles, Jackson's Lakers won the title. And then they did it again, and again. So yes, the right coach can make all the difference.

Coaching Styles

NBA coaching styles cover a wide spectrum. On one end there's the fiery intensity of coaches like Pat Riley, while on the other end you'll find the relaxed style of a player's coach such as Larry Bird. In between are the Zen approach of Phil Jackson and any number of other coaching styles, all of which seem to work to some degree or another.

> **Tip-In**
>
> "[Larry] Bird was a little bit more laid back. His assistants [Dick Harter and Rick Carlisle] had a big input in a lot of decisions. Ultimately Larry had final say. [Isiah] Thomas is a little bit more hands-on, a little bit more direct."
>
> —Reggie Miller on the coaching styles of two of his coaches

Indeed, two of the most respected coaches of our era, Phil Jackson and Pat Riley, couldn't seem to have more dissimilar styles. Riley has a reputation for being a tough, demanding taskmaster, while Jackson is the laid-back, intellectual Zen master.

However, according to Jackson, the two coaches "have more similarities than differences." In fact, Jackson says, although "I have more desire for a basketball team to regulate their own selves out there, organize themselves, and run what they do with reading the defense, Riley calls a few more things from the bench. But both of us run systems and have a lot of control."

Pat Riley has always been an intense competitor.

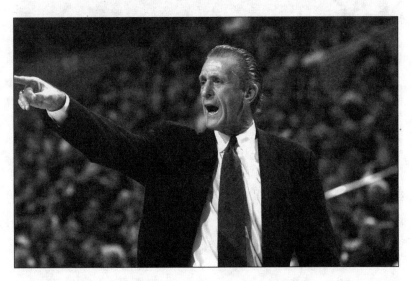

The difference is that the great coaches, like Jackson and Riley, use their system and control to coax the best from their players individually and collectively.

Lenny Wilkens is one of the all-time great coaches, and in fact is the winningest coach in NBA history. According to Wilkens, the best coach ever was Red Auerbach. Why?

> "The reason Red remains a legendary coach is that yes, he had great players, but they also attained greatness playing together. They did it year after year after year. He won titles in each of his last eight seasons, an amazing accomplishment ....
>
> Red had those guys ready to play in big games. He fought off complacency .... Give Red credit for motivating his players and keeping them striving for excellence." (From Unguarded, by Lenny Wilkens.)

Lenny Wilkens has won more regular season games than any other NBA coach.

That is what the great NBA coaches do. They bring out the best in their players, and in so doing, inspire an amazing loyalty in the process. That is why Michael Jordan famously declared that he would rather retire than play for any coach other than Phil Jackson.

That is also why Magic Johnson said, "The Lakers were successful because Coach Riley was able to draw the best effort out of each player. Everything we had to give, he was able to get. Before he came along, we were a group of good players. Pat Riley made us a team."

So styles only matter insofar as they produce, or fail to produce, results. You could be the nicest guy in the world, espousing a positive mental attitude, but if you can't get your team to win, if you don't inspire your players to excellence, it is so much hot air.

> **Technical Foul** _____
>
> Red Auerbach won 938 career games. In 1995, Lenny Wilkens passed him to become the winningest coach in NBA history. Did Wilkens have to coach a lot more games than Auerbach to accomplish that feat? You bet. But consider this, too: The player who played the most games for Red Auerbach was Hall-of-Famer Bob Cousy. The player who played the most games for Lenny Wilkens was Craig Ehlo.

Where Do They Come From?

Finding someone who embodies leadership, flexibility, intelligence, and affability is difficult in any workplace. Finding someone in the NBA who has them, along with basketball know-how, coaching insight, the ability to relate to today's player, and the ability to win, is tougher still. So where do most NBA coaches come from?

The College Ranks

Head-coach hirings in the NBA tend to run in cycles with hiring ex-players as the latest trend. At one time, it was thought that a successful college coach would make for a successful NBA coach, and a slew of college coaches hit the pros.

> **Tip-In** _____
>
> "Those who work the hardest are the last to surrender."
>
> —Rick Pitino

Thus in the mid-'90s, for example, P.J. Carlesimo from Seton Hall was hired to coach the Portland Trail Blazers, while Rick Pitino came from Kentucky to take over the helm in Boston. In 2000, Lon Kruger from the University of Illinois was hired to replace Lenny Wilkens. Pitino did have previous NBA experience serving as an assistant coach with the New York Knicks.

Only Kruger is coaching in the NBA today. It turns out that coaching college ball and coaching in the NBA are two very different animals. Aside from the fact that the rules are different, the skills necessary to get the best out of some very eager sopho-mores is vastly different than the ones necessary to get the best from superstars.

Consider the NBA record of these recent standout college coaches:

Recent College Coaches in the NBA

Coach	College Record	NBA Record
*Rick Pitino	219–50 (.814) at Kentucky (National Champs, 1996)	102–146 (.411) at Boston
John Calipari	193–71 (.731) at UMass (Final Four, 1996)	72–112 (.391) at New Jersey
Tim Floyd	81–47 (.633) at Iowa St. (Sweet 16, 1997)	49–190 (.210) at Chicago
P. J. Carlesimo	212–166 (.561) at Seton Hall	183–222 (.452) at Portland and Golden State
Jerry Tarkanian	509–105 (.829) at UNLV (National Champs, 1990)	9–11 (.450) at San Antonio (resigned after 20 games)

Rick Pitino also coached the New York Knicks (1987-89).

Although the record of recent college coaches is anything but stellar, there have been some notable exceptions.

Back in the 1970's, Dick Motta was coaching at Weber State before joining the Bulls. Motta was very successful in Chicago, and won an NBA Championship with Washington in 1978. Similarly, Jack Ramsay coached at St. Joseph's before leading the Portland Trail Blazers to the title in 1977. Chuck Daly did the same thing in Detroit after coaching at Boston College and Penn.

But because the NBA is cyclical, and because the recent rash of college coaches per-formed so poorly, it will likely be awhile before they get another chance.

The NBDL

A far more likely place for a head or assistant coach to emerge from these days is the National Basketball Development League (NBDL). Play in that league is more like the NBA than is college-level play. Players heading both into and out of the NBA play there, and the travel schedule is more closely akin to that in the NBA (save for the style and mode of transport). Thus, coaching there makes for a good NBA-type experience.

Ex-Players

The most common place to find an NBA coach these days is from the ranks of ex-players. It is believed that ex-players know what present players will listen and respond to.

That ex-players such as Larry Bird, Byron Scott, Rudy Tomjanovich, Phil Jackson, Pat Riley, Don Nelson, K.C. Jones, and Jerry Sloan have had so much success as coaches has solidified this belief.

Tricks of the Trade

Although it's difficult to pinpoint exactly what separates the good from great NBA coaches, it's easy to identify the traits they share.

They Have a "System"

Excellent NBA coaches have thought a lot about professional basketball; they have tinkered with offenses, broken down defenses, and designed countless plays. They know what works and what doesn't work, and they have created a plan of action—a system—designed to maximize strengths and minimize weaknesses.

Some coaches have a name for their system, others simply implement their offensive and defensive schemes. Either way, the distinguishing characteristic is that the coach expects the players to adapt to his system, not vice versa. The coach is in charge.

Phil Jackson gets a lot of credit, deservedly so, for having a system that his players buy into. That system combines many things, but it is centered on the Triangle Offense.

Tip-In

"All really successful coaches have a system."
—Coach Jim Valvano

According to former Chicago Bulls guard John Paxson, "A system offense is made for someone who doesn't have the athletic skills that a lot of the guys in the league have. It played to my strengths. But it tightened the reins on guys like Michael and Scottie. It was the job of Phil to sell us on the fact we could win playing that way."

It is to Jackson's everlasting credit that he was able to sell his product, his system, and that it worked. Doing so enabled him to get the next requirement necessary to become a special head coach: respect of your players.

Respect

There are 29 teams in the NBA, and every year, only one wins the championship. Needless to say, the coach of that team gets the respect due to him. But what about the other 28 coaches? Do they have the respect of their players? Some do, and some don't.

Quite often—in fact, very often—when a coach is fired, the rationale is that he lost control of the team, that the players stopped listening to the coach. Lack of respect is the death knell of NBA coaches.

When a new coach comes on the scene, he undoubtedly gets the benefit of the doubt. The new coach is replacing a coach who, for whatever reason, wore out his welcome, so the new guy is usually a relief. Respect is assured, at least for a while.

The problem for many coaches is that the NBA is a players' league, and maintaining that respect often proves difficult. The players make amazing amounts of money, they are the ones the fans pay to see, and thus have a lot of power. Lose your players, lose your job. But win your players over, and you just might stick around for a while.

Larry Brown wins wherever he goes.

How do you do that? There are many ways. Stand up to a popular player and show him you mean business. Implement a system that utilizes the players' skills. Have a sense of humor. Be tough but fair. Give them a day off. Make them work extra hard. Bench the lazy. What works for some doesn't work for others, but the savvy coach is able to pull just the right strings to make the instrument sound beautiful.

Preparation

All coaches prepare, most probably overprepare. They break down game videos, run statistic after statistic, know the weaknesses of the teams coming in, have a plan, and practice the plan.

The difference is that with some coaches, all of that work makes little difference; the team plays the same no matter what he does. The better coaches have figured out a way to turn that work into results.

Here's an example: In his autobiography *My Life*, Magic Johnson describes the practices that he used to have with Coach Pat Riley when they were winning all of those championships together. Magic says that "each practice had a specific goal .... He [Riley] always knew where he wanted to take us." Magic continues,

> "It helped a lot that every practice had a purpose. If we were preparing to play a great passing team like Denver, Riley would set up drills where the bench players would execute a running offense without ever taking a shot."

But even more than that, Riley's work was intended to make the team better, not just prepared. So, Magic says, for example,

Tip-In

At practices, Riley would remind his players, "Basketball is a business. If you want to have fun, go to the YMCA."

> "We were a great running team, but Riley thought our fast break could be even faster. So he brought in a running coach, an Olympic sprinter named Henry Hines. Henry showed us how to use our arms more effectively, among other things. Just as Riley intended, our transition game went up another notch."

The exceptional coaches practice and prepare with specific results in mind, and usually attain them.

The Great Coaches

Despite the challenges, NBA coaching is one of the premier jobs in all of sports, and those who succeed at this level would probably have succeeded wildly no matter what profession they chose; these are exceptional leaders and people.

The 10 Best Ever

In 1996, as part of the NBA's 50th anniversary, a panel of experts (coaches, players, and media) convened to determine the 10 best coaches in NBA history. This was their conclusion, presented in alphabetical order:

Red Auerbach: Guiding your team to nine titles in 10 years and creating the greatest dynasty in professional basketball history are the sorts of things that cause people to consider you the greatest NBA coach of all time.

According to Lenny Wilkens, "Red Auerbach was like a basketball god when I was [in college]." Red's total number of wins—938—became the gold standard for coaches, a number that was seemingly untouchable.

And although it has been surpassed (by Wilkens), Red remains the standard by which all other coaches are judged. His teams won, and won big. They played a great and exciting brand of basketball, they were stimulating and dominating, and he was egotistical and gifted.

Chuck Daly: By the standards of some of the NBA lifers on this list, Chuck Daly wasn't a head coach for all that long—only 13 years total. It proves then what a great coach he was, that in that short a period of time, he established himself as one of the top five coaches of all time.

Coaching first in Cleveland, and then in Detroit, New Jersey, and Orlando, Daly won two NBA titles with the Pistons, and his teams made countless playoff appearances. As one of his sayings is, "The first shot does not beat you." Chuck Daly teams usually played great defense for all 24 seconds.

Daly's Piston teams averaged 49 wins a year, and he was selected to coach the first Dream Team in the 1992 Barcelona Olympics. Chuck Daly was enshrined in the Hall of Fame in 1994.

Bill Fitch: Fitch is one of the rare college coaches who succeeded greatly in the NBA. After spending a dozen years coaching tiny college teams in Iowa and North Dakota, Fitch got his big break when he was asked to become the head coach of the expansion Cleveland Cavaliers in 1970. When he retired from coaching 25 years later, he had 944 career wins, the third-most ever.

In 1981, he led the Celtics to their first championship with Bird, McHale, and Parish on board. Fitch is also a two-time Coach of the Year.

William "Red" Holzman: Red Holzman was one of only 10 people ever to win championships as both a player and a coach. As a player with the Rochester Royals, he won the NBL Championship in 1946 and the NBA Championship in 1951.

As a coach, he guided a great Knicks team to the title in 1970 and '73. Those Knicks teams were defensive-oriented, team-first squads, featuring Hall of Famers Willis Reed, Walt Frazier, Dave DeBusschere, and Bill Bradley. Holzman's motto was, "If you play good, hard defense, the offense will take care of itself."

Holzman was named NBA Coach of the Year in 1973, and was enshrined as a coach in the Hall of Fame in 1986.

Phil Jackson: Like Riley, Phil Jackson once had the almost-unenviable task of coaching a great team with great individual players. "Anyone could win with Jordan and Pippen" said the naysayers, but of course, they were wrong.

It wasn't until Coach Jackson came to the Shaq and Kobe Lakers—a team that hadn't lived up to its lofty expectations—and won three championships, that the doubters were finally quieted. No one had taken that Laker team to a championship, except for Jackson.

Tip-In

John Kundla coached six future Hall of Famers during his career: Elgin Baylor, Clyde Lovellette, Slater Martin, George Mikan, Vern Mikkelsen, and Jim Pollard.

Inside Stuff

As a general manager, Don Nelson has drafted All-Stars Marques Johnson (using a pick he had acquired for Swen Nater), Sidney Moncrief, Mitch Richmond, Tim Hardaway, Tyrone Hill, Chris Gatling and Latrell Sprewell. Nelson is also responsible for plucking John Starks, Sarunas Marciulionis, and Mario Elie from later rounds of the draft.

Over the course of his career as a player and coach, Jackson has run out of fingers with which to wear championship rings. In a league where even a single championship makes the difference between a great coach and a run-of-the mill coach, that is a remarkable feat.

John Kundla: Maybe you have never heard of Coach Kundla, but basketball historians sure have. Kundla was the man behind the first NBA dynasty, the Minneapolis Lakers. Just as Michael and Scottie needed Phil, just as Magic and Kareem needed Riley, just as Russell and Cousy needed Auerbach, George Mikan and Jim Pollard needed John Kundla.

Enshrined in the Hall of Fame in 1995, Kundla won championships in the NBL, the BAA, and the NBA, and is one of only three coaches to have guided teams to a three-peat (Red Auerbach and Phil Jackson are the others.)

Don Nelson: Nelson is probably the most creative coach in league history, always willing to create a mismatch or tweak a rule to get an advantage. Nelson is the third-winningest coach in NBA history with a record of 1,036–806 (.562) entering the 2002-03 season. He and Pat Riley are the only coaches ever to be named Coach of the Year three times.

Coaching in Milwaukee, Golden State, New York, and Dallas, Nellie also coached Dream Team II to a gold medal in 1994. Affable and intense, Don Nelson always seems to find a way to make his team better.

Jack Ramsay: Dr. Jack has come a long way from coaching high school basketball in 1949. By 1955, Ramsay was coaching at his alma mater, St. Joseph's, and led the team to a 23–6 record his first year, winning a Big 5 championship.

In 1966, Ramsay jumped to the pros, becoming the general manager of the Sixers. But Ramsay wanted to become a basketball coach, and soon was on the sidelines again. In 1977, he led the Portland Trail Blazers into the playoffs, and the championship, for the first time. He retired from coaching in 1988 and has gone on to have another successful career as a basketball commentator and analyst.

Pat Riley: When Riley was winning four championships in Los Angeles during the '80s, the conventional wisdom was that "anyone could win with Magic and Kareem," but that simply was not so. Right before Riley showed up, the Lakers were in disarray. He molded the team and he made it click.

He has since gone on to coaching success in New York and Miami, and it is now the conventional wisdom that Riley is a superb, albeit challenging, coach. With his legendary tough practices and high expectations, Riley demands a lot from his players, but gives back a lot in return.

Tip-In

"If you couldn't put up with Riley's intensity, and a few players couldn't, you didn't last very long with the Lakers."

—Magic Johnson

Of his coach, Magic Johnson once said, "Riley was a strong leader, but he wasn't a dictator. Like most good leaders, he knew how to follow. He listened to his players, and paid attention to our ideas. He understood our emotions. Under Riley's leadership, good players became better, and average players became good."

Lenny Wilkens: As previously noted, Wilkens is the all-time winningest coach in NBA history. That's a pretty amazing accomplishment, considering he never coached one of those special teams—the Celtics, Lakers, or Bulls. In fact, Wilkens says that one thing that makes him "very proud" is the fact that he won as many

Tip-In

"A lot of people don't understand the nature of coaching in the NBA. The measure of any coach is not his final victory total; it's how his players performed compared to their talent. Did the team improve from the year before? Did the players improve?"

—Lenny Wilkens

games as he did as a coach "without any players named Russell, Bird, Magic, Jordan, Chamberlain, or Abdul-Jabbar."

Dignified and unassuming, Wilkens is considered a great teacher *and* a great strategist. Winning the title with Seattle in 1979, and coaching the Olympic team in 1996, Wilkens was inducted into the Hall of Fame as both a player and a coach.

The Least You Need to Know

♦ Coaching in the NBA is a tough calling.

♦ Many coaches are former players.

♦ Great coaches get respect, prepare with a purpose, and have a system.

♦ The top 10 coaches of all time are in a league by themselves.

Chapter 17

The Making of a Referee

In This Chapter

- ◆ What it takes to be a referee
- ◆ Refereeing in an earlier era
- ◆ Refs today, what's the matter with refs today?
- ◆ Unwritten ref rules

Fans love to boo officials, and NBA fans are no exception; booing the refs is almost as popular as cheering the players.

What Makes a Ref a Ref?

Refereeing a professional basketball game is no easy thing. On the same court as some of the world's biggest, best athletes, NBA refs are charged with setting the tempo, calling a fair game, keeping egos in check, and making sure that the game runs smoothly. It's a tall order.

And by and large, the refs do a pretty good job. Perfect? Nope, but pretty darn good. They know what to call, and maybe more importantly, what *not* to call. Keeping Shaq in check for example, and keeping those who defend Shaq honest, are but two of the many of issues that today's referee has to deal with.

Tip-In

"It's the referee's job to make sure the game's played right, and if we do our job well, that's going to *allow* superstars to do their thing."

—Hall of Fame referee Earl Strom

Where do they learn it? Where does a referee wanna-be learn the rules, learn the intangibles, and hone his or her craft? It all starts in places far, far from New York, L.A., and Boston, that's for sure.

A Long Time Ago in a Galaxy Far, Far Away

One of the most famous referees in NBA history was Earl Strom. In his book *Calling the Shots*, Strom recounts his 30 years as a ref, including the story of why he first considered becoming a basketball referee.

Strom explains how, although he loved sports, he was not much of an athlete. One night, while playing in a semipro basketball game, Strom was mouthing off to the refs and was finally ejected from the game. Afterwards, the ref who had tossed Strom out of the contest came up to him and said, "Look, you're not much of a player and you've got a pretty good mouth on you, so why don't you think about taking up refereeing?"

While today's NBA ref has much less chance to be as colorful and "mouthy" as their earlier counterparts like Strom and Mendy Rudolph, the point is well taken. A good ref has to be strong and confident, assured and knowledgeable.

Like many NBA refs, Strom started out refereeing high school games. After a few years there, establishing his skill and style, he began to ref high school playoff games. And once he proved himself there, he was offered a chance to referee college games.

Tip-In

Mendy Rudolph was an old-style ref whose charisma and personality made him a crowd favorite. He was the first NBA referee in history of officiate 2,000 games.

After doing that for a while, Strom simply picked up a pen one day in the late 1950s and wrote to the then-supervisor of NBA officials, Jocko Collins, asking Collins how one would become a ref in the NBA (rest assured, the process is a bit more complicated today). He got a letter back from Collins that said, in part:

Dear Earl:

Please fill out the enclosed data sheet and return.

Also, as a tip, I would suggest that you be more EMPHATIC with your VOICE (make it strong and loud) and give BETTER and more DECISIVE SIGNALS. (Study the book signals.) You run good and your judgment looked good, but you must strive for ABSOLUTE CONTROL of players and coaches. This is a very important requisite for NBA officials. Awaiting your reply.

Sincerely,

Jocko

Jocko's analysis and suggestions make a lot of sense for any wanna-be NBA ref. Refereeing an NBA game does indeed take good judgment. You can't call every foul, and yet you have to earn the respect of the players and coaches. The athletes are obviously bigger and stronger, the coaches are more glamorous and richer, but it's the referee who must own the court.

Technical Foul

In days gone by, refs used to be part of the NBA show. They considered themselves entertainers, too, and their personality often had much to do with how they officiated a game.

Maybe the biggest showman of the all was Matthew "Pat" Kennedy. Animated and affable, Kennedy began officiating in 1928 at age 20, and worked nearly 4,000 games during his career. He retired in 1946 and then served as the NBA's supervisor of referees until 1950. After that? Kennedy officiated Harlem Globetrotter games.

As the legendary ref Mendy Rudolph once told Strom, "These guys will take all the rope you give them. You might as well cut it short." The idea is not so much that the players and coaches don't get any slack—they most certainly do—but rather that the ref has to let them know who is boss.

Rudolph shared the following words of wisdom with Strom:

"Draw your parameters early. Let them know you are only going to take so much and no more. These guys are going to really test you here, but just ignore the little stuff and nail them if they go to far."

What's too far? That's the $64,000 question. Refereeing is an art as much as it is a science, as Strom's first night refereeing in the old Boston Garden illustrates. Before the

Hoopology

In basketball, a player going to the hoop can legally take one and a half steps after he stops dribbling. If he takes more than that, it is called **traveling**.

Inside Stuff

Earl Strom was inducted into the Basketball Hall of Fame in 1995. He officiated in the pros for 32 years (29 NBA, 3 ABA) and called 295 playoff games, including 29 games in the Finals, as well as seven All-Star Games.

game, Strom met with the captains, and Bob Cousy held that position for the Celtics back then. Cousy found out that Strom was from Pottstown, Pennsylvania, and said "Well, Earl, how's everything in Pottstown? Good to have you in the league. Good luck!" Mendy Rudolph warned Strom that Cousy was playing with him.

The game was a Boston blowout. Late in the fourth quarter, Cousy came down on a fast break and whipped the ball around and behind his back, not once but *twice*, and passed to Russell, who jammed it home. Strom whistled Cousy for walking with the ball.

Cousy was outraged, ran up to Strom, and said, "You know, Earl, in the Pottstown YMCA that might be walking, but in Boston Garden, when I do that, it isn't walking." Strom told the Cooz that walking is walking, whether it's in Pottstown or Boston. Cousy cursed the new ref, and Strom hit him with a technical.

Earl Strom is a Hall of Famer.

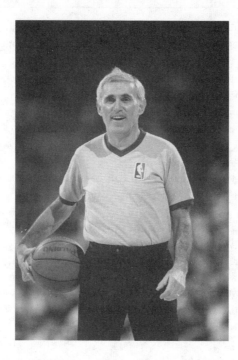

The crowd went wild, and Strom told Cousy to get away before he was tossed from the game. Cousy replied, "You don't have the guts." Strom did—he gave him another technical, and tossed Cousy out of the game. Strom believes that he earned Cousy's respect that night.

So that is the balancing act a ref must perform. Do the right thing, control the players, earn their respect, but don't go overboard with the whistle.

NBA Referee Danny Crawford discusses on-court action with Sacramento Kings head coach Rick Adelman.

The Road to Becoming a Referee

Today, refs who want to make it to the NBA have a far more arduous road than the one Earl Strom took. The path takes longer, and the goal is harder to reach.

In the 2001–02 season, for example, there were only 61 NBA referees. Making the cut as a ref isn't much different than making it as a player: Only the best of the best need apply.

According to Ed T. Rush, the NBA director of officiating, the league only hires two to three new refs each year, and the process of making it through the interviews and tryouts takes years. "It's a four- to six-year process for any one candidate," says Rush.

The ability to clearly communicate is another important attribute.

Take Gary Zielinski, for instance. Zielinski was a rookie official in the NBA during the 2001–02 season. How did he get there? After starting out in the amateur ranks, he refereed for seven seasons in the CBA and four in the summer for the WNBA, before finally making it to the show.

<table>
<tr><td colspan="1">**Inside Stuff**</td></tr>
</table>

In 2002, the NBA conducted four different summer pro leagues:

- The Southern California Summer Pro League (Long Beach)
- Shaw's Pro Summer League (Boston)
- The Rocky Mountain Revue (Salt Lake City)
- The Orlando Summer Professional League (Orlando)

Along the way, there are countless clinics and training sessions new refs must attend. Refs who make it to the NBA have to be ready for the pressure, the far more physical play, the egos, and the superior athletes they will encounter when they get there.

One place they hone these skills is at the Rocky Mountain Revue and other similar summer leagues that NBA players participate in during the off-season. The Rocky Mountain Revue is a summer league that provides various teams a chance to watch some draft picks and young players in action for a week in Salt Lake City.

Not only do the teams use the summer leagues to scout out new talent, but so does the NBA. Fifty officials got to strut their stuff for the NBA during the summer leagues. The refs are culled from the WNBA, the college ranks, and the new NBA Developmental League (the NBDL).

The referee brass watch the new refs to see which ones might make the best candidates for promotion. In addition, they conduct classes for the new refs every day, teaching them all they can about the nuances of refereeing big-time basketball. The things they cover include …

- Relationships with coaches.

- Handling players.

- Conflict resolution.

- Being challenged.

- Body language.

- Rules interpretation.

- Language.

The point isn't just to evaluate officiating talent, but to teach it, too. Games are videotaped, and the work of the refs dissected. Everything each ref does, both right and wrong, is subject to comment and review. Essentially, it's basketball boot camp for referees!

If it sounds like a lot of pressure, it is. Says Director of Officials Rush, "Frankly, there should be pressure. If you get to this level, there's going to be a lot of pressure every night, and we want to see how [they] will respond to it."

Inside Stuff

"I really like to talk to the refs. I have trouble remembering their names, keeping them all straight, but they're fun to talk to. In a line going back to Mendy Rudolph, Darrell Garretson, Earl Strom, up through Jake O'Donnell, now with the likes of Joey Crawford, Dick Bavetta, … Steve Javie, the whole lot.

They do talk back to me, you know. I may yell, 'How can you call that?' They might say, 'Don't ask if you don't know.' I'm ready for one of them to say, 'If you don't know, you better ax somebody.'"

—Spike Lee, renowned movie director and avid Knicks fan, in his book, *Best Seat in the House*

Referee Summer Camp

George Toliver has been an NBA referee since 1998. In 2002, he spoke with Hoopsref. com and explained how he went from bystander to NBA referee. It is both an instructive and fascinating tale, showing how a ref today breaks in and learns his craft.

According to Toliver, his first game ever was "in the industrial league and I was the only referee. You had the loading dock versus the accountants and all the emotions going on. So I had to learn about game management and the human emotions right away."

Toliver went from there to refereeing high school games, and soon attended his first summer camp for referees in 1982. He says that the camp was "a very interesting experience. They had a lot of good veteran referees and a lot of the ACC [Atlantic Coast Conference] staff and they were very helpful in teaching the game and giving guidance. There were 82 of us at the camp and my goal going in was just to learn and get better. I was picked up by the ACC from that camp in 1982."

Toliver spent six years refereeing ACC games, and then was picked up by the NBA in 1988. One thing that amazed Toliver most was the difference between the college and pro game:

> "It is like night and day. I thought that working in the ACC was the highest level you could work. The NBA is leaps and bounds above that level in terms of speed, quickness, aggressive players and the overall environment. I was amazed at how different the game was at the pro level. I focused on rules and the mechanics. I didn't realize that a greater skill needed was game management. Being able to step in and earn the respect and take charge of the game."

Tip-In

The life of an NBA ref isn't much different than the life of an NBA player, save for the fact that the player is paid a bit better. Consider George Toliver's average game day:

"I get up and go work out first. I like to do it early in the morning. Then I will have a light breakfast. I will then start to prepare for the morning meeting. We [he and the other refs working that night] will meet around 11:00 A.M. and then we go have lunch. After lunch, I will usually work on something in the afternoon and then I will take a nap. Usually a nap for me is 45 minutes to an hour at the max. After that, I get up, shower and meet the guys to go to the arena."

Leroy Richardson is a seven-year veteran NBA referee, and his experience mirrors that of Toliver. Richardson began officiating games while he was in the Navy, and then attended one of these now all-important summer camps—ironically, George Toliver's camp.

The camp gave him the chance to ref college games, where he learned more and proved himself to be a top-notch referee. By 1995, the year the NBA had a shortened season due to an owner lockout, Richardson was hired to referee NBA games on a part-time basis.

Richardson has since become a full-time ref and loves his job. The best part of being an NBA official, he says, is "to be able to be on the floor in a contest with the best athletes in the world. It is the best feeling out there."

They Still Wear Stripes, but ...

Since the days of Earl Strom and Mendy Rudolph, the NBA has made some significant changes to the way its games are refereed.

Adding a Third Referee

From the inception of the league in 1946 until the late 1980s, the NBA always had two refs calling the game. But as players got bigger, stronger, and faster, the NBA Board of Governors realized that two refs were having a hard time controlling the game and seeing everything that was happening on the court.

As such, in the 1988–89 season, the Board of Governors voted to add a third official to the crew. According to Rush, "With the type of athlete you have today, the strength, size, and speed, you just have to have that extra pair of eyes."

> **Inside Stuff**
>
> The NBA reviews officials daily. At the end of each season, the league rates each official. Using a numerical ranking system, the refs are evaluated by a committee that includes the NBA's head of operations and the supervisor of officials. They also get input from coaches and general managers.

Adding new refs also meant that those refs had to be trained properly, and so the NBA has continuously strived to improve its development and training of its officials (despite what some fans might think.)

NBA referees, new and old alike, are constantly evaluated and graded. Their games are taped for review, and they are required to watch those tapes and have their performance evaluated.

Breaking the Glass Ceiling

Although the NBA is a sport played by men, the league was progressive enough to become the first professional sports league to hire women referees.

In 1997–98, the NBA hired its first two women referees, one of whom is Violet Palmer. Although some players were skeptical, the two women were certainly well qualified. Palmer had been an official in the WNBA, and had also refereed college women's games.

Yet not all players gave the new refs a warm welcome. Charles Barkley was quoted at the time as saying, "I hope they don't bring 'em. That's my opinion. I don't have to give you a reason why. I treat all officials the same—like dogs. It's the principle of the thing. I wouldn't want a man doing a WNBA game."

But most players and coaches were supportive of the move. Indiana Pacers President Donnie Walsh said, "I don't see any difference in the female and male referees."

Instant Replay

The NBA decided after the 2001-02 season to add instant replay to the arsenal of referee tools. Here are some instances that helped prompt such a decision.

- In an April playoff game between the Hornets and the Magic, Baron Davis made an improbable shot that should have won the game. The shot was called off, saying it was released too late.

- In the series between the Nets and Pacers, a shot by Reggie Miller sent a game into overtime, even though the videotape showed that the clock had already reached 0:00.

- Most glaringly, in the hard-fought Western Conference Finals between the Lakers and Kings, a desperation three-pointer by the Lakers' Samaki Walker at the end of the first half counted, even though the shot came after the buzzer, providing the margin of victory for the Lakers at the end of the game.

Because of these instances, the NBA decided to allow referees to review an instant replay of any shot that goes in as the clock expires in any quarter, as well as using it to determine if a player had his foot on the three-point or out-of-bounds line, again only on shots at the end of periods.

Tip-In

"I think there's an overwhelming consensus, perhaps even unanimous ... that we should institute next season an instant replay for last-second shots," NBA Deputy Commissioner Russ Granik said after the playoffs were over. "I think we've finally come to the conclusion that you're not really asking a referee to make that call, good or bad. You're just asking him to guess and hope that he guesses right. So if instant replay can help in that, then we ought to be using it."

According to Stu Jackson, the NBA vice president of operations, "There have been a number of incidents where, quite frankly for any human being, it would have been nearly impossible to determine if the shot got off in time. We felt it was time to take advantage of the available technology."

The Unwritten Rules

While games are called according to the official rulebook, to deny that there is an "unofficial" rulebook would be naive. The question is, does that other rulebook interfere with the game?

Changes in the Game

If you think NBA games are called differently today than in years past, you're right. The game today is far more physical, and today's players are stronger, especially down in the block. They seem to get away with more. Ironically, and by the same token, it also seems as if there are more whistles now than ever before, slowing down the beautiful game.

No less an expert than Stu Jackson seems to agree. "The flow of the game needs to be better," Jackson told *The Sporting News*. "It's a very artistic game with gracefulness and athleticism," he said. "It has to have a flow to it that isn't always there today."

Certainly scoring is down from the days when 120–118 was your typical nail-biter. Why is that? NBA observers have a number of different theories. Yes, defensive schemes have gotten better, and the third referee also means that there are more whistles being blown, but that alone can't account for the significant change in game styles and scoring levels.

Tip-In

The average score for the 1965 NBA Finals between the Celtics and the Lakers was 123–110. In the 2001–02 Finals between the Lakers and the Nets, average score was 106–97.

The NBA has endeavored to respond to this situation by tinkering with the rules—getting rid of the illegal defense rule, for example—with a modicum of success.

Although games with triple-digit scoring are few and far between now, don't be surprised if they actually make a comeback. Like much of the rest of life, the NBA runs in cycles. Big men once dominated the league, and then big guards did. Offense was once supreme, lately defense is. It will likely come around again.

The Star Treatment

Another sore subject is the alleged special treatment that the superstars seem to get from the refs. A whistle blown on a regular player might never get blown on, say, Shaq. Why is that?

The reason is twofold, and neither is nefarious.

Tip-In

"Most [fans] think that we cheat for the home team, that we cheat for the superstar," referee Joey Crawford has said. "That's all bull. It has always been bull. Many aren't going to believe it. They think we cheat anyway."

Tip-In

"A Dr. J or Jordan taking off from the free-throw line and slamming the ball might take an extra hop before going airborne, but he's done enough spectacular things to cause people to give him the benefit of the doubt."

—Earl Strom

According to Earl Strom, stars do get favored treatment to "some slight extent." But, he continues, "the edge goes to superior talent. It is imperative that the referee make sure that the super talent isn't taken out of the game by desperate defense."

In Strom's opinion, so-called coddling of superstars by the refs isn't a "matter of protecting the privileged few as it is ensuring that the guys with the great skills, the guys with all the flair and finesse and touch, can play their game."

So superstars get super calls in part because they can naturally do things that less gifted players cannot, and the keen-eyed refs can see the difference.

Another reason for seemingly unfair calls is that the NBA is entertainment—it's a league built on superstars. Strom tells of the time when a player for the Hawks undercut MJ as he was going for a dunk. Strom called a flagrant foul on the guy. A fan from the stands yelled out, "Ah, you're just protecting the superstars." Strom replied, "Damn right I am. You eliminate these guys from the game and we're all out of work." Dominique Wilkins took his teammate aside and said, "Amen."

To think that the players who are the very, very best don't sometimes get the benefit of the doubt would be unrealistic. As Stu Jackson told the *Orlando Sentinel*, "the product must be one that does not turn off the public."

The Least You Need to Know

◆ Earl Strom was one of the best referees ever, but started out in a much different era.

◆ Refs today have to work their way up from the bottom.

◆ When they get to the NBA, refs are constantly evaluated.

◆ Yes, there are unwritten rules, but they make sense.

Chapter 18

The Best Teams of All Time

In This Chapter

- ◆ Judging the best team ever
- ◆ The Celtics have two different teams on the list
- ◆ The Lakers have two, too
- ◆ Some one-hit wonders

You've already read about the great franchises in NBA history. And I've regaled you with stories of legendary players from yesterday and today. But what about the best team ever? The greatest group of players ever to set foot on a basketball court in a single season or string of seasons? Is it Wilt Chamberlain and the 1967 Philadelphia 76ers, who won a then-record 68 regular-season games and the NBA title? Or how about Michael and the Chicago Bulls, circa 1996, a team that won a record 72 regular-season games? Perhaps it is Shaq, Kobe, and the L.A. Lakers of 2002? Although it's hard to say, that won't stop us from trying.

The Usual Suspects

This challenge—deciding which team was the best ever—is rhetorical, as no consensus has ever emerged. The good news is that by and large, what teams should be considered the best ever has been narrowed down to a select few. Here are the most likely candidates deserving of the mantle "Greatest Team of All Time," in chronological order:

1. **The 1964–65 Boston Celtics:** This is best of the Celtic teams that won a record eight championships in a row (and 11 in 13 seasons!).

2. **The 1966–67 Philadelphia 76ers:** This team, built around Wilt, stopped the Celtics' run and is often considered the best ever.

3. **The 1969–70 New York Knicks:** Any team that fields a starting lineup of Willis Reed, Dave DeBusschere, Bill Bradley, Dick Barnett, Walt Frazier, and Cazzie Russell is one of the greatest.

4. **The 1971–72 Los Angeles Lakers:** Another team built around Wilt, but this time with an aging Jerry West, this team won a record (at the time) 69 games and 33 in a row. Pretty good credentials, at that.

5. **The 1982–83 Sixers:** This team, starring Moses Malone and Dr. J, lost only one time in the playoffs, going 12–1.

6. **The 1985–86 Celtics:** This team was so deep that future Hall of Famer Bill Walton was coming off the bench and won the NBA's Six Man of the Year Award.

7. **The 1986–87 Lakers:** Magic, Kareem, and Co. had many good years, and so it's hard to pick out just one team, but this rendition was a well-oiled, fast-breaking basketball machine.

8. **The 1988–89 Detroit Pistons:** Isiah Thomas, Joe Dumars, Bill Laimbeer and Co. won back-to-back titles.

9. **The 1991–92 Chicago Bulls**: When Michael Jordan, Scottie Pippen, and Phil Jackson started clicking, theirs was a team for the ages.

Tip-In

The only teams to have won five or more championships are the Minneapolis Lakers of the '50s, the Boston Celtics of the '60s, the Los Angeles Lakers of the '80s, and the Chicago Bulls of the '90s.

10. **The 1995–96 Bulls:** This was Michael's first full year back after his first retirement, and he, Scottie, and Phil went on to win a record 72 games in the regular season.

11. **The 2000–01 Lakers:** Shaq, Kobe, and Phil steamrolled through the playoffs, losing only one game in the process (15–1).

Conspicuous by their absence on this list are the old Minneapolis Laker teams. While there were undoubtedly great, they were not voted as one of the ten best teams of all time during the NBA at 50 anniverary season.

So, which is the best? Let's find out.

Determining the Best Ever

When deciding which of the teams deserves the title "Greatest Team of All Time," various factors come into play, including the following:

◆ How many championships did they win?

◆ How much better were they than other teams of the era?

◆ How would they compare to teams of other eras?

◆ What special accomplishments did the team achieve, and how do they compare to those of other teams on the list?

◆ How good were the players individually, and collectively?

1964–65 Boston Celtics

If pure domination and the number of championships are the standard by which the greatest team is to be measured, the Celtics of the early '60s were the best team ever, and the 1964–65 version was the best of the best.

Boston won its first NBA title in 1957, and then won 10 more over the course of the next 12 years. While the makeup of these teams necessarily changed over the course of time, the one thing they had in common was Bill Russell. Not even Coach Auerbach was there for every one of these championships.

Along the way, these Celtics fielded some great teams, and it is difficult to say which of these was the greatest. The 1962–63 team, for instance, boasted eight future Hall of Famers. But if forced to, it might be the 1964–65 version. This team had Russell, the greatest defensive player ever, anchoring the middle, and Sam Jones, John Havlicek, Tom Sanders, and Tom Heinsohn. They broke their

Tip-In

"You need a dominant big man to get to the [NBA] Finals. Chicago did it [without one]. But they were an aberration."

—Phil Jackson

own league record for most victories in a season. This team was in the middle of not repeating, not three-peating, but *eight-peating!*

The only team that has come close to this feat was the Chicago Bulls, and of those teams, the 1995–96 team is on this list. So how would these Celtics do against those Bulls?

Both teams were great on defense, but with no center to match Russell, the Bulls begin the game at a significant disadvantage, both on the offensive and defensive end (Russell could score 20 points a night without a hitch). Jordan might be able to drive to the basket, but when he gets there, what does he see? Bill Russell, who could have had his way with Bull's center Luc Longley, no matter how hard the Bulls practiced.

Although they had one of the best players ever, the rest of those Celtic teams had very good players, but no superstars. Yet as a team, they won, and kept on winning—11 titles in 13 seasons. It is hard to argue with those 11 championships.

> **Inside Stuff**
>
> "I decided early in my career the only really important thing is to win the games. I wanted my career to be such that people would say, "He won championships," and that's a historical fact, that's not anyone's opinion."
>
> —Bill Russell

1966–67 76ers

The 76ers of the '60s had such a hard time beating the impenetrable Celtics that they finally decided to build a team specifically to defeat the greatest dynasty of all time. The 1967 team was the result.

The team was "centered" around Wilt Chamberlain, who was in the midst of the greatest scoring run the league would ever see. From 1962, when he averaged a never-to-be-repeated 50.4 points per game, and on through the '60s, Wilt was asked to score, and score he did.

In the 1966–67 season, new Philadelphia coach Alex Hannum asked him to score less and to be more of a team player. He did, and the results were impressive. That he had a lot of other impressive players around didn't hurt the matter, either, as the points per game stats reveal:

- Chet Walker averaged almost 20 ppg that season
- Billy Cunningham averaged 18.5 ppg
- Guard Hal Greer averaged more than 22 ppg
- Wilt averaged 24.1 ppg

But what was even more important than their individual play was how they played together, and together they were simply astonishing. They won 45 of their first 49 games en route to a regular-season record of 68–13.

The Sixers accomplished their mission when they beat the Celtics 4–1 in the Eastern Conference Finals, and then whipped the Warriors 4–2 for the championship, Wilt's first.

The team that finally beat the Celtics: Front row (L-R): Wilt Chamberlain, Dave Gambee, Lucious Jackson, Billy Cunningham, Chet Walker. Back row: Trainer Al Domenico, Head Coach Alex Hannum, Wali Jones, Billy Melchionni, Matt Guokas, Hal Greer, Larry Costello, Owner Irv Kosloff, G.M. Jack Ramsay

When comparing them to any of the great teams that came later, it is hard to say how they would do. Wilt could match Jordan point for point, but his supporting cast was better than MJ's ever was. Against the Celtics of the '80s, Wilt would be matched against Robert Parish, while Bird and McHale would do damage in the middle.

Against the Lakers of the '80s, however, it's hard to see Wilt's team winning. Kareem could always score off of Wilt, the Sixers would have no answer for Magic, and Worthy was as good as any forward who ever played.

1969–70 Knicks

One of the best passing teams ever, the 1969–70 Knicks featured Willis Reed, Walt Frazier, Dick Barnett, Dave DeBusschere, Bill Bradley, and Cazzie Russell. They won 60 games and the championship that year, and won it again three years later with essentially the same cast.

The epitome of teamwork, these Knicks passed, played, and defended with precision. When looking at the all-time best team, however, it is hard to see how these guys would match up well against some other teams on this list.

Reed was only about 6' 10", and he would be badly outmatched by either Kareem or Shaq. The rest of the Knicks crew was special, but they are not in the same league as Bird and McHale, Magic and Worthy, or Michael and Scottie.

Inside Stuff

Knicks highlights, 1969–70:

- ◆ **Willis Reed:** Regular-season NBA Most Valuable Player, All-Star Game MVP, and NBA Finals MVP
- ◆ **Reed, Frazier, and DeBusschere:** NBA All-Stars
- ◆ **Reed and Frazier:** All-NBA First Team
- ◆ **Red Holzman:** NBA Coach of the Year

1971–72 Lakers

Here we have another team built around Wilt, one that is actually quite similar to his great Sixer squad. Like that team, this Laker team was built to win a championship; like that one, Wilt was asked to score less but do more; and like that one, a great guard scored a lot of points (here, Jerry West, there, Hal Greer.) And like that Sixer team, this Laker team was a great *team*; the whole was greater than the sum of its parts.

 Tip-In

Before Game 5 of the finals, Jerry West told friends that that he had suffered from insomnia after the second game (a Lakers victory.) Why? He was trying to figure out how he would act when he finally won a championship (this being his seventh trip to the NBA Finals without ever having won).

The 1972 Lakers started slow, but became one of the most dominant single-season teams ever. Roughly 10 games into the season, when Elgin Baylor retired, the Lakers went on that remarkable 33-game winning streak, something that alone qualifies them as the one of the best ever.

The team also posted the best-ever record in NBA history up until that time, going 69–13. Their run through the playoffs was equally impressive, beating the Knicks in the NBA Finals, 4–1.

Although both West and Chamberlain were at the twilight of their careers, this team was special. On paper, they probably would have been a pretty even match for their Laker brothers of the '80s, although stopping Magic would have been almost impossible for anyone in any era.

Against the Bulls, these Lakers might have had more luck. The Bulls' center was Luc Longley; Wilt would have had his way with him. In the backcourt, West and Goodrich would have matched up well against Jordan and Ron Harper. Hairston and McMillian would have given Rodman fits.

1982–83 Sixers

Like many teams on this list, the '83 Sixers boasted two of the greatest players ever at their respective positions. With Moses Malone in the middle (an MVP season for him) and Julius Erving on the wing, the team was dominant. Adding in Maurice Cheeks, Andrew Toney, and Bobby Jones made it a fantastic starting five. This team can certainly lay claim to the title of best ever.

Moses Malone took the 1983 Sixers over the top.

The team also had an impressive record, both during the season and in the playoffs. Going 65–17 in the regular season, the Sixers had every reason to think that this was their year, and it was. Said Bobby Jones, "Everybody had a sense that this was our opportunity."

Malone probably put it best when asked how the team would do in the playoffs. He replied, "Fo, fo, fo"—they would sweep each series. And he was just about right, too. The Sixers swept the Knicks, lost one game to Milwaukee, and then swept the Lakers.

For the city of Philadelphia, this was an especially sweet championship, given that it had waited so long. And for Julius Erving, it was even sweeter: His first and only NBA Championship after losing in three previous tries.

1985–86 Celtics

With the best frontcourt ever in Bird, McHale, and Parish, and Walton and Scott Wedman coming off the bench, the 1985–86 Celtics team had incredible depth and a great passing game. They caused matchup problems with whomever they went up against.

Larry Bird was at the peak of his remarkable career. Winning the MVP trophy for the third time in a row, he was fourth in the league in scoring (25.8 ppg), fourth in three-point field-goal percentage (.423), and first in free-throw percentage (.896).

Inside Stuff

"I remember sitting in the stands at Madison Square Garden one night when the Celtics were in town. The New York fans were riding Bird unmercifully, calling him a hick and chanting "overrated" repeatedly during warm-ups. Bird never changed expression, never let on that he heard a word. Then he went out and put on a clinic. He seemed to make every jumper on offense, anticipate every pass on defense.

Late in the game, he cut down the lane, took a pass from a teammate and in the same motion flicked a no-look pass over his right shoulder to Kevin McHale for a dunk. It was such a beautiful play that there was an audible gasp from the crowd, and then a burst of applause. Bird had won the tough New York fans over, and they simply had to give him his due."

—Phil Taylor in *Sports Illustrated*

But statistics don't say what Bird did best. He was a clutch player, a gifted passer, and a tough defender. He made his teammates, as they say, better. The team went 67–15, winning an amazing 40 out of 41 games at home. This very deep team beat the Rockets in six games to win the championship.

It helps their standing that the Bird-led Celtics won three titles. It also helps that they had a great bench, something those Chicago teams never really had. We know how these Celtics would do against the Lakers of the '80s—in the three NBA Finals they played against each other, the Lakers won two and Boston one.

Against the older Boston teams, the matchup would likely end in a draw. Both teams were deep and well rounded. Great players were teamed up with great role players. This Celtic team was as good as any previous one, if not better; and that is saying a lot.

1986–87 Lakers

These Lakers boasted two legendary players in Magic and Kareem, and James Worthy would have been the franchise player on any other team. The supporting cast was no less impressive: Byron Scott and Kurt Rambis knew their roles, and Michael Cooper and Mychal Thompson did great things coming off the bench.

The core players won five championships in nine years, and played together for 10 years. They met challenge after challenge, even beating their nemesis, the Boston Celtics, in Boston, in 1985.

Magic: The essence of Showtime.

The 1987 team won the championship again, and is considered best version of this era of the Lakers. Proof came again the next year when, for the first time in a generation, they won it again for back-to-back titles. Consisting of the same core group, that team was also as focused, as possessed, as any team ever. They were on a mission. As Riley explained to each player on that team before the season began:

> "[This] year is not about winning another championship or having one more ring, or developing bigger reputations. It's about leaving footprints.

> After four championships in eight years, we have arrived at a point in this team's history where there is just one thing left for us to accomplish. That is to become a team for the ages and eras, the greatest basketball team ever.

> We do not merely want to be considered the best of the best. It is time to separate ourselves from the pack .... The future is now, fellas."

The team played up to Riley's expectations, but, as Magic says, "it was the hardest championship of all." Yet even so, even he thinks "we already knew that we were the best team in the league. And looking back now, I think we were probably the best Laker team ever." That's a pretty lofty place to be.

Tip-In

New Jersey Nets coach Byron Scott played starting 2 guard on that Lakers team and says, when comparing that Lakers team to the one with Shaq and Kobe, "We had a lot more weapons, our teams in the '80s. This [Laker] team is great. They're a great team, but I tell everybody that if we had played them in a seven-game series, we would have beaten them four out of five, four out of six."

1988–89 Detroit Pistons

The Detroit Pistons had been knocking on the championship door for some time, but it had never been answered, at least not until the 1988–89 season. That team started the season strong, but even so, three days after the All-Star break, they traded high-scoring Adrian Dantley for high-scoring Mark Aguirre. And it worked. The team won a league best 63 games.

Indicative of what a good *team* they were, no Piston finished in the top 20 in scoring. Point guard Isiah Thomas was ninth-best in assists, and center Bill Laimbeer was ninth-best in rebounds. Dennis Rodman, it must be noted, was a rebounding monster. As a team, they meshed well and played great.

Meeting the defending champion Lakers in the Finals, the Pistons nevertheless proved their mettle, sweeping the Lakers 4–0.

1991–92 Chicago Bulls

In 1990–91, Michael Jordan and the Chicago Bulls won the first of what would turn out to be six championships in eight years. Although these Bulls teams changed around the fringes, the core of Michael, Scottie Pippen, and coach Phil Jackson were the nucleus that made it all happen. In fact, these Bulls teams were so good that two versions of it makes it to the all-time best list.

The first is the 1991–92 team. Although they had won the championship the year before, NBA observers were not sure if these Bulls were for real. They were not yet, as *Saturday Night Live* once put it, *Da Bulls!*

But in 1991, they had made it back to the NBA Finals, against the Portland Trail Blazers. Up three games to two, the Bulls nevertheless found themselves down by 15 points at the start of the fourth quarter and a deciding Game 7 seemed imminent. But Pippen and bench players Stacey King, Bobby Hansen, B. J. Armstrong, and Scott Williams started the quarter and went on a 14–2 run. Jordan then entered the game, and he and Pippen scored the Bulls next 19 points, cementing the win and back-to-back championships. Yes, they most certainly were for real.

Scottie Pippen was an essential element of the Bulls success.

1995–96 Bulls

The 1995–96 Bulls were on a mission to prove they were the best ever. The team had some new faces in the likes of Steve Kerr and Dennis Rodman, but they gelled quickly and lost rarely. Their record in November was 12–2, and in December, they went 13–1. In January, they were perfect: 14–0. No team had ever won 70 games before, but this Bulls team looked like they could do it.

No less an authority than Jerry West stated that the Bulls looked like they could surpass the Lakers' mark of 69–13 set in 1971–72. When Jordan was asked to compare this team to other great teams in NBA history, he said "I look at the Celtics back in '86 .... Those guys were tough to deal with. Those guys played together for a long time. We're starting to learn how to play together."

When asked about the Bulls' lack of a truly dominating center, and how most great teams had that, he replied, "I think Pippen compensates for that. I don't think any of those teams, other than maybe the '86 Boston Celtics, had a small forward that was as versatile on offense and defense as Scottie Pippen is."

In the end, the team won 72 games and lost only 10, a record that is likely to stand for some time. They romped through the playoffs, too, losing only three times.

Tip-In

Among the Bulls' accomplishments that season:

♦ The Bulls' .878 winning percentage is the best in NBA history, eclipsing the marks set by the 1971–72 Los Angeles Lakers, who had an .841 percentage.

♦ The Bulls finished 39–2 at home and 33–8 on the road, their 33 road victories are the most ever.

Are they the best team ever? Michael Jordan thinks so. "What other team has won 72 games?" he asks. Good point.

2000–01 Lakers

In 1999–2000, the Lakers with Shaquille O'Neal and Kobe Bryant won the NBA title. The next season seemed like an ordinary one. The team was bickering, Phil Jackson was publicly chastising his players. Nothing out of the ordinary, really.

And then, just before the season ended, the team seemed to flip a switch. Unbeatable for the last month of the season, they barreled through the playoffs, sweeping the Western Conference, unstoppable. They met the Sixers in the NBA Finals, lost but once, and desired then to lay claim to the "Best Ever" title. Statistically speaking, they make a strong case. The team's 15–1 mark is the best in NBA Playoff history.

These Lakers won it all again the next year, further bolstering their case. Says starting point guard Derek Fisher, "We have a lot of respect for the history of this game. Every guy on this team respects guys who came before us. So we don't want to try to step over anyone. But obviously, winning three championships in a row puts us closer to the top of the list."

How would they fare against some other teams on this list? Maybe not so well. Yes, Shaq and Kobe are unique talents, but every team on this list has at least two such players, and some have three. And certainly, the bench of this team cannot compare to some of those Celtics benches, or even those of earlier Lakers teams.

Inside Stuff
"As far as all-time NBA teams, I'd take the mid-'80s Boston Celtics with Larry Bird, Kevin McHale, and Robert Parish over this year's Lakers [2001]. I'd also take the Lakers with Magic Johnson, Kareem Abdul-Jabbar, James Worthy, Byron Scott, and Michael Cooper and the 76ers with Dr. J and Moses Malone over these 2001 Lakers. Obviously, if these current Lakers grab a few more titles, I might have to reconsider. But right now, I don't see them beating these other teams."   —Dan Patrick, ESPN

Says Byron Scott, "As strong and physical as Shaq is, I try to imagine Kareem guarding this guy. I was shaking my head," acknowledging that Shaq would be able to score off of the skinnier-than-Shaq (isn't everyone?) Kareem. But, Scott also states, "The other thing I know is that [Kareem] would have scored on him, too."

Scott added, "They're right up there. I mean, they have two of the greatest players in the game today, and they have a great, great coach in Phil Jackson. [But] if you're trying to compare them to the teams we had in the '80s, I still think we had a better team."

So?

It's impossible to say with any certainty which of these teams is the best of all time. Perhaps Byron Scott put it best when he quipped, "It's just a test of time."

The Least You Need to Know

- ◆ Judging the best team ever is a difficult task.
- ◆ The Celtics of the '60s and '80s can both lay claim to the title.
- ◆ The Lakers of the '80s have a good argument, too.
- ◆ Don't forget about 1990s Bulls.
- ◆ There is simply no easy way to answer the "greatest ever" debate!

Chapter 19

Buzzer Beaters

In This Chapter

- Two-pointers that beat the buzzer
- Three-point magic
- Defensive gems

There are two kinds of players in the league: Those who don't want the ball at the end of a pressure-filled game, and those who do. And of the latter, there are also two kinds of players: Those who can hit the big shot, and those who can't. Jerry West, Michael Jordan, and Reggie Miller are the types who can. Many others, of course, cannot. Will the ball go in the basket? That's why we watch the game!

One of the things that makes sports in general, and basketball in particular, fun is that the outcomes of games can change at the very last second. This is even truer in the NBA after the advent of the three-point shot. You never know when some wild, crazy shot or event will change the outcome of a seemingly already determined game.

NBA history is filled with dramatic moments, some of which have been retold in this book already—Michael Jordan hitting "The Shot," John Havlicek stealing the ball—and there's no need to repeat them in this chapter. Here, then, are some other memorable buzzer beaters from the annals of the NBA.

Two-Pointers That Made the Difference

Every kid in his driveway who has ever pretended to play in the NBA has his or her share of hits and misses of buzzer-beating shots. The drill usually goes something like this: "Three seconds left, Jeff has the ball, two seconds left, he is being guarded by MJ, one second, Jeff lets fly a 20-footer—bzzzzzz—there's the buzzer … and its GOOD! It's good! Jeff wins the game!!"

The difference is these guys did it for real.

Mr. Clutch at His Best

Long before Michael Jordan became one of, if not *the*, greatest clutch players of his generation, there was another guard out of the East Coast who could make the basket when the pressure was on and his team needed him most. Jerry West, a.k.a. Mr. Clutch, earned his nickname for a reason.

Inside Stuff

In 1962, before he was Mr. Clutch, Jerry West faced the Boston Celtics in the NBA Finals for the first time. In Game 7 in Boston, the score was tied 100–100 with but a few seconds left and the ball and their fate in the L.A. Lakers' hands.

Point guard Hot Rod Hundley had the ball and saw 29-year-old, two-time NBA All-Star Frank Selvy wide open not far from the basket. Hundley whipped the ball to him, and Selvy tossed up an easy 8-footer. It bounced off the rim, the buzzer sounded, the game went into overtime, and the Celtics beat the Lakers in the NBA Finals for the first of many times.

Jerry West's skill at hitting the big-time, gutsy clutch shot was never more evident than in the 1970 NBA Championship series.

Now, you may recall that '70 series is remembered for Willis Reed's dramatic, out-of-the-locker-room gimp and shot, but the series has an equally, if not more, dramatic moment.

With the series tied 1–1, the Knicks had a 102–100 lead with three seconds to play in Game 3. The Lakers, out of timeouts, in-bounded the ball at the far end of the court to West. Mr. Clutch dribbled a few times and let fly a desperation 60-foot shot.

Swish. Nothing but net. The crowd roars, the game is tied, and we're going to over-time. Unfortunately for L.A., in the extra period, the Knicks came out fighting and eventually won the game 111–108, and eventually the series, 4–3.

Had West made that same shot today, it would have been a three-pointer and the Lakers would have won the game, and maybe the series.

Laker fans never forgot it. For years afterward, at the point on the floor where West hit the shot, there was a dab of paint, marking the moment.

Ralph Sampson Beats the Clock

Long before seven-footers Tim Duncan and David Robinson took to the floor together in San Antonio, the Houston Rockets originated the "twin towers" concept by teaming up another pair of gigantic frontcourt players: Ralph Sampson (7'4'') and Hakeem Olajuwon (7'0'').

Although Sampson towered above his opponents, his strength was not just in his size, but in his skill as well. Sampson played like a small forward—agile, lean, able to handle the ball and pass, and blessed with a sweet jumper.

Although Sampson's career was cut short by knee injuries, he did have a moment for the ages. In Game 5 of the 1986 Western Conference Finals, Sampson and the Rockets were playing the defending-champion, 62–20 Los Angeles Lakers in the Forum. The Rockets had a surprising 3–1 edge in the series.

The game was tied with one second left as the Rockets' Rodney McCray in-bounded a pass from near half court. Sampson, guarded by none other than Kareem Abdul-Jabbar, saw the ball coming his way.

One second is no time at all in a basketball game, and especially in that situation. Sampson would have to catch and shoot the ball in an instant if he was to beat the clock. And, as Sampson was facing away from the basket when the pass was made, he would also have to turn while shooting, almost a physical impossibility given the amount of time remaining.

Almost. As the pass came in, Sampson leapt, caught the ball, twisted in midair, and let rip a

 Tip-In

Ralph Sampson was the College Basketball Player of the Year while playing ball at Virginia and was the No. 1 pick in the 1983 draft. He retired after only playing eight seasons in the NBA due to knee injuries.

Today he lives in Georgia with his wife and four children. He runs a program called Winner's Circle that teaches basketball and academics to children.

 Tip-In

"It's probably the best experience I've ever had in my basketball career."

—Ralph Sampson, referring to his last-second shot

desperation 15-footer from the side of the key. In it goes, the crowd roars. Sampson won the game and the Rockets are headed to the Finals.

Heating Up

In 1990, Detroit's Vinnie "Microwave" Johnson hit one of the most dramatic game-winners in NBA history. The Pistons were playing the Portland Trail Blazers in the Finals, and Detroit was hoping to win back-to-back championships.

They had taken a 3–1 series lead, but Game 5 in Portland was proving to be very tough. The Blazers were up by seven with three minutes to go when the Pistons exploded and tied the game up with 20 seconds left.

Detroit had the ball, and Isiah Thomas was running down the clock, waiting for the last shot. With six seconds left, he made his move, heading toward the hoop. At the last second he saw teammate Vinnie Johnson mismatched against a slower player. Thomas passed Johnson the ball.

They don't call him Microwave for nothing—when he's hot, he's hot. Johnson drove, stopped short, pulled up for an awkward, quick-release J, and swished it going home. With 00:0.7 left on the clock, the Pistons were champions again.

In Houston, We Have a Problem

In 1999, the New York Knicks were an average team at best. Battling just to make the playoffs, New York won six of its final eight games to capture the eighth seed in the East. And whom would they meet in the first round of the playoffs? None other than their old nemesis, the top-ranked Miami Heat.

Recall their history: Miami coach Pat Riley used to coach the Knicks. Knicks coach Jeff Van Gundy used to be Riley's assistant. Van Gundy's brother *was* Riley's assistant. Miami had blown playoffs to New York. New York had blown playoffs to Miami. And brawls and suspensions had become almost commonplace between these two teams.

Tip-In

In the playoffs, every series but the opening round is a best-of-seven format. In the first round, it's best of five.

And here they were again—the eighth-seeded Knicks against the first-seeded Heat. The records went out the window. In a hard-fought series (natch), the teams were all tied up 2–2, with a deciding fifth game scheduled in Miami.

With 24.9 seconds to play, Miami was up 77–76, and the Knicks had the ball. They called timeout, ran a play that was broken up, the ball got loose, and Terry Porter of the Heat knocked it out of bounds with 4.5 seconds to play.

New York took the ball out, got it in to Allan Houston, and he put up a runner as time was running out. It hit the front of the rim, the backboard, and then fell through with 00:0.8 left on the clock.

For only the second time in NBA history, an eighth seed had knocked off a one seed in the first round. Needless to say, Houston called that "the biggest shot of my life."

Allan Houston was the hero of Game 5 of the 1999 first-round series versus Miami.

It seemed as if the Knicks would never be able to top that moment, but they did, and it was during that same playoff run, in the Eastern Conference Finals against the Indiana Pacers.

At the end of Game 3, with the series tied 1–1, Indiana was up by three with six seconds remaining. That was when New York's Larry Johnson let rip a three-pointer, hit it, and a foul was called against the Pacers' Antonio Davis. Johnson went to the line, nailed the free throw, and the Knicks won the game (and later the series) with an improbable, very rare, four-point play.

As Jeff Van Gundy said, "First time I have ever seen a four-point play decide a game. [It] was a miracle."

Kerr Cans the Jumper

The casual NBA fan primarily thinks of Jordan, Pippen, and head coach Phil Jackson when remembering the Chicago Bulls' six championships in the '90s, but the committed fan knows that two of those titles might never have happened had it not been for two unsung role players.

In 1993, John Paxson hit a big shot to help the Bulls get their first three-peat (discussed later in this chapter). In 1997, it was Steve Kerr's turn.

That year in the NBA Finals, the Bulls were up against a tough Utah Jazz team. John Stockton and Karl Malone had made it to the NBA Finals at last. With the Bulls up 3–2, Game 6 was pivotal, even potentially decisive. The score was tied 86 all with about 20 seconds to play when Chicago got the ball and called timeout. Everyone knew that the ball would be coming to Jordan and that he would take the shot; everyone, that is, except Jordan and Kerr. In the huddle, Jordan turned to Kerr and said, "I know Stockton is going to come over and help and I am going to come to you."

Hoopology

Those players who go from team to team, the ones that never seem to latch on anyplace for too long, are called **journeymen**.

It says much about Michael that he was so confident in his teammate, Kerr, a *journeyman* player. But Jordan by then had learned that one man does not a basketball team make, that teamwork is the key to ultimate success.

With five seconds left, Jordan the decoy was doing his job. Bryon Russell was guarding him and John Stockton came over to double team as the clock wound down. MJ faked a shot, faked a pass to Toni Kukoc, and then flipped the ball to Kerr, who was by then wide open.

Inside Stuff

At Chicago's victory parade a few days later, Steve Kerr took the microphone and said:

"A lot of people have been asking me about the shot the other night, and there have been some misperceptions about what actually happened and I want to clear it up.

When we went into the huddle, Phil told Michael, "Michael, I want you to take the last shot." And Michael told Phil, "You know Phil, I don't feel real comfortable in these situations, so maybe we ought to go in another direction." And Scottie said … "Why don't we go with Steve?" And I thought to myself, "Well, I guess I've got to bail Michael out again, but I've been carrying him all year anyway, so what's one more time?"

Anyway, the shot went in, that's my story, and I'm sticking to it!"

Kerr calmly swished it on home: Game, set, and match. Kerr later said, "[Michael] is so good that he draws so much attention. His excellence gave me the chance to hit the game-winning shot in the NBA Finals. What a thrill."

Three-Pointers at the Buzzer

Nothing beats a three-pointer at the buzzer for pure dramatic effect. It is what makes NBA basketball great.

Miller Time: 8 points in 8.9 seconds!

If there has been one player who embodies the crunch-time clutch ethic, it's Reggie Miller. In a league where everyone wants to be the hero, Miller doesn't mind being the villain. On the road, in hostile arenas, with crowds booing, that's when Miller shines brightest.

His deadly shot, which seems to get more accurate the farther away from the basket he gets, allows him to put the dagger in, in most dramatic fashion.

Like Michael Jordan, Reggie Miller has hit so many big, game-winning shots that it would be difficult to catalog them all. Most are from beyond the arc, but not all are. Either way, this one is probably his best:

Of all the places Reggie loved to play, of all the fans he loved to torment, it was in New York's Madison Square Garden where Miller did the most damage. And no moment was tougher on the Knicks fans than Reggie's explosion at the end of Game 1 of the 1995 Eastern Conference Finals.

Tip-In

The title of Reggie Miller's autobiography is *I Love Being the Enemy.*

With 18.7 seconds left, the Knicks had a comfortable six-point lead, 105–99. Indiana called time out, and Larry Brown urged his players to score quickly, foul, and get the ball back. But, as the coach later admitted, "Realistically, I thought we had no chance."

Point guard Mark Jackson inbounded the ball to Reggie, behind the arc, and Reggie let fly a perfect jumper. With 16.7 seconds left, the Knicks had the ball and a 105–102 lead.

Anthony Mason had a hard time getting the ball in play, before finally passing it toward teammate Greg Anthony. Miller stole the ball, stepped back behind the three-point line, and nailed a second trey. With 13.3 seconds left, the game was tied, 105 all. Unbelievable!

New York got the ball back, missed, and Reggie got the rebound. He was fouled with 7.5 seconds left to play. He calmly stepped to the line, ignoring the bedlam that had become Madison Square Garden, and sank both free throws. Pacers win.

Stockton Comes Through

The Utah Jazz were so good for so long that everyone expected that they would sooner or later win the title, or at least get to the big show. But as the years went on, it became obvious that it would be later, if at all.

In 1997, their moment was at hand. The Jazz were up against the Rockets in the Western Conference Finals, vying for the chance to take on the Bulls. It was Game 6, and the Jazz were up three games to two as the clocked ticked down and the scored was tied 100–100.

John Stockton has always been a big-game player, able to do what the team needed when they needed it most, whether it be making the pass, getting a rebound, or hitting the shot. This guy was clutch. Game 6 was no exception.

In the last few minutes of the last quarter, Stockton caught on fire. Houston had a double-digit lead when Stockton started raining down jumpers, scoring 13 points in the final three minutes of play to tie the game up.

Stockton hits the Game 6 winner!

With seconds to play, the Jazz had the ball when they found Stockton open behind the three-point line near the top of the key. Stockton got the ball and shot a picture-perfect jumper that hit nothing ... but net. The Jazz won the game 103–100 and finally made it to the finals, if not the championship.

Memorial Day Miracle

In Game 2 of the Western Conference Finals, Memorial Day 1999, a determined Blazers squad was up against a tough Spurs team in San Antonio. The Blazers were clinging to a two-point lead with about 10 seconds left.

Spurs guard Sean Elliott had already had a great game, making five of six three-pointers and having scored 19 points. With time winding down, the Spurs needed a miracle if they were to pull out the game. The Spurs called timeout and Elliott told his teammates, "I've got one more three in me."

Mario Elie inbounded the ball to Elliott, who was camped out on the far, far right side of the basket, behind the arc, almost out of bounds, in fact. Elliott caught the ball on his tiptoes ("If his heels had gone down it would not have counted," Spurs coach Gregg Popovich later admitted) and Elliott gathered himself, and shot the ball.

Portland's Rasheed Wallace was covering Elliott and leapt in the air to block the shot. The ball danced just above Wallace's outstretched arms, floated above the crowd, arced toward the basket, and went straight in the hole.

The 35,260 fans in attendance at the Alamodome went crazy, the Spurs won the game 86–85 and the series (in four straight), and finally the NBA Championship, beating the Knicks in five games—thanks to the Memorial Day Miracle that spurred them on.

Tip-In

Sean Elliott needed a kidney transplant after the NBA Finals, but finding a match is no easy feat; even harder than hitting the game-winner.

Luckily for Sean, his brother Noel turned out to be a perfect match, and on August 16, 1999, Noel gave one of his kidneys to Sean. Of his sacrifice, Noel Elliott said slyly, "I told Sean that I was going to have to have tickets to all the Spurs' games *and* a book deal!"

Paxson for the Three!

In 1993, the Bulls were on the unlikely quest to three-peat. No team had won the NBA Championship three years in a row since the Celtics had done it in the 1960s, so Chicago's pursuit seemed both difficult as well as improbable.

Yet championships in 1991 and 1992, and an amazing run in 1993, brought Michael and the Bulls to the cusp of their quest. But in the finals that year against the Phoenix Suns, the Bulls uncharacteristically lost Game 5 at home. Thus, although the Bulls still led the series 3–2, the Suns now held home-court advantage.

With about two minutes left in Game 6, the Suns were up by four, hoping to force a seventh and deciding game. Jordan stole the ball with a little more than a half a minute left and cut the lead to two. Phoenix failed to score on their possession, and the Bulls got the ball back with 14 seconds left to play.

The whole world—including the Suns—expected that MJ would take the final shot. Jordan inbounded the ball, and over the next 10 seconds, the whole team touched it at one time or another as the Bulls passed the ball around the horn, looking for the open man, and then finally found him.

John Paxson, a guard with a great eye, was open behind the arc on the left side of the key. Horace Grant hit the open man with the pass, Paxson caught the ball and shot it in one fluid motion, the ball sailed in the basket with 3.9 seconds left, and the Bulls won the game and the title.

Said Paxson after the game, "It was like a dream come true. You're a kid out in your driveway, shooting shots to win championships. When you get down to it, it's still just a shot in a basketball game. But I think a lot of people could relate to that experience."

Defensive Gems

While shots at the buzzer are the stuff of legend, great defensive plays can be just as remarkable. Havlicek did, after all, steal the ball.

A Block by Hakeem

It's the 1994 NBA Finals, Knicks versus Rockets. The Knicks are up three games to two and time is running out. New York knows too well that championship moments don't come along very often, and so that when they do, you have to capitalize.

The last thing the Knicks wanted was to let Houston back in the series. They wanted to close the game out, and so relied on the pony they had been riding the whole game: John Starks.

Chapter 19: Buzzer Beaters   **263**

Starks is one of those amazingly streaky shooters who could light up the scoreboard instantly when he got hot. In Game 6, Starks was red hot. He had scored 27 points by the time the game was almost over, 16 of them in the fourth quarter alone.

With six ticks left on the clock, the Knicks were down by two, 86–84. The plan was to get the ball to Starks behind the three-point line and let 'er rip. The way he was shooting, that one shot could have given the Knicks their first title since 1973.

Hakeem was a great defensive player.

The play was executed perfectly and Starks got a good look at a three-pointer. But just as he let it go, Hakeem Olajuwon, all 7 feet of him, came bounding over, leapt into the air, and blocked the shot. The Rockets won the game, and then the series, and thus the championship.

"There's a Steal by Bird!"

In 1987, the Larry Bird Celtics were running out of gas just as the Isiah Thomas Pistons were beginning to play at full throttle. Meeting in the Eastern Conference Finals, the two teams seemed evenly matched, with the series tied 2–2.

With five seconds left on the clock in Game 5, the Pistons had a tenuous 107–106 lead, but they also had possession of the ball. Isiah Thomas was taking the ball out on the side across the Celtics bench when Larry Bird saw Thomas eye Piston center Bill Laimbeer in the low post.

Thomas passed the ball in toward Laimbeer and Bird moved into the passing lane. Here's what happened next, according to Bird: "At the last instant, I reached in and just barely tipped it. I was trying get control of the ball while practically falling out of bounds ... when I saw a blur, a white jersey streaking down the lane. The blur was Dennis Johnson."

> **Tip-In**
>
> Dennis Johnson averaged 14.1 points, 5.0 assists, and 3.9 rebounds during his 14-year NBA career. He won three NBA Championships (Seattle in 1979—where he was the MVP of the Finals—and Boston in 1984 and 1986.) A defensive specialist, Johnson was also named All-Defensive First Team six times.

Here's how it looked to Celtic announcer Johnny Most: "And, now there's a steal by Bird! Underneath to D.J., who lays it in! We might have one second left. What a play by Bird! Bird stole the in bounding pass, laid it off to D.J., and D.J. laid it in and Boston has a one-point lead with one second left! Oh my, this place is going crazy!"

And that, folks, is how you become one of the 50 Greatest Players in NBA History.

The Least You Need to Know

- ◆ MJ, Jerry West, Ralph Sampson, and Steve Kerr have all hit memorable game-winning 2-point shots.

- ◆ Reggie Miller is the king of the 3-point dagger.

- ◆ Bird stole the ball.

Part 5

Inside Stuff

It's time for a close-up look at two of the premier showcases for NBA players—the NBA All-Star Game and the Basketball Hall of Fame. We also examine the growth of the league. From NBA Entertainment to the league's global expansion, from the emergence of a new and exciting breed of international player to NBA.com and other media outlets for the game, the league stands poised to reach even greater heights.

Chapter 20

NBA All-Star Game

In This Chapter

◆ The evolution of the All-Star Game

◆ The Slam-Dunk Contest

◆ The Three-Point Shootout

Being named to the NBA All-Star Game is a highlight in any player's career. It is an indication of what fans, coaches, and the league generally think of him. It is an honor.

The All-Star Game is also a hoot. The NBA All-Star break has become the traditional halfway point in the season, a time players can relax a bit and fans can watch some fun, exciting, high-scoring, slam-dunking, three-point-shooting NBA basketball. Besides the All-Star Game, there's a week-long celebration of basketball, music, and reading fun that is housed at the massive Jam Session—featuring tons of activities and games.

How It All Got Started

The frolicking game that is the NBA All-Star Game today is a far cry from what it was even 20 years ago, not to mention 50 years ago when it all started.

The First NBA All-Star Game

Basketball in 1951 was a very unpopular sport. A rash of scandals had tarnished the college game, and the stench had permeated the pros. NBA publicist Haskell Cohen thought he had a solution. Taking a page from Major League Baseball, Cohn conceived of a midseason game pitting the best players from the East against the best players from the West—an NBA All-Star Game.

Few people liked the idea, but Boston Celtics owner Walter Brown was behind it. "Things were going so badly that even my wife wanted me to get out of the business. But I thought the All-Star Game would be a good thing," Brown said. "I told the league I would take care of all the expenses and all the losses if there were any."

The conventional wisdom was that the game wouldn't attract enough interest to be worth the effort. According to Brown, "Even up until the last week, the game was in doubt. A few days before the game, Maurice Podoloff, the NBA commissioner, called me on the phone and asked me to call it off. He said that everyone he had talked to said it would be a flop, and that the league would look bad."

But Walter Brown didn't get to his station in life by not trusting himself. It's a good thing he stuck with it, too. More than 10,000 fans came to the old Boston Garden and saw the East whip the West 111–94.

Tip-In

The first MVP of the NBA All-Star Game was "Easy" Ed Macauley, who scored a game-high 20 points and limited George Mikan to four baskets.

NBA All-Star Game Highlights Through the Years

Since that first matchup between the best of the East and West, the NBA All-Star Game has seen some great moments.

The fourth NBA All-Star Game was remarkable in that the originally named MVP was not given the trophy. Near the end of regulation, a vote was taken and Jim Pollard was the choice for Most Valuable Player. However, the game went into overtime and Bob Cousy wowed the crowd, scoring 10 points in five minutes. A revote was demanded and Cousy was named MVP.

In 1957, with time winding down in the first half, Bill Sharman attempted a full-court pass to teammate Bob Cousy. Sharman's pass was off, landed in the basket, and he thus recorded the longest shot in NBA All-Star Game history—70 feet.

In 1960, rookie Wilt Chamberlain let the league know that a new man was in town by scoring a game-high 23 points and pulling down 25 rebounds. It was his first, and only, NBA All-Star MVP trophy. In the 1962 game, Wilt set an NBA All-Star Game scoring record by netting 42 points.

In 1966, a little-known, late addition to the East squad named Adrian Smith scored 25 points and led the East to a convincing win over the West, 137–94. (The West only scored 36 points in the first half.) Smith was a career 11.8 point-per-game man. The next year, Rick Barry scored 38 points in 34 minutes and was the game MVP.

Larry Brown receives the MVP Trophy after the ABA's first All-Star Game in 1968. George Mikan, the first ABA Commissioner, and Rick Barry flank Brown.

In the 1970 game, the West was down 106–85 after three quarters. Led by Jerry West, the West went on a rampage, scoring an NBA All-Star Game record (at the time) 15 points in the fourth quarter, only to lose the game, 142–135.

1972 was the year of redemption for Jerry West. Not only did he finally win an NBA championship that year, but the All-Star Game was played in L.A., and he thrilled the hometown crowd. With the game tied and time winding down, Mr. Clutch hit a 20-footer at the buzzer to win the game and MVP honors.

In 1977, in his first appearance as an NBA All-Star, Dr. J scored 30 points and grabbed 12 rebounds, earning him MVP honors—something he never had accomplished in five

Tip-In

In 1978, at the end of the first quarter, Buffalo's Randy Smith hit a 30-foot shot at the buzzer, and then topped that with a 40-footer just before halftime. His 27-point performance earned him MVP honors, although he also committed five fouls in one half.

ABA All-Star Games. Erving was only the second player in NBA history to earn MVP honors while playing on a losing All-Star team. Bob Pettit of the St. Louis Hawks was the first player to accomplish this feat in 1958.

In 1980, the game went into overtime for only the second time in its 30-year history. That was when rookie sensation Larry Bird took over, sealing a victory for the East. Although George Gervin won the MVP that year, Bird won it two years later.

The NBA All-Star Game has always been a high-flying affair.

In 1984, the Doctor won the MVP award for the second time after scoring 34 points. Also notable was Magic Johnson's record 22 assists. But the 1984 game will be remembered for something much more lasting—the introduction of the Slam Dunk contest and *All-Star Saturday.*

In 1987, the NBA All-Star Game saw its highest score ever. In a quadruple-overtime thriller in Seattle, the West beat the East 154–149. Seattle's Tom Chambers was the official MVP after scoring 34 points, and Magic Johnson was the unofficial MVP as he made sure that hometown hero Chambers got the ball often.

In 1988, Michael Jordan was named All-Star MVP for the first time, after scoring 16 points in the final 5:51 to assure a victory for the East in Chicago Stadium.

In 1990, Magic Johnson scored 22 points, pulled down six rebounds, and dished out four assists for the losing West squad. He became only the third player in All-Star history to win the All-Star Game MVP trophy while playing for the losing team.

The 1992 game may have been the most emotional one ever. Earlier that season Magic Johnson had stunned the world by announcing he was HIV positive and was retiring. But his name had already been printed on the NBA All-Star ballot, and he was overwhelmingly voted to start the game by the fans. Though some players were hesitant about playing in the game with Magic in the end, Magic played.

It turned out to be a joyous game, one where Magic scored 25 points and earned his second NBA All-Star Game MVP Award. The end of the game, with he and buddy Isiah Thomas playfully egging each other on near the end of the game. Magic hit his last shot with 14 seconds to play—a very deep three—and was overwhelmed by players on both teams. As he later said, "It's the only game that's been stopped on account of hugs."

For many years, Sacramento's Mitch Richmond was the best player never to play in an NBA All-Star Game. Finally, in 1992, that omission was corrected, and in the 1995 game, Mitch scored 23 points in 22 minutes, earning him the MVP. Richmond eventually played in six NBA All-Star Games.

In 1997, Jordan became the first player in NBA All-Star Game history to record a triple double: 14 points, 11 rebounds, and 11 assists. The MVP of the game that year was Glen Rice, who caught fire and scored 20 points in the third quarter, an All-Star record.

In 1998, Jordan had been sick with the flu a few days before the All-Star Game, and it was

Hoopology

The NBA All-Star Game is held on Sunday. However, starting in 1984, the NBA began expanding the festivities to include a slam-dunk contest, a three-point shootout, and other similar events. Later, other events were added, such as the Rookie Challenge, a game between the top first- and second-year players. They are now all a part of **All-Star Saturday.**

Tip-In

Also at the 1988 game, 40-year-old Kareem Abdul-Jabbar appeared in a record 17th NBA All-Star Game, and broke the career All-Star scoring record with 10 points for a total of 247, topping Oscar Robertson's 246.

Inside Stuff

At the 1993 game at the Delta Center in Salt Lake City, Utah's Karl Malone and John Stockton played brilliantly, leading the West to a victory, and were named co-MVPs.

unclear whether he would even play. But the game had been built up as a match between MJ and first-time All-Star Kobe Bryant, and if there is anything Michael loves, it's a challenge.

So what was the East's strategy? "Give it to Michael and get out of the way," said Larry Bird, the Eastern Conference coach. They did. Jordan scored 23 points, grabbing six rebounds and dishing a team-high eight assists, including three during a 20–1 run early in the fourth quarter that blew the game open. The East won and Jordan was named MVP.

Inside Stuff

The highest per-game scoring averages in NBA All-Star history are as follows:

- ◆ 20.8: Kobe Bryant
- ◆ 20.5: Oscar Robertson
- ◆ 20.4: Bob Pettit
- ◆ 20.2: Michael Jordan
- ◆ 20.1: Julius Erving
- ◆ 19.8: Elgin Baylor

* Entering 2002–03 season.

After the game, Jordan said, "I've been in bed for three days, basically. I didn't expect to come out here and win the MVP. I just wanted to fit in, to make sure Kobe didn't dominate me. The hype was me against him. I was just glad that I was able to fight him off."

The 2002 game was the changing of the guard. Held on February 10 in Philadelphia, fans and the media thought that it might be a homecoming, of sorts, for Philly native Kobe Bryant. Michael Jordan had come out of retirement that season (2001–02) and was also in the game, and no one was sure what to expect.

Kobe upheld his end of the bargain, scoring 31 points and leading the West to victory. Bryant was the first player to score 30 points or more in an All-Star Game since Michael did it in 1993. Kobe was named game MVP, but was surprised when the Philadelphia crowd booed him. They apparently hadn't forgotten that Kobe's Lakers had beaten the Sixers in the NBA Finals less than a year earlier.

Jordan was merely mortal this game. Orlando's Tracy McGrady more than made up for it, though, ramming down some spectacular dunks. Commenting on McGrady's moves, Jordan wistfully remarked, "I remember when I used to be like that. It's truly a great thing to see."

The Slam-Dunk Contest

The NBA All-Star festivities have become much more than the Sunday All-Star Game. It is now a full week of events that includes a slam dunk contest and three-point shootout. These extra events began years ago.

By the 1976 ABA All-Star Game, there were only seven teams left in the league; it was limping to the finish line. Ever inventive, the ABA decided to have a dunk contest. The contestants were ...

- 7' 2" Artis Gilmore
- 6' 7" George Gervin
- 6' 9" Larry Kenon
- 6' 4" David Thompson
- 6' 7" Julius Erving

Tip-In

Larry "Special K" Kenon played in the ABA and NBA for 10 years, averaging 17 ppg and 7.8 rebounds per game. He appeared in one All-Star Game.

Fans wondered who would win, the creative Dr J. or the high-jumping David Thompson. Thompson was indeed spectacular, performing the first 360-degree dunk. But the Doctor's second dunk was one for the history books as he ran the length of the floor and swooped in from the free-throw line to slam it home. The first slam-dunk contest was a rousing success.

The NBA adopted the idea in 1984 and slated its first slam-dunk contest for the Saturday before the All-Star Game. The rules of the contest are simple: Each dunk is worth a total of 50 possible points, and players have to make a certain number of dunks in each round. A jury of their peers judges the contestants. Special credit is given for originality and degree of difficulty. High scorers move on to the next round, and by the last round, the player who scores the most, wins.

It seemed to make sense to have Julius Erving inaugurate the new event, since he had participated in the last one during his ABA days. Erving was the prohibitive favorite and was joined in the contest that first year by Larry Nance, Dominique Wilkins, Darrell Griffith, Edgar Jones, Ralph Sampson, Orlando Woolridge, Clyde Drexler, and Michael Cooper.

Erving, Nance, Wilkins, and Griffith made it to the second round, and then the Doctor and Nance met in the final round. In an upset, Nance won, with a combined score on

Tip-In

Larry Nance played in the NBA for 13 years. He appeared in three NBA All-Star Games.

his three dunks of 134 to Erving's 122. (And now you have the answer to a great trivia question!)

The slam-dunk contest soon became one of the most anticipated events of the NBA season, as the best dunkers of the era would compete for a title that carried with it a lot of bragging rights. For the next few years, Michael Jordan and Dominique Wilkins would have the contest to themselves, almost.

In 1985, Wilkins and Jordan were joined by reigning champ Larry Nance, as well as by returning contestants Drexler, Griffith, Erving, and a couple of others. Not surprisingly, Air Jordan and the Human Highlight Film (Wilkins) made it to the final round.

Dominique Wilkins after winning the 1985 Slam Dunk Contest.

Wilkins exploded, getting two perfect scores of 50 in the final round, and beating Jordan 147–136. Two 50s is pretty amazing, but it would happen again the next year, performed by the most unlikely of suspects.

Jordan was absent from the 1986 contest because of injury, and so Dominique Wilkins was considered the favorite going in. His only real competition seemed to be his brother, Gerald Wilkins. But it was 5' 7" Spud Webb, Dominique's diminutive teammate in Atlanta, who gave him fits.

Spud led after the first round, and the crowd was clearly behind him. He and Wilkins tied in round two, but in the final round, Spud scored not one, but two perfect 50s to become the shortest man to win the slam-dunk contest.

In 1987, Michael Jordan took a page out of Julius Erving's book to finally win the contest. He and Portland's Jerome Kersey were in the finals. Jordan had already scored two 48s when he went to the other end of the court, started running, and took off from the free-throw line before jamming it in for a perfect 50.

The next year, 1988, in the highest-scoring finals ever in the slam-dunk contest, Jordan was again up against Dominique Wilkins. One thing that makes the contest frustrating for some is that it is necessarily subjective. That year, many people thought that Wilkins should have won, but just a few more thought Jordan did, and so he did. Jordan scored 147 to Wilkins' 145, to the delight of the hometown crowd at Chicago Stadium.

Tip-In

At the 1988 All-Star Game, Michael Jordan was named MVP after scoring 40 points, the second-highest point total ever, behind Wilt's 42 in 1962.

In 1990, Dominique decided to enter the contest one last time. The semis pitted Wilkins against Kenny "The Jet" Smith, Shawn Kemp in his prime, and returning champ Kenny "Sky" Walker. Dominique edged out Smith in the finals, with a score of 146.8 to 145.1.

In 1992 Cedric Ceballos had one of the more memorable dunks in slam-dunk-contest history. In the final round he put a blindfold over his eyes, and ended up scoring a 50. He won, defeating Charlotte's Larry Johnson.

In 1995, Isaiah Rider battled Harold Miner and Jamie Watson in the finals. In 1997, a new kid named Kobe Bryant beat Chris Carr and Michael Finley.

After its two-year hiatus, a whole new cadre of high-flyers began to emerge, exciting players like Kobe, Vince Carter, and Tracy McGrady. So in 2000, the NBA brought the slam-dunk contest back, by popular demand.

Inside Stuff

Vince Carter and Tracy McGrady are cousins.

The contest was shortened to two rounds, five dunks total. That year, in only two rounds, Vince Carter, Air Canada himself, had three scores of 50 and won the contest decisively. The slam-dunk contest was back.

The Three-Point Shootout

A thought arises: If the dunkers had their own contest to show off their skill, what about the long-ball shooters? Shouldn't they have a contest, too? You bet.

In 1986, a three-point-shooting contest was added to NBA All-Star Saturday. The rules are similar to the slam-dunk contest, except there is no subjectivity involved; either you nail the shot or you don't.

Contestants have 60 seconds to shoot 25 balls, which are placed on racks in groups of five at different locations around the arc. The buzzer buzzes, and the player begins to shoot from one corner. Each ball is worth one point, except the last one in each rack. The "money ball" is worth two points. After finishing the first rack, the player moves to the next, which is located above the *elbow*, then to the top of the key, and back down the other side.

That first contest in 1986 found Larry Bird pitted against the following players:

Hoopology

The area to the left or right of the free-throw line is called the **elbow**.

Tip-In

Larry Bird won the regular season MVP in 1984, 1985, and 1986. He is one of only three players in NBA history to achieve the feat three seasons in a row.

- ◆ Craig Hodges
- ◆ Trent Tucker
- ◆ Dale Ellis
- ◆ Sleepy Floyd
- ◆ Kyle Macy
- ◆ Leon Wood
- ◆ Norm Nixon

The confident Bird said he would win, and did. He beat Craig Hodges in the final round 22–12, although in the first round, Hodges found the zone and had scored an amazing 25.

Bird defended his crown and won the next year, too, beating Detlef Schrempf of Seattle, 16–14. He then went for a three-peat in 1988 and won, retiring undefeated after beating Dale Ellis 17–15. The lasting image of that contest was Bird raising his index finger in the air before the winning shot from the corner went in. There was no doubt who the number-one three-point shooter in the NBA was.

The 1989 contest was wide open the next year without Bird competing, and runner-up Dale Ellis won it, defeating Craig Hodges 19–15. Hodges had another amazing first round that year, too, scoring a 20.

But Hodges was not to be denied the crown for much longer. He came back again the next year, saved something for the final round (although he did score another 20 in the first round), and hung on to defeat Reggie Miller 19–18.

Hodges then decided to defend his title, and in 1991, he won it again. He won *again* in 1992, but lost in the first round in 1993. Even so, he became the only other player besides Larry Bird to three-peat the event.

In 1994, Mark Price of the Cavaliers scored 24 points in the final round—a record for that round. In 1998, Jeff Hornacek won, and then took the title again in 2000.

In 2002, Peja Stojakovic of the Kings defeated Wesley Person in the first overtime shootout. In the process Peja became the first international player to win the contest and staked his claim to the unofficial title of best shooter in the NBA.

Peja Stojakovic of the Sacramento Kings won the three-point shootout in 2002.

The Least You Need to Know

- ◆ The NBA All-Star Game has been a big success since it was introduced in 1951.
- ◆ The Slam Dunk contest features NBA players showcasing their best moves and dunks.
- ◆ The three-point shootout has always been a fan favorite.

The Growth of the NBA

In This Chapter

- ◆ David Stern to the rescue
- ◆ NBA TV
- ◆ NBA.com
- ◆ Books and videos
- ◆ Marketing and merchandising

It wasn't so long ago that the NBA was a blip on the media screen. Interest in the league had faded in the late '70s, and the overall economic growth of the league was bleak at best. During these "Dark Days of the NBA," talk centered more on contraction—teams going out of business—rather than expansion.

Fortunately, two forces were instrumental in forever changing the direction, fortunes and visibility of the NBA. The first was the emergence of Magic Johnson and Larry Bird on the NBA scene in 1979–80 and the parallel re-emergence of the Los Angeles Lakers–Boston Celtics storied rivalry. The second was the deft appointment of David J. Stern as fourth commissioner in league history in 1984. These on- and off-the-court forces combined to help turn the once-stagnant league into a global media and basketball giant.

Difficult Times

Although Magic and Bird re-ignited interest in the NBA, and the league was starting a comeback, it was still experiencing problems before David Stern became commissioner in 1984:

♦ The 1980 NBA Finals between the Lakers and the Philadelphia 76ers were shown on tape delay on CBS at 11:30 P.M. in the East.

♦ Seventeen of the 23 teams were losing money.

♦ In 1980, average attendance was 10,021 (in contrast, by the start of the 1997 season, it was 17,252).

♦ There was a perception that drug abuse was a major problem among the players.

Dramatic change was needed, and the NBA Board of Governors found the answer in David Stern.

David Stern to the Rescue

David Stern was born on September 22, 1942, in New York. His first job was working behind the counter in his family's delicatessen, Stern's Deli. He learned many valuable lessons while working at the restaurant, especially those that pertain to customer service and making sure the paying consumer is completely satisfied. (Valuable lessons that he would apply in his future job as NBA commissioner.) He played basketball for fun, and grew up watching the New York Knicks.

> **Tip-In**
>
> "Others talk about working as clerks for Supreme Court justices or federal judges, but I enjoy saying that my first clerkship was at Stern's Delicatessen."
>
> —David Stern

Stern attended Rutgers University where he studied political science, and received his B.A. in 1963. He continued to work at the family deli through his first year of law school at Columbia, graduating in 1966.

As fate would have it, Stern's first law job in 1967 was with the New York firm Proskauer Rose Goetz Mendelson, whose clients included the National Basketball Association. Stern served as outside counsel to the league before moving over full-time in 1978 to become the NBA's first general counsel. In 1980, he was named Executive Vice President of the league.

During those years, Stern had a hand in virtually every matter that would shape the league, including the landmark 1976 settlement between the NBA and its players leading to free agency, the collective bargaining agreement that introduced the salary cap, revenue sharing and a drug policy—all firsts in professional sports.

NBA Commissioner David Stern.

By 1984, the league was growing thanks to the revival of interest in its new stars. After a nearly nine-year run, NBA commissioner Larry O'Brien was ready to step down. David Stern was elected unanimously to be the commissioner of the league, and began his tenure on February 1, 1984.

Inside Stuff

Lawrence O'Brien captained the NBA through some turbulent times. He became commissioner in 1975, after having been Postmaster General of the United States, and Special Assistant to Presidents John F. Kennedy and Lyndon B. Johnson, as well as the chairman of the Democratic Party.

His NBA credentials were also impressive:

◆ The league expanded from 18 to 23 teams during his tenure.

◆ He coordinated the absorption of four ABA teams in 1976.

◆ He was selected as *The Sporting News'* "Sportsman of the Year" in 1976.

Since becoming commissioner, Stern has guided the NBA to unprecedented growth. Among his many other attributes, David Stern understands sports marketing and promotions. When he became commissioner, he knew he had a valuable commodity—an exciting product played by the world's greatest athletes. So he set about selling that product. Stern was responsible for the development of NBA Properties as the league's marketing arm, and the creation of NBA Entertainment, a television and multi-media production company that has been telling the NBA story in award-winning fashion for nearly two decades. In recent years, the NBA launched its own 24-hour network—NBA TV—and is the only professional sports league that can boast that claim.

His extraordinary vision helped the NBA increase its revenue by some 500 percent since he took over, and the franchise market values have increased correspondingly. For example, when the Ackerly group bought the Seattle SuperSonics in 1983, it paid $16 million. In 2001, it sold the team to a group headed by Starbucks Coffee founder Howard Schultz for $200 million—not a bad return on his investment.

By 1984, the Magic-Larry/Lakers-Celtics rivalry was in full swing, Michael Jordan had entered the NBA via the University of North Carolina, and Kareem Abdul-Jabbar and Dr. J were still exciting fans with their All-Star play. The NBA began to showcase and promote its many star players. The Finals were also exciting again, and so it is no surprise that the slogans of the league soon became: "The NBA—It's Fan-tastic!" and "I Love This Game!"

As the 1980s continued, interest in the league grew exponentially and it only increased during the '90s as Michael Jordan led the Chicago Bulls to six NBA championships. Ratings soared and the league didn't miss a beat when Bird and Johnson retired.

Tip-In

The 1998 NBA Finals between Chicago and Utah earned the highest TV ratings of any NBA Finals ever.

Tip-In

David Stern serves or has served on the boards of Columbia University, Beth Israel Medical Center, the Rutgers University Foundation, the National Association for the Advancement of Colored People, the Martin Luther King Jr. Federal Holiday Commission and the Thurgood Marshall Scholarship Fund, among others.

Stern's vision also fueled the global popularity of the sport of basketball and the NBA in particular when NBA players represented the United States in the 1992 Olympic Games in Barcelona. The Dream Team's success and popularity helped the NBA truly become a global brand.

Under NBA Commissioner Stern's guidance, the league has enjoyed unparalleled success:

♦ The NBA grew from 23 to 29 teams.

♦ The league expanded internationally into Canada (1995).

♦ The league launched the WNBA and the NBDL.

♦ NBA players participate in the Olympics.

♦ The league opened international offices in Barcelona, Beijing, Cologne, Hong Kong, Mexico City, Miami, Paris, Singapore, Taiwan, Tokyo, and Toronto.

- The league has become a leader in professional sports by implementing the salary cap.

- The league's web sites—NBA.com, WNBA.com and NBDL.com—attract more than one million visitors a day, with one third of the traffic coming from outside the United States.

Entertainment, NBA Style

NBA Entertainment (NBAE) was created in 1982 to license and promote all things NBA. Today, it covers all aspects of the business of the NBA:

- Coordinating sponsorships and marketing

- Handling merchandising

- Overseeing television opportunities

- Managing e-commerce

And it all starts with television.

The NBA on TV in the United States

Since its inception in the 1940's, the NBA has seen an incredible growth in its television business, and today there are a variety of television avenues that allow fans to watch games and other programming to learn more about the game of basketball and the NBA.

One reason the league has continued to grow over the years is because of its ability to bring fans the best basketball action in the world—through either live in-arena games or through presenting games on television. The league recently saw tremendous continued growth throughout the 1990s, its great partnerships with NBC on network television and Turner Sports (TBS/TNT) on the cable side. NBC's partnership began with the 1990–91 NBA season and Turner's partnership began with the 1984–85 season. Both partnerships were great outlets to promote the NBA's stable of stars.

Previous to NBC's partnership, CBS had broadcast NBA games for the 17 years before. When NBC took over, they saw the NBA as a potential profit center and bid $600 million for the rights to broadcast NBA games for four seasons (the previous CBS deal, for four years, was for $173 million). As executive Vice President at NBC

Sports, Ken Schanzer said at the time, "Right now, we think the NBA can be enormously profitable for us." He was right. The NBA on NBC saw great successes throughout its long relationship.

As the NBA became more and more popular and more stars were born, the league's popularity continued to thrive and more partnerships were created, more advertising revenue came in, and the ratings increased correspondingly. It was a symbiotic relationship, with both NBC and Turner, from which everyone benefited.

Two more four-year deals between the NBA and NBC would emerge, but all good things must come to an end. After 12 successful seasons of broadcasting NBA basketball, NBC no longer had the rights after the 2001–02 NBA season. Beginning with the 2002–03 NBA season, and continuing through the 2007–08 season, NBA games are televised on ABC and ESPN and continue on TNT. The overall value of the six-year deals totaled a reported $4.6 billion dollars.

International TV

The NBA's television business in the United States is continuing to thrive, but what some fans may not know is that NBA games and programming are also seen in more than 210 countries around the world in more than 42 different languages. The league has international television partnerships with more than 140 international telecasters, including deals in places like China, Spain, France, Germany, and even Egypt, Croatia, Mongolia, and more! Customized versions of the league's *NBA Inside Stuff* and *NBA Jam* programs are distributed overseas, and more than 14 international co-productions currently exist overseas, including shows like *Eddy Time* (France); *NBA Dei Di* (Hong Kong); and *Above the Rim* (Russia).

NBA TV

To add to the television exposure the NBA provides fans, in 1999 the league launched NBA TV, a 24-hour television network for the true basketball junkie. NBA TV offers fans real-time statistics, scores, news from NBA.com, with live studio-based programming, live "look-ins" of games in progress, highlights, vintage NBA games and additional programming from the award-winning archives of NBA Entertainment. The network is also planning to start televising live NBA games during the 2002–03 NBA season.

During the off-season, NBA TV continues to be an oasis for the starved hoops junkie by delving into the NBA archives to offer some of the greatest games of all time, NBAE programs, international play, summer league games and off-season league transactions.

With the launch of NBA TV in 1999, NBA fans no longer need a remote control to get their fix.

A related venture is NBA LEAGUE PASS, a package that allows subscribers to watch several NBA games per week from areas outside of their local viewing areas.

NBAE Programming

NBA Entertainment, in addition to airing NBA games and programming with network and cable partners in the United States and around the world, also produces a variety of ancillary programs for fans.

NBA Inside Stuff, one of the league's longest running programs, is the weekly youth-oriented news magazine program of the NBA that launched in 1990. The show is hosted by Ahmad Rashad (also executive producer) with co-host Summer Sanders. *Inside Stuff* recently moved from NBC to ABC as part of the league's new television deal, and introduced a new interactive, fun-filled set for the 2002–03 season. NBA stars, WNBA stars and even celebrities and political icons, have appeared regularly on *Inside Stuff.*

Other NBA Entertainment-produced programs include *NBA Matchup, NBA Action, NBA Jam, Vintage NBA* and more.

NBA.com

Launched in November of 1995, NBA.com offers a multitude of NBA-related information for the fan. One of the most successful Internet launches ever, NBA.com attracted more than 200,000 visitors in its first week and now boasts more than 1 million visitors *per day*. Of those, more than 40 percent live outside the United States.

Shanghai, China, June 26, 2002: Yao Ming follows the action on NBA.com after being chosen first in the 2002 NBA Draft by the Houston Rockets.

Among other things at NBA.com, you will find …

- Official home pages for all 29 teams, including news, stats, histories, biographies, profiles of players, latest transactions, and other background information.

- Exclusive video and audio highlights and photo galleries.

- Extensive coverage of All-Star Weekend, the NBA Playoffs, the NBA Finals and the NBA Draft.

- Schedules, standings and complete statistics.

- Polls, contests, and auctions.

- Fantasy games, including NBA Virtual GM, and NBA Triple-Double.

- The NBA.com store, which sells merchandise from all 29 teams.

One of the great things about the site is the special features that give in-depth analysis of important NBA events. So, for example, when the NBA turned 50, the site offered a complete retrospective of the league, and when Michael Jordan retired for the second time in 1998 visitors could access an MJ retrospective that included a video archive, facts, analyses, and photo galleries.

NBA.com has proven so popular that there are now specific versions of site designed for residents of Canada, China, Japan, and Great Britain, as well as NBA.com/Español.

Books and Video

The NBA has partnered with some of the world's leading publishers to offer books such as the *NBA Encyclopedia* and *At the Buzzer: The Greatest Moments in NBA History*—and this book!

NBA Video is a leader in the sports video and DVD field, offering a wide variety of titles for sale, including the following:

- ◆ *Ultimate Jordan* (two-disc DVD set)
- ◆ *The NBA at 50*
- ◆ *Allen Iverson: The Answer*
- ◆ *The Annual Championship Home Video*

The NBA also produces two magazines: *Hoop* and *Inside Stuff*.

NBA Marketing and Merchandising

NBA Entertainment may be best known for its impressive marketing arm. A main reason that the league has grown as it has is that a great product was marketed well.

By creating strategic partnerships with other global brands like Coca-Cola, McDonald's, Reebok, and Nike, the league has been able to extend the NBA brand into new markets, and make it known to more people around the world.

The Dream Team

NBA marketing was able to go global in a big way after the 1992 Olympics. In 1989, the International Basketball Federation (FIBA), the body that governed international basketball competition, decided for the first time to allow professional athletes to play in international competitions.

This allowed the NBA to join the American counterpart—USA Basketball—and send NBA players to the Olympics for the first time. As noted previously, the 1992 Dream Team crushed everything in its way and amazed fans worldwide with the basketball

Tip-In

The gold medal game at the 1992 Olympics pitted the U.S. against Croatia. The Dream Team won the game 117–85.

prowess of its players. Fans across the globe fell in love with Michael Jordan, Magic Johnson, and company.

The Dream Team was the undeniable hit of the Barcelona Olympics, and in the process of changing the way the world thinks about hoops, it allowed the NBA to expand internationally in ways that were not previously possible. (See Chapter 23.)

After those Olympics, the league was flooded with international requests for NBA games, television rights, and merchandise. The NBA became a global brand.

The 1992 USA Men's Basketball Olympic Team (The Dream Team): Seated front row (L-R): David Fischer, Scottie Pippen, Christian Laettner, Patrick Ewing, Head Coach Chuck Daly, David Robinson, Karl Malone, Charles Barkley. Standing (L-R): Assistant coach Mike Krzyzewski, Assistant coach Lenny Wilkens, Michael Jordan, Larry Bird, Magic Johnson, Chris Mullin, Clyde Drexler, John Stockton, Assistant coach P.J. Carlesimo and trainer Ed Lacerte.

Sports fans around the globe point to the 1992 Olympic Games as the springboard for the sport of basketball truly becoming the global game it is today. In 1989, the International Basketball Federation (FIBA), the body that governed international basketball competition, decided for the first time to allow open competition in international basketball.

While pro players from countries such as Russia, Yugoslavia, Brazil and many others were permitted to play in prior Olympics, NBA players were not eligible. When

FIBA voted in 1989, the U.S.-based basketball federation immediately focused on '92 for the debut. This allowed the NBA to join the American counterpart—USA Basketball—and make the preparations for sending NBA players to the Olympics for the first time. When the Barcelona Olympics began, the original Dream Team crushed anything and everything in its way, and amazed fans worldwide with their basketball prowess. Fans worldwide had fallen in love with Michael Jordan, Larry Bird, Magic Johnson and company.

Tip-In

The Gold Medal game at the 1992 Olympics pitted the United States against Croatia. The Dream Team won the game 117-85.

The Dream Team was the undeniable hit of the Barcelona Olympics, and in the process of changing the way the world thinks about hoops, it allowed the NBA to expand internationally in ways that were not previously possible. (See next chapter.)

After those Olympics, the league was flooded with international requests for NBA games, television rights and merchandise. The NBA had became a global brand.

NBA Global Merchandising

The NBA's marketing arm works hard to promote all of its stars. It helps various stars land shoe endorsement deals, parts in movies like *Space Jam* and *Like Mike*, television gigs, and other similar contracts.

The NBA's Global Merchandising Group works with its licensees to distribute products such as NBA apparel, electronic games, and sporting goods. These sorts of goods are now available at stores around the world.

And if you think the NBA is big now, you haven't seen anything yet. This is a league poised for even more worldwide dominance and popularity.

The Least You Need to Know

- ◆ NBA Commissioner David Stern picked up where Larry O'Brien left off.
- ◆ The NBA is seen around the world.
- ◆ NBA.com is one of the Internet's leading sites.
- ◆ The NBA excels in marketing and merchandising.

The Basketball Hall of Fame

In This Chapter

- ◆ Hall of Fame history
- ◆ A Hall of Fame for the new millennium
- ◆ The hallowed library

It is the pinnacle of a career. Making it into the Basketball Hall of Fame (the actual name is the Naismith Memorial Basketball Hall of Fame) is the epitome of personal achievement for someone associated with basketball.

When Alex English made it into the Hall of Fame in 1997, he said, "There is no greater validation of your career. It's one of the great days of my life." When told that he had been elected into the Hall, Magic Johnson said, "Once we won all those championships, I thought I had a good chance to get in. The Olympics was probably my biggest thrill to date. This is bigger."

But the Hall isn't just for the NBA; it is dedicated to basketball generally and so has many constituents: USAB, Womens, NCAA, FIBA, overseas players, college coaches, really anyone making a mark on the game is eligible for induction.

Located in Springfield, Massachusetts, the birthplace of basketball, the Hall is a great place to visit for anyone who wants to learn more about the game of basketball.

History of the Hall

It should be no surprise that the Hall of Fame is named after the inventor of basketball, James A. Naismith, but getting the Hall of Fame built would actually prove to be more difficult than inventing the game of basketball itself.

Tip-In

Invented in the winter of 1891, basketball had become one of the world's major sports by the start of World War I in 1917. The Hall of Fame would take considerably longer to come to fruition.

By 1936, the game was being introduced as a new sport in the Olympics. Dr. Naismith was present in Berlin for the event, thanks to the National Association of Basketball Coaches (NABC.)

Dr. Naismith died three years later. His death, combined with the success of the sport at the Olympic Games, fostered a desire by the members of NABC to build a memorial to the game and its inventor. But plans for such a memorial would have to wait; the world was careening toward global war and more pressing matters took center stage.

Genesis

After World War II, the NABC appointed a committee to examine the possibility of creating a basketball hall of fame. Bill Chandler head coach of Marquette University, headed the committee. He has called the undertaking "the greatest endeavor our Coaches Association has ever attempted."

Inside Stuff

Legendary University of Kansas coach Phog Allen founded the NABC in 1927 during a basketball crisis. The joint Basketball Rules Committee had just passed a rule eliminating the dribble, and Allen wanted to create a unified voice in opposition to the new rule. They succeeded.

Since then, the NABC has referred to itself as the "Guardians of the Game," instituting educational programs that focus attention on the group's four core values: Advocacy, leadership, service, and education. Aside from establishing the first Hall of Fame, the NABC is also responsible for creating the NCAA Basketball Tournament format.

The NABC committee concluded that a basketball hall of fame was an idea whose time had come. Even though in 1949 there was no building, no artifacts, and no inductees, the NABC formed the Hall of Fame anyway.

Ed Hickox, the hoops coach at Springfield College (the place where basketball began, although it was a YMCA at the time) was chosen as the first executive secretary of the Hall. The college gave Hickox an office, which was known as the "little red house next to the football field," thus earning the distinction as the first home of the Hall of Fame.

Hickox volunteered his time and began to solicit artifacts and funds to construct a real Hall of Fame. Finding memorabilia was the easy part, as interest in the nascent Hall had grown rapidly. Balls, photographs, hoops, and other pieces from the early days of basketball were donated. But finding the money to build a place to house it all proved far more difficult.

Technical Foul

Later in life, Dr. Naismith became the first basketball coach ever at the University of Kansas. He is the only coach in Kansas's basketball history to have a losing record.

The first 24-second clock is part of the permanent collection of the Naismith Memorial Basketball Hall of Fame.

Even though it didn't have a place to display its emerging collection, the Basketball Hall of Fame inducted its inaugural class in 1959. Seventeen members were enshrined as part of that first class, including the following:

◆ **James A. Naismith**—the inventor of the game.

Harvey Pollack, the recipient of the 2002 John Bunn Award, speaks at the 2002 Hall of Fame induction ceremony. Behind him is a portrait of James Naismith.

◆ **The "First Team"**—Participants were members of Dr. Naismith's 1891 physical education class. According to the Hall of Fame records, they were "a group of 18 incorrigibles [who] had already disposed of two previous instructors, and initially scoffed at the idea. Frank Mahan, the leader of the group, remarked doubtfully, 'Huh! Another new game!' Undaunted by their statements, Naismith remained unfazed and developed 13 rules for the game." But the 18 incorrigibles" liked the new game and word spread. Spectators began to fill the gymnasium to watch the two teams of nine play. For their efforts in creating the new game, the First Team became an original member of the Hall of Fame.

◆ **Forrest "Phog" Allen**—Phog Allen is often called the "Father of Basketball Coaching." He learned the game while playing at the University of Kansas under James Naismith, and went on to coach college ball for 48 years. He retired with a 746–264 record and was the all-time winningest coach in collegiate basketball history.

◆ **Luther Gulick**—Gulick was the head of the physical education department at the Springfield YMCA, and he is the one who persuaded Dr. Naismith to invent a new game. Gulick went on to chair the Basketball Rules Organization, serve on the Olympic Committee, and is credited with starting both the Boy Scouts and the Camp Fire Girls.

◆ **The Original Celtics**—In 1918, two promoters, Jim and Tom Fuery, put together a barnstorming team that they named the Original Celtics (no relation to the Boston Celtics). The Original Celtics, based in New York City, were one of the best teams of the era and instituted innovations that would change the game: zone defenses, passing the ball into the pivot (the center), and contracts for individual players.

Inside Stuff

There were several great barnstorming teams during this era. The Buffalo Germans once won 111 games in a row (take that, Lakers!) and had an astounding 792–86 record between 1895 and 1929. Eddie Gottlieb, the genius behind what would later be the Harlem Globetrotters, helped create another barnstorming team, the SPHAs (South Philadelphia Hebrew Association). The SPHAs won championships in three different leagues.

But of all the barnstorming teams out there, it was the Original Celtics who were considered the best and who had the most lasting impact on basketball. Playing in the Seventy-First Regiment Armory in Manhattan every Sunday night when they weren't touring the country, the team had some great showmen. One lasting play that they developed was when Nat Holman would fake getting hit harder than he actually did, and thereby drawing a foul. That play is called "the flop."

The Original Celtics tried joining various leagues now and then, but were so overpowering, they soon withdrew. In 1922 for example, they joined the Metropolitan League, but after winning their first 13 games, dropped out.

The Hall Finds a Home

Groundbreaking began on the Hall of Fame on November 6, 1961, the seventieth anniversary of Dr. Naismith's invention. A two-wing, $860,000 building would go up on the Springfield campus. But almost from the start, construction and fund-raising snafus delayed completion of the building.

In 1963, the City of Springfield decided to join the project and it set up the Naismith Hall of Fame Fund, Inc., raising $200,000 in the process. In 1966, the unbuilt Hall suffered a big loss. With cost overruns and fund-raising problems still hampering the project, the NABC decided that it could no longer afford to continue with its efforts to build a basketball hall of fame.

But on July 1 of that year, a new group took over the dream. Naismith Hall of Fame Fund, Inc., hired ex-NABC president Lee Williams to spearhead the project. As Williams tells it, "When I came here, the [Hall of Fame] was still a hole in the ground." At the time, he continued, "there was a sign at the future building site that said 'Hall of Fame.' Well, in our local paper, a reporter took the liberty of referring to our site as the 'Hole of Fame.' That was all the inspiration I needed."

Williams immediately instituted a plan of action. The design for the building was scaled down, the budget was trimmed back, and Williams began to travel extensively, raising funds for the project. It worked.

On February 17, 1968, the Naismith Memorial Basketball Hall of Fame finally opened its doors to the public, more than 30 years after the idea had first been conceived.

Interest in the new Hall of Fame grew slowly and then picked up steam. It took five years before the Hall saw its one hundred thousandth visitor, but it then started getting more than 100,000 visitors *each year*. The small building was not ready for such an onslaught.

Inside Stuff

When told that he was going into the Hall of Fame, Coach Larry Brown said, "To get into the Basketball Hall of Fame is an unbelievable feeling. When I got into the game, this is nothing I ever expected could happen. I love the sport so much, but you never stay in it as long as I have thinking your career will wind up in the Hall of Fame.

"I look at the Hall of Famers who I played for and learned from, Coach McGuire at North Carolina, Coach McClendon, Coach Iba, Coach Wooden, Alex Hannum, Dean Smith, and to be joining them in the Hall of Fame is remarkable. It's hard to believe it's true."

By 1978, although the paint on the first building was hardly dry, plans were underway to build a bigger and better facility. Part of the plans included moving the building to a more prominent address (the original building was in an out-of-the-way location); considering that the building was already attracting a lot of tourists to its site on the Springfield campus, it seemed to make more sense to move it into a bigger facility closer to Springfield's business district. The State of Massachusetts kicked in $8 million, private fund-raising netted another $3.4 million, and construction for a new structure began in 1984.

Tip-In

With the opening of the new Hall of Fame, Executive Director Lee Williams retired, after 19 years at the helm. Williams noted, "How many people are fortunate enough to be around and have had a hand in the building of two Halls of Fame? It was a labor of love and I got paid for it!"

The Hall Finds a Second Home

In 1985, the Naismith Memorial Basketball Hall of Fame moved from the Springfield campus into a new three-story, state-of-the-art facility. It was just in time, too; the explosion in interest in the game due to the rise in popularity of the NBA was just beginning. The new Hall would have many, many visitors from around the globe. In 1988, the Hall had record attendance, attracting 173,898 people.

By expanding its programming, offering interactive experiences, and transforming the enshrinement weekend (the three day event where new inductees enter into the Hall) into a world-class event, the Hall of Fame became one of the preeminent sports museums in the world.

A Hall of Fame for the New Millennium

The global explosion of interest in basketball generally, and the NBA specifically, created a need for an even bigger and better Hall of Fame. In 1995, David Gavitt became chairman of the Hall of Fame and began to look at creating yet another facility to house the Hall's ever-expanding collection and activities.

Gavitt decided that the Hall needed to be completely revamped, and that an expansion would not work. "the problem," Gavin noted, was that "the Hall had become such a static thing. We needed to bring it alive."

To do so, the Hall of Fame's Board of Directors would need to raise the necessary funds. However, this time it would be infinitely easier than in the time of Lee Williams, since it was necessary for the government and the constituents to contribute. The plan was to turn the old Hall into a children's museum, include a mix of retail space in the new facility, revamp the Springfield waterfront, revitalize the local economy, and build the world's best sports museum. Because of the extensive plans, state and local governments were involved, and the Hall also relied on constituent contributions.

A Game Plan

"Dave Gavitt told us he wanted to have a postcard picture of the Hall of Fame, without having to write underneath what it was," says Andrew Crystal, vice president of design and construction for O'Connell Development, the local Springfield group that worked on the project.

And that is just what they got. The architectural firm of Gwathmey Siegel & Associates, which also helped design the Guggenheim Museum in New York, created an immediately identifiable building.

Most notable is the giant basketball-like sphere that anchors the building. Eight stories high and 120 feet in diameter, the sphere contains 850 tiny multihued, computer-controlled lights that can be illuminated in a variety of ways, in accordance with the occasion. When Magic Johnson was enshrined, they shined Laker purple and gold, and when Michael Jordan is enshrined, they will shine Bulls' red and black.

Inside Stuff

According to Hoopshall.com (the web site for the Basketball Hall of Fame), the goals for the new Hall of Fame were to ...

- ◆ Revere the Enshrinees.
- ◆ Provide a unique, educational, and enjoyable visitor experience for fans of all ages.
- ◆ Design a building that takes advantage of the prominent site to attract visitors.
- ◆ Use reliable high-end technology.
- ◆ Preserve the museum collection.
- ◆ Support local and regional community involvement.

It's Good!

On September 28, 2002, the new Hall of Fame opened, just in time for the enshrinement ceremonies of that year's class, which included ...

- ◆ Earvin "Magic" Johnson
- ◆ Drazen Petrovic
- ◆ NBA/college coach Larry Brown
- ◆ Coach Lute Olson
- ◆ Coach Kay Yow
- ◆ The Harlem Globetrotters

At the ceremonies, guests were treated to one of the most amazing museums on the planet.

Visitors enter the new Hall via a retail concourse, and then enter a lobby that is patterned after an arena, with famous photos, videos of games, and other interactive experiences bringing the excitement of the game to life.

A fan compares his armspan to that of Chris Webber of the Sacramento Kings at the Basketball Hall of Fame.

Once inside the new Hall of Fame, visitors find a plethora of things to see and do, including the following areas of interest:

- **Center Court:** On a full-sized basketball court, fans can view permanent exhibits, participate in trivia games, try their hand at various basketball skills, participate in live clinics, and engage in shooting competitions.

- **The Honors Ring:** The centerpiece of the Hall of Fame is suspended from the ceiling of the basketball-shaped dome: The large glass plaques that honor all Hall of Fame enshrinees. Each display has a picture of the member etched in the glass along with a biography, and also contains displays and videos showing them in action.

- **The Game:** Here you'll find displays dedicated to all aspects of the game of basketball, including its invention, the great barnstorming teams, the origins of the rules, changes in equipment, styles of shooting, the great basketball dynasties, and much more.

CAUTION

Technical Foul

On March 2, 1962, Wilt Chamberlain scored 100 points against the Knicks. What you don't know is that these two teams played again the next night. When Knicks center Darrall Imhoff was taken out late in the game that night, he was given a standing ovation. Why? Because on this night he had "held" Chamberlain to only 54 points.

The history of the game is explored in three sections: The Pioneer Years (1891 to the 1930s), the Formative Years (1930s through the late '60s), and Basketball Comes of Age (mid-1960s to the present.)

♦ **Players:** This interactive area allows visitors to compare their skills to those of the all-time greats. Hands-on activities (like testing your vertical leap) are interspersed with players' personal artifacts, home movies, and a minitheater in which visitors can watch great moments, games, and moves.

♦ **Media:** Overlooking Center Court, visitors get a media-eye view of the game. Here again, interactive exhibits, such as simulated broadcasts, and vintage artifacts tell the history of the media's coverage of basketball, from newspapers, through radio, and on to the Internet.

♦ **Contributors:** Here, visitors to the Hall of Fame are able to watch the game through the eyes of a ref, make their own calls (a fan's dream!), and then compare them to how a ref actually called the play.

♦ **Coaches:** This "locker room" uses text, graphics, videos, sound, and displays to recreate the space where coaches do most of their work. Visitors are able to devise their own game strategy and compare that to the coaches.

♦ **Teams:** All-time great teams are memorialized here, and teamwork, winning, and creating a cohesive unit are the themes explored. Great moments in basketball history captured on video can be found here as well.

♦ **Fans:** Photo opportunities with team mascots, fan support, and an analysis of the game's global audience are all covered here.

Inside Stuff

Since 1946, Harvey Pollack has been involved in almost all facets of the NBA, and he has been witness to some of the game's greatest moments (he scribbled the "100" sign that Wilt holds in that famous picture, for example.)

Pollack was the head of public relations for the Philadelphia 76ers for years, and then became the director of statistical information for the team. He is responsible for introducing the statistical categories that are now commonplace—things like rebounds, blocked shots, field goals made, and so on.

For his long and distinguished service to the game, the Naismith Memorial Basketball Hall of Fame presented Pollack with the John Bunn Award in 2002. The Bunn Award is the highest honor that an individual in basketball can receive, outside of actual enshrinement in the Hall. The Bunn Award is named in the memory of John Bunn, the first chairman of the Hall of Fame Committee. It is intended to honor those who have contributed in a significant way to the game of basketball.

The Edward J. and Gena G. Hickox Library

Also inside the Hall of Fame is the most extensive collection of basketball-related information in the world. The library's collection dates back to the very beginning of basketball and documents the game on every level—from high school on up through the pros.

The library was founded in 1959 and is dedicated to preserving, displaying, and making accessible to the public its considerable collection.

Not only does the library house an amazing collection of books about basketball (the entire collection numbers more than 5,000 volumes), but it also is home to ...

♦ Oral histories

♦ Encyclopedias

♦ Directories

♦ Media guides

♦ Magazines and other periodicals (more than 100 titles)

♦ Film and movies

♦ Photographs

The archive includes histories and scrapbooks of the old barnstorming teams like the Buffalo Germans, as well as an abundance of other documents such as press releases, ticket stubs, scorecards, yearbooks, clippings, photographs, and programs.

Inside Stuff

As part of its charge to document the history of the game of basketball, the Naismith Memorial Basketball Hall of Fame has undertaken to record the oral histories of people associated with the game.

The Oral History Program preserves the history of the game through taped interviews with players, coaches, and others who have made a significant contribution to basketball.

The tapes, transcripts, and related material are housed in the library and are available for research purposes.

For more on the Hall of Fame, check out Appendix A.

The library, indeed, the entire Naismith Memorial Basketball Hall of Fame, makes available in a single space those things that make basketball so special.

The Least You Need to Know

♦ It took many years to get the Hall of Fame off the ground.

♦ Three different locations in Springfield, Massachusetts, have housed the Hall.

♦ The newest Hall is an interactive showcase that allows visitors a chance to have a hands-on experience with the game and its history.

The Game Goes Global

In This Chapter

- ◆ The globalization of the NBA
- ◆ The emergence of worldwide clinics
- ◆ The International Invasion
- ◆ The future of the NBA

The NBA has come a long way from the mom-and-pop league that began over 50 years ago. It survived low-scoring games prior to the invention of the 24-second shot clock, uninspired offenses, a general lack of interest, the complete domination of the league by one team, rival leagues, and tape-delayed NBA Finals to become the preeminent professional sports league on the planet.

As a result, the NBA has expanded internationally, and international players have contributed to the NBA. The future of the league is global.

The Globalization of the NBA

The governing body for international basketball in the United States is USA Basketball—the organization that sends the American team to the Olympics every four years. Until 1989, though, it did not have jurisdiction over professional players. But, FIBA, the international basketball governing body, voted to allow NBA players to play in international competitions. This allowed NBA players to participate. That decision would have many long-term benefits for the NBA.

You Deserve a Break Today

FIBA's acceptance of NBA players in 1989 is in no small part due to NBA Commissioner David Stern. Stern had a global vision for the league, one that included international play for NBA players. So in 1987, Stern and FIBA (the International Basketball federation) worked together to stage an event in which NBA players competed in a global club competition: the first McDonald's Open, held in Milwaukee. The door was finally cracked open.

> **Tip-In**
>
> In 1987 the Milwaukee Bucks finished third in the Central Division with a record of 50–32. Michael Jordan lead the league in scoring that year, averaging 37.1 points per game, and Charles Barkley led the league in rebounding with 14.6 rebounds per game.

The open was a three-team tournament that pitted the Soviet National Team, Tracer Milan of Italy, and the Milwaukee Bucks in a round-robin battle. The Bucks beat the Soviets 127–100 in the final, and Terry Cummings was the tournament MVP.

At the second McDonald's Open, held in 1988, the Boston Celtics met the Yugoslavian National Team, Spain's Real Madrid, and Scavolini Pesaro of Italy in Madrid, Spain. The Americans won again, beating the hometown favorites as Larry Bird was named MVP. NBA players, getting their first dose of international competition in Europe, lived up to their ever-growing popularity in ensuing competitions:

- In 1989, the Denver Nuggets won the tournament in Rome.
- In 1990, in Barcelona, the New York Knicks won.
- In 1991, the tournament was staged in Paris, and the L.A. Lakers won.

In 1992, with the Olympics looming, FIBA and the NBA decided to hold the event every odd year, to account for the Olympics and the World Championships, which were staged in even years. In 1993, the Phoenix Suns won in Munich.

The NBA upped the ante in 1995 when it committed to sending the reigning NBA champion to the tournament. So in 1995, with the name now changed to the McDonald's Championship, the NBA champion Houston Rockets were pitted against five other international league champions in London and won. In 1997, the NBA champion Chicago Bulls beat Greece's Olympiakos Pireo, 104–78. Guess who the MVP was? If you guessed MJ, you're right.

The MVP of the McDonald's Championship received the Drazen Petrovic Trophy. The trophy is named for the Croatian star who played four seasons in Portland and New Jersey before dying in an automobile accident in Germany at the young age of 28 in 1993. He was elected to the Hall of Fame 2002.

NBA Commissioner Stern said of Petrovic, "Drazen was a pioneer in our sport, having been a star in European basketball, the NBA, and the Olympics. He demonstrated that basketball is truly a global sport."

Drazen Petrovic

Arigato

As a natural outgrowth of the worldwide interest in the NBA, the league began to schedule games overseas. The first Japan games occurred in 1990 when the Utah Jazz and Phoenix Suns opened their regular season schedules in Tokyo. The NBA thus became the first professional sports league to play regular season games outside of North America.

The success of that first Tokyo game allowed the NBA to schedule the event again and again. NBA teams played in Japan in 1992, 1994, 1996, and 1999.

Attendance at the Japan games was impressive. In the 1990 Japan game, attendance was 10,111 for both games (two games are played because it takes so long to get there.) At the 1992 games in Yokohama, attendance was 14,544 for both games. At the 1994 games in Yokohama, attendance was 14,239 for each game. In 1996, the venue was moved to the Tokyo Dome, where 38,639 people each night watched the Orlando Magic take on the New Jersey Nets for a pair of games. (A typical NBA game draws about 19,000 people on opening night, depending upon the arena.)

The 1999 games between the Minnesota Timberwolves and the Sacramento Kings were an unqualified hit. About 35,000 fans squeezed into the Tokyo Dome each night to watch the two games between the two popular NBA teams. Good seats went for about 40,000 yen, or about $400.

The fans were incredibly enthusiastic. It was, according to Minnesota's Kevin Garnett, "like being a rock star." Sacramento's Chris Webber agreed, stating that the Japanese "were so into the NBA game" and thus "welcomed us with open arms."

Those two games were a media bonanza as well:

- ◆ The games were broadcast to a record 131 countries in 13 languages.

- ◆ The telecast was broadcast in English, Japanese, Arabic, Bahasa Indonesia, Bahasa Malaysia, Cantonese, Hindi, Korean, Mandarin, Portuguese, Spanish, Tagalog, and Thai.

- ◆ An astonishing 639 media credentials were issued at the Tokyo Dome for the two games.

Inside Stuff

As a result of the terrorist attacks on the United States in 2001, the NBA canceled all preseason games outside the country that season, including …

- ◆ An October game between the Toronto Raptors and Telekom Baskets Bonn of Germany, and a game between the Minnesota Timberwolves and Scavolini Pesaro of Italy.

- ◆ An October game between the Toronto Raptors and the Timberwolves scheduled for Cologne, Germany.

- ◆ The Japan Games between the Lakers and the Golden State Warriors.

- ◆ A game between the Los Angeles Clippers and the Magic in Mexico City.

Gracias

Aside from Japan, the NBA has also staged a number of games in Mexico. The NBA's Mexican arm—NBA Mexico—has presented NBA games in Mexico City since 1992. According to NBA Commissioner Stern, "Staging international preseason games gives the NBA an opportunity to showcase the best basketball in the world. The games provide our loyal and enthusiastic fans in Mexico ... some of the NBA's most exciting young stars."

In 1992, the Houston Rockets and the Dallas Mavericks were the first to play in Mexico City before a crowd of 20,635, a record attendance for a basketball game in Mexico. Buoyed by the success of the Mexican venture, the NBA expanded the format in 1994, creating the NBA Challenge. The San Antonio Spurs, Houston Rockets, Seattle SuperSonics, and the L.A. Clippers played four games over two days to enthusiastic crowds.

NBA Mexico 1997 found the NBA playing its first (and so far only) regular season game south of the border, as the Rockets and Mavericks staged a Texas-style shoot-out. Houston won, 108–106.

In 2002, the NBA expanded its efforts in Mexico even further by creating the NBA 3 x 3 League, the first-ever league in Mexico backed by the NBA. The new league comprises Mexican players from three cities. It kicked off play in September, the finals were held in December, and the winning team attended the NBA All-Star Game in Atlanta the following February.

Inside Stuff

The growth of NBA basketball in Mexico and throughout Spanish-speaking communities led the NBA to partner with Telemundo, the fastest-growing Spanish-language television network in the United States. The agreement made Telemundo the official Spanish-language network of the NBA, as Telemundo agreed to carry 15 NBA games a year on its network.

It isn't surprising that the NBA and Telemundo struck a deal; the Hispanic fan base is one of the fastest-growing segments for the league. According to a 2001 ESPN sports poll, 64 percent of Hispanics in the United States consider themselves NBA fans, and they make up fully 13 percent of the NBA's total domestic fan base.

One reason for this is the emergence of Hispanic players in the NBA. By 2001, seven Hispanic players were on NBA rosters: Pau Gasol, Felipe López, Eduardo Nájera, Oscar Torres, Milt Palacio, Raul Lopez, and Emanuel Ginobili.

In 2002, the NBA played its first game in the Dominican Republic as the Heat and T-Wolves staged a preseason game, the 19th time the NBA had organized an event in Latin America since 1992.

Given the success the NBA enjoys in Mexico and Latin America, and that NBA Commissioner Stern has said that the future of the NBA is partly in international expansion, don't be surprised to see an NBA franchise popping up in Mexico City in the distant future.

NBA Clinics and Programs Around the World

As part of its internationalization effort, the NBA has teamed up with various organizations to help create a variety of programs designed to spread goodwill and understanding.

NBA Jam Session: It may help to think of Jam Session as the NBA's traveling theme park. It is an interactive basketball experience that combines games, activities, and entertainment.

Fans of all ages can meet NBA and WNBA players, dunk the ball, learn to pass, test their basketball knowledge, listen to music, and more. Jam Session has traveled to Canada, England, Italy, Australia, Mexico, Spain, Japan, and Taiwan.

NBA Basketball Challenge: This annual international event is open to players of all ages and offers 5-on-5 basketball along with activities and shows, including a slam-dunk contest. In 2002, the event was held in Germany, and Dirk Nowitzki judged the dunk contest.

Tip-In

In 2001, the United Nations Drug Control Program (UNDCP) and the NBA picked Mexican-born Eduardo Nájera of the Dallas Mavericks to be the UNDCP Goodwill Ambassador for Sports Against Drugs. Sports Against Drugs is a program that reaches out to young people worldwide and encourages them to live drug-free lives.

Goodwill Ambassadors: Every summer the NBA sends some of its brightest stars overseas to represent the league at a variety of functions, including youth basketball programs.

During the summer of 2002, for example, Vince Carter went on a goodwill tour of Asia, playing with Yao Ming in China before heading off to conduct clinics in Hong Kong and Taiwan.

Basketball Without Borders: In 2001, the NBA teamed up with FIBA and several corporate sponsors to create a summer camp for kids aged 12 to 14 that promotes friendship, understanding, and peaceful conflict resolution.

The first camp was held in Italy with Vlade Divac and Toni Kukoc heading the effort. Along with five other NBA players, the stars worked with 50 children from the war-torn provinces of Bosnia, Herzegovina, Croatia, Macedonia, Slovenia, and Yugoslavia.

The 2002 Basketball Without Borders camp found stars like Peja Stojakovic and Hedo Turkoglu of the Kings working with Turkish and Greek children in Istanbul, Turkey. "This has been a great experience," said Antonis Fotsis, an NBA player of Greek descent. "This camp brings these kids together and teaches them tolerance of different cultures."

The International Invasion

The NBA is truly a global league. At the beginning of the 2002–03 regular season, NBA team rosters featured 68 international players from 36 counties and territories, including reigning NBA MVP Tim Duncan (U.S. Virgin Islands); "got milk?" Rookie of the Year Pau Gasol (Spain); 2002 All-Stars Dikembe Mutombo (Congo), Steve Nash (Canada), Dirk Nowitzki (Germany) and Peja Stojakovic (former Yugoslavia); and China's Yao Ming, the No. 1 pick in the draft. The number of international players comprise 19 percent of the total number of NBA players. Among them:

> Dikembe Mutombo (Congo)
> Dirk Nowitzki (Germany)
> Felipe Lopez (Dominican Republic)
> Hedo Turkoglu (Turkey)
> Patrick Ewing (Jamaica)
> Peja Stojakovic (former Yugoslavia)
> Rick Fox (Canada)
> Steve Nash (Canada)
> Tim Duncan (U.S. Virgin Islands)
> Todd MacCulloch (Canada)
> Toni Kukoc (Croatia)
> Tony Parker (France)
> Vitaly Potapenko (Ukraine)
> Vlade Divac (Yugoslavia)
> Yao Ming (China)

And the trend will only continue. But it wasn't always so easy for international players to join the NBA.

Timeout

Prior to 1989, there had been very few international-born basketball players in the NBA for a very good reason. Had any international star crossed the "global baseline" to play professionally in the NBA, they would have been banned from international play by existing FIBA rules.

So only players who didn't particiapate for their country's national teams tried to make it in the NBA. Most of these players had come to the United States to attend college in hopes of getting drafted into the league.

Among those early pioneers were Hakeem Olajuwon from Nigeria, drafted first by Houston in 1984 when he was known as Akeem; Manute Bol from Sudan, drafted thirty-first by Washington in 1985; and Detlef Schrempf from Germany, drafted eighth by Dallas in 1985. Arvydas Sabonis was drafted twenty-fourth by the Blazers in 1986, but didn't come to play in the States until almost a decade later.

Tip-In

Arvydas Sabonis is considered by many to be the greatest player in the history of European basketball. The 7' 3" Lithuanian has a soft jumper, can hit the three, is thick as a brick, and can run the floor and pass like Magic Johnson. He may well be the best passing center of all time, on any continent.

Sabonis is a six-time recipient of the Euroscar, an annual award presented to the "best" European basketball player. He is the all-time winner of that award, getting it in 1984, '85, '88, '95, '97, and '99.

Note: Sabonis was drafted *twice* by the NBA. In 1985, a 20-year-old Sabonis was drafted in the fourth round by the Atlanta Hawks, but the selection was voided because Sabonis had not yet reached the age of 21, the rule at the time.

But the change in FIBA's rules in 1989 heralded a new era in international basketball. Suddenly, the United States was free to field its best team to play overseas, and world's best players could see if they could make it in the NBA.

A New Sort of NBA Player

International players have both attributes and detriments for NBA-type play as compared to Americans. On the positive side, they tend to be more well rounded on the offensive end. Unlike American players who usually learn one position, international players often are taught all aspects of the scoring game. A center knows how to pass, shoot a jumper, and run the floor, in addition to being able to hit a jump hook, box out, and rebound.

On the downside, they don't play defense nearly as well as U.S.-born players, and that usually slows down their transition into the league considerably. Yet even so, a few brave Euros ventured across the pond after the FIBA rule change to try their luck.

Sarunas Marciulionis: "Rooney" had as sweet a jump shot as you ever saw, and he was a tough-as-nails competitor to boot. In 1989, Marciulionis joined the Golden State Warriors and made an immediate impact with his offensive prowess. His knees started to give out after a few years, but Rooney endured the pain and made an impact, playing in the league seven years and retiring with a 13 ppg average.

Drazen Petrovic: Petrovic came from Croatia and joined the Blazers the same year. It was soon apparent that this guy might someday be a superstar in this league. He had the total package, making his untimely death that much harder for everyone.

Alexander Volkov: A talented gold medalist from the Soviet national team, Volkov came over and played two seasons for the Hawks, averaging 6.8 ppg.

It is not surprising that the Hawks drafted Volkov, as they had been courting international players longer, with more foresight, than any other team. General Manager Stan Kasten and Coach Mike Fratello understood early that there were many countries with plenty of basketball talent to choose from besides the United States.

Aside from Volkov, the Hawks drafted Valery Tikhonenko from the Soviet Union, Augusto Binelli from Italy, Song Tao from China, Theo Christodoulou from Greece, Jose-Antonio Montero from Spain, Ricardo Morandoti from Italy, Franjo Arapovic from Yogoslavia, and Jorge Gonzalez from Argentina. And that was just in 1986 and 1987.

Although none of these players really stuck, the Hawks were onto something. The rest of the league began to take notice.

Tip-In

Vlade appeared in the 1991 NBA Finals with the Lakers against the Chicago Bulls. He averaged 12.9 ppg and 7.7 rpg. In 2002, as a member of the Sacramento Kings, he was selected to participate in the All-Star Game for the first time.

Tip-In

Players taken before Dirk Nowitzki in the 1998 draft:

1. Michael Olowokandi
2. Mike Bibby
3. Raef LaFrentz
4. Antawn Jamison
5. Vince Carter
6. Robert Traylor
7. Jason Williams
8. Larry Hughes

One person who definitely was paying attention to this emerging trend was Jerry West, then the GM of the Lakers. With the 26th pick of the 1989 draft, West picked the 7' 1" Serbian center Vlade Divac. Vlade brought that exciting, pass-first, shoot-second euro-mentality to the Lakers, and in the process he became one of the best centers of his generation.

In 1996, Sacramento Kings Executive Vice President Geoff Petrie used the four-teenth pick in the draft to select a player out of Serbia named Predrag "Peja" Stojakovic. Fans watching the draft inside Arco Arena were not pleased with the selection, but Petrie soon had the last laugh.

Similarly, Don Nelson was able to land a first-round pick in the 1998 NBA Draft to snag German Dirk Nowitzki. Nowitzki quickly became one of the best big men in the league, showing that European combination of agility, range, and passing ability.

The Effects of the Invasion

Of the influx of international players into the NBA, Milwaukee coach George Karl said, "I find it kind of sad, but the fundamental play of the European players is a lot more sound than the players coming up in this country."

The general consensus, though, is that an unintended benefit of the arrival of so many quality foreign players is that American high school players may be far less likely to declare for the draft, as most clearly don't have the skills that the new pool of older, more experienced foreign players possess.

By the same token, it may also mean that college kids in the United States may stay in school a bit longer, again because the international player is usually a better, more well-rounded player than say, a college freshman. According to Joe Dumars, president of the Detroit Pistons, "European players … master the fundamentals of the game. They pass, dribble, and shoot. At the same time, American players have gotten away from fundamentals."

For his part, Dirk Nowitzki warns that we all better get used to this change, whatever its consequences: "This is just the start of [international] players coming to the NBA."

> **Inside Stuff**
>
> Tom Meschery was born in Manchuria, China, the son of Russian immigrants. In 1963 he became the first international player to play in the All-Star Game.

What's Next for the NBA?

The international invasion is only the latest in a long line of events that has changed the league and helped it evolve. It is to be welcomed.

In the early 1970s, the NBA was engaged in a bitter rivalry with the upstart ABA, a league with a flashier style. But within a few years, the NBA absorbed what was left of the ABA, adopted the best aspects of that league (the three-point shot and the All-Star Weekend, if not the red, white, and blue ball), and became a better, more exciting, stronger league.

In the 1980s, an infusion of new talent brought a new level of interest to the league, and that was compounded in the '90s. Revolutionary labor agreements, television deals, and a host of world-class partners are propelling the NBA to even greater heights in the new millennium.

The future is no less bright. Foreign players will bring a new style of play to the league, keeping it fresh and exciting, and globalization of the NBA generally will add flair and interest to the game. The world's best athletes will continue to flock to the world's most exciting sport and play in the world's best professional sports league.

And that's why fans around the globe will continue to say, "I love this game!"

The Least You Need to Know

- The NBA has a growing presence around the world.
- The NBA stages clinics and events around the globe.
- A new crop of international players is changing the league.
- The future of the NBA is bright indeed.

The Basketball Hall of Fame

Enshrinement into the Naismith Memorial Basketball Hall of Fame is the epitome of individual achievement for an NBA player. For the fan, it is a great place to spend some time, learn more, and have some fun.

General Information

Contact Information

Naismith Memorial Basketball Hall of Fame
1000 West Columbus Avenue
Springfield, MA 01105
Phone: 413-781-6500 or 1-877-4HOOPLA
Fax: 413-781-1939
www.hoophall.com or www.basketballhalloffame.com

Hours

10 A.M. to 6 P.M. (Sunday through Thursday)
10 A.M. to 8 P.M. (Friday and Saturday)
(Hours subject to change)

New Hall of Fame Admission Prices

(Effective September 28, 2002)

Adults	Seniors 65+	Youths 5–15	Under 5
$15.00	$12.50	$10.00	Free

For group rates: Please call 413-781-6500

Directions

From the East (Boston):

Take the Massachusetts Turnpike (Route 90) to Exit 4, 91 South. Take Exit 7. Continue straight off Exit 7 for 1 mile. The Hall of Fame appears on the right. Approximate driving time: 2 hours.

From the West (Albany):

Take the Massachusetts Turnpike East (Route 90) to Exit 4, 91 South. Take Exit 7. Continue straight off Exit 7 for 1 mile. The Hall of Fame appears on the right. Approximate driving time: 1½ hours.

From the North:

Vermont

Take 91 South, Exit 7. Continue straight for 1 mile. The Hall of Fame appears on the right. Approximate driving time from Brattleboro: 1¼ hours.

Maine

Take 95 South to 495 South to the Massachusetts Turnpike West (Route 90) to Exit 4 (91 South). Take Exit 7. Continue straight off Exit 7 for 1 mile. The Hall of Fame appears on the right. Approximate driving time from Augusta: 5 hours.

New Hampshire

Take 93 South to 495 South to the Massachusetts Turnpike West (Route 90) to Exit 4 (91 South). Take Exit 7. Continue straight off Exit 7 for 1 mile. The Hall of Fame appears on the right. Approximate driving time from Concord: 2¼ hours.

From New York City and South:

Take 95 North to Exit 47, 91 North (New Haven). Continue straight on 91 North for 60 miles until Exit 4, Broad Street exit. Go to your second light and take a left. At the next light, turn left. The Hall of Fame appears on your right. Approximate driving time from New York City: 3½ hours.

Members of the Hall of Fame

There are 246 individuals and five teams enshrined in the Hall of Fame. I've listed only those associated with the NBA. (Those with a * were also named one of the 50 Greatest Players in NBA History.)

Players:

Kareem Abdul-Jabbar*	Gail Goodrich	Bob McAdoo
Nate Archibald*	Hal Greer*	Dick McGuire
Paul Arizin*	Cliff Hagan	Kevin McHale*
Rick Barry*	John Havlicek*	George Mikan*
Elgin Baylor*	Connie Hawkins	Vern Mikkelsen
Walt Bellamy	Elvin Hayes*	Earl Monroe*
Dave Bing*	Tom Heinsohn	Calvin Murphy
Larry Bird*	Robert Houbregs	Drazen Petrovic
Bill Bradley	Baily Howell	Bob Pettit*
Al Cervi	Dan Issel	Andy Phillip
Wilt Chamberlain*	Harry Jeannette	Jim Pollard
Bob Cousy*	Magic Johnson*	Frank Ramsey
Dave Cowens*	Neil Johnston	Willis Reed*
Billy Cunningham*	K.C. Jones	Oscar Robertson*
Bob Davies	Sam Jones*	Arnie Risen
Dave DeBusschere*	Bob Lanier	Bill Russell*
Alex English	Joe Lapchick	Dolph Schayes*
Julius Erving*	Clyde Lovellette	Bill Sharman*
Walt Frazier*	Jerry Lucas*	Isiah Thomas*
Joe Fulks	Ed Macauley	David Thompson
Harry Gallatin	Moses Malone*	Nate Thurmond*
George Gervin*	Pete Maravich*	Jack Twyman
Tom Gola	Slater Martin	Wes Unseld*

Bill Walton*

Bobby Wanzer

Jerry West*

Lenny Wilkens*

George Yardley

Coaches:

Red Auerbach

Larry Brown

Pete Carril

Chuck Daly

Alex Hannum

Red Holzman

Doogie Julian

John Kundla

Ken Loeffler

Frank McGuire

Jack Ramsay

Lenny Wilkens

Contributors:

Danny Biasone

Clair Bee

Walter Brown

Wayne Embry

Lester Fleisher

Eddie Gottlieb

Lester Harrison

Ned Irish

J. Walter Kennedy

Bill Mokray

Pete Newell

Larry O'Brien

Harold Olsen

Maurice Podoloff

Fred Zollner

Referees:

Jim Enright

Pat Kennedy

John Nucatola

J. Dallas Shirley

Earl Strom

Glossary

2-guard   In basketball, each position is assigned a number, and a player of that position is often referred to by that number. The point guard is a 1, the shooting guard is a 2 (or 2-guard), the small forward is a 3, the power forward is a 4, and the center is a 5.

24-second clock   The device that saved the NBA! Danny Biasone's invention was originally called the 24-second clock. As time went by, however, it was given another, informal name: the shot clock.

.500 ball   .500 ball means that a team is winning as many games as it is losing. In a typical 82-game season, a .500 team won 41 games and lost 41 games. It's nothing to brag about.

ACL injury   The main ligament that holds the knee in place is the anterior cruciate ligament, or ACL. Tearing it, or suffering an ACL injury, used to be a career-ending injury for hoopsters.

All-Star Saturday   The All-Star Game used to be held on a Sunday, and that was that. However, starting in 1984, the NBA began expanding the festivities to include a slam-dunk contest, the three-point shootout, and other similar events. They are now all a part of All-Star Saturday.

All-Star starters   The starting five for the NBA All-Star Game are voted on by the fans. The top vote getters in the East and West, for each of the five starting positions, start the game—they are the All-Star starters. The rest of the squad is picked by the coaches.

antidrug policy   The NBA has an antidrug policy that limits the use of certain substances, including marijuana. The policy includes random testing, confidentiality, a voluntary treatment program, and, in extreme cases, suspension or banishment from the league—three strikes and you are out.

banger   In basketball parlance, a player who is willing to fight for rebounds, set up on the block, and battle it out beneath the basket is known as a banger. Big men acting physical.

Boston Garden   The Celtics played in the Boston Garden from 1946 until 1995. With its fabled parquet floor and rafters full of championship banners and retired numbers, the Garden was one of the most difficult places for opposing teams to play. The building only enhanced the "Celtic Mystique."

cagers   Early players used to play in a mesh cage, which explains why basketball players are still sometimes called cagers.

center jump   There was a time in basketball when, after every basket, the centers of the opposing teams would go to midcourt and face off for a jump ball. In the NBA, the center jump occurred only at the beginning of each quarter. Later, the league all but abandoned the center jump altogether, having one jump to start the game, and then alternating possessions at the beginning of each quarter.

collective bargaining agreement   Every six years or so, the league, the team owners, and the players negotiate the contract that governs their business, called the collective bargaining agreement.

Community Assist Award   Each month, all 29 NBA teams nominate a player for the Community Assist Award. The award goes to that player whose community involvement is exceptional. The award emphasizes the NBA's commitment to programs that improve reading and on-line literacy initiatives for children.

dog days   The NBA season begins in late October and lasts until the NBA Finals in June. As such, the middle part of the regular season, occurring during the end of winter, is sometimes referred to as the dog days.

draft lottery   Every year, the 13 teams that had the worst records in the league compete for the right to pick first in the draft lottery, the method by which college and foreign players are brought into the league. The lottery is weighted in favor of the teams with the worst records.

Dream Team   In 1992, the greatest basketball team of all time represented the United States in the Barcelona Olympics. That was the first year that professional basketball players could represent their country, and USA basketball wasted no time in putting together its Dream Team.

Dr. J   Julius Erving, one of the greatest to ever play the game, is usually called by the nickname he earned while at the University of Massachusetts—Dr. J, or simply, the Doctor.

elbow   The area to the left or right of the free-throw line is called the elbow.

finish   On a fast break, you've got to get the ball in the hole. The highest percentage way to do that is to dunk, but a layup will work just fine, too. Either way, the key is to finish the play and get the points.

first round   When players want to join the NBA, they enter a draft. The NBA drafts players based on team records from the year before, with the worst teams getting the best chance to draft first in the lottery for draft position. The best players available are, obviously, taken in the first round of the draft. Lesser players are drafted in the second and last round.

foul shot   When a player is fouled, he gets a free shot from a line 15 feet from the basket, hence the name free throw, or foul shot.

home-court advantage   Playoff series are always odd numbers, either best of five or best of seven. That means that one of the two teams will get to play at least one more game on its floor. That is called home-court advantage. The team that gets it is the team that won more regular season games of the two.

inside the paint   The area inside the key is painted a different color than the rest of the floor. Players who can score in that area, inside the paint, are valuable because it's a tough zone with a lot of bodies and elbows flying around.

journeymen   Those players who go from team to team, the ones who never seem to latch on anyplace for too long, are called journeymen.

leprechaun   Boston Celtics' lore has it that a lucky leprechaun graced the fabled parquet floor of Boston Garden, tapping in errant shots and otherwise helping the boys in green win.

MJ   Michael Jordan has been given many nicknames over the years; MJ, Air Jordan, and His Airness are the most common.

NBDL   The National Basketball Development League is a relatively new NBA-related league where players who are not quite ready for the NBA can work on their skills.

Never underestimate the heart of a champion   In 1994, the Houston Rockets won the NBA championship. The next year, the team stumbled badly in the regular season. They entered the 1995 playoffs as a sixth seed, and most of the talking heads had written off the team's chances of repeating. But when the Rockets did in fact roar back to win back-to-back championships, their coach, Rudy Tomjanovich, uttered words that live on in the NBA lexicon: "Never underestimate the heart of a champion."

overtime   An NBA game is 48 minutes long. If the score is tied at the end of that time, the teams play a five-minute overtime period. They continue to do so until one team wins.

player-coach   A phenomenon of the early NBA was that some players not only played, but coached the team as well. Aside from Bill Russell, these player-coaches included Lenny Wilkens, Buddy Jeannette, and Al Cervi.

post-up players   On offense, the prototypical center or power forward will get set up down low with his back to the basket, called "posting up." When he gets the ball, he will use a variety of moves to fake out his man and try to score. This is a post-up player.

Red Auerbach Trophy   Every year, one coach is named the NBA Coach of the Year. The name of the trophy he receives is the Red Auerbach Trophy.

set shot   Today when a shooting guard shoots from the outside, he is likely to leap up and shoot the ball at the top of the arc of his jump, using mostly his strong hand. This is called a jump shot. But back in the day, at the dawn of the NBA, most outside shooters would plant their feet, grab the ball on either side, and let it fly. Some of the game's greatest players—Dolph Schayes, Bob Davies, and Bob Wanzer—were great set shooters. By 1950, the jump shot gradually became the shot of preference.

shooting the J   When a player shoots a jump shot, it is sometimes referred to as shooting the J.

sign   A player must sign a contract with a team before he can set foot on the court. When he does put his name on the dotted line, he is said to have signed, and can now officially play for that team.

sixth man   One of Red Auerbach's great inventions was that of the sixth man. While the five best players on the team usually start the game, Red realized another great player waiting on the bench was necessary. This would have to be a player who was as good as a starter and could come off the bench and ignite the team versus the other team's subs. That was the sixth man. During the '60s, the sixth man gave Boston the advantage when a great player entered the game versus the other team's not-so-great substitutes. Two star sixth men were Frank Ramsey and John Havlicek.

skyhook   Prior to Kareem, a hook shot was shot with an arc—up, then down. But because of his size (7' 1''), and the fact that he jumped when he shot it, Kareem's hook shot was often going down toward the basket from the moment he released it. It was this dubbed the skyhook because it looked like it was coming down from the sky.

Sportsmanship Award   The annual Sportsmanship award honors those players who foster the ideals of sportsmanship—ethical behavior, fair play, and integrity.

taking the ball to the rack   When a player drives hard to the basket, it is also called taking the ball to the rack.

three-peat   When the Lakers were winning all of those championships, guard Byron Scott coined the term *three-peat* for when a team that won three champion-ships in a row. Coach Pat Riley liked the term so much that, rumor has it he trademarked it.

triple double   When a player scores 10 or more points, assists, blocks, steals or rebounds, he is said to be in double figures in that category. When that player has double figures in three categories in one night, he is said to have a triple double. It is the sign of an all-around great game. The great Oscar Robertson once averaged a triple double during an entire season! He did this in the 1961–62 season.

walking with the ball   In basketball, a player going to the hoop can legally take one and a half steps after he stops dribbling. If he takes more than that, it is called traveling, or walking with the ball.

Index

U–V

W–X–Y–Z